# Assessment *for* Learning
## An Action Guide for School Leaders

Stephen Chappuis, Richard Stiggins, Judith Arter, and Jan Chappuis

Assessment Training Institute
Portland, OR

# Assessment *for* Learning

## An Action Guide for School Leaders

© 2004 Assessment Training Institute
Portland, OR

Project Coordinator: Barbara Carnegie
Editor: Robert L. Marcum
Cover Design: Brass Design
Page Layout: Anita Jones

The authors and publisher have made every effort to identify and cite the copyright holders of all material reproduced from other sources, and to obtain permission for their reproduction. Anyone identifying outstanding copyright attribution issues is invited to contact the publisher, who will be happy to make any necessary corrections in future editions or reprints of this work.

Many of the Activities and Resources in this book appeared, some in substantially different form, in J. A. Arter and K. U. Busick, *Practice with Student-Involved Classroom Assessment,* Portland, OR: Assessment Training Institute, 2001. Reprinted and adapted by permission.

The material appearing on pages 137–138, 149–152, 155–162, and 275–278 is reproduced or adapted from J. A. Arter and B. Nutting, *Student Assessment Mini-lessons for Your Staff,* Portland, OR: Northwest Regional Educational Laboratory, 1998. Reprinted and adapted by permission of Northwest Regional Educational Laboratory and Bill Nutting.

Library of Congress Control Number: 2003106332

ISBN 0-9655101-4-X

Printed in the USA

# Acknowledgements

This guide has been years in the making. It represents over a decade of research and development that has helped us (1) refine our vision of excellence in assessment, and (2) understand the nature of assessment change and how to help school districts attain that vision of excellence. Along the way we have benefited from those who have worked to understand sound assessment more clearly, those who applied our ideas and shared successful implementation stories, and those who have helped us teach others about quality assessment. We wish to thank you all.

Those who have helped us deepen our own understanding of quality assessment and school leadership include Paul Black and Dylan Wiliam and their associates in the Assessment Reform Group of the United Kingdom, Kathy Busick, Anne Davies, Rick DuFour, Linda Elman, Heidi Hayes-Jacobs, Jim Popham, Janet Barry, and Ruth Sutton.

Practicing school leaders who have implemented our ideas and permitted us to watch and learn include Kathi Bell of West Palm Beach, Florida; Bob Nielsen of Bloomington, Illinois; Jay Linksman of the Professional Development Alliance in Illinois; Bill Parrett of Boise State University, Idaho; Steve Price of Middletown, Ohio; Doug Christensen and Pat Rochewski of the Nebraska Department of Education; and Bruce Herzog and Joni Heutink of Nooksack Valley.

To help us share our ideas with practitioners, we thank ATI associate trainers Carol Commodore, Ken O'Connor, Leslie Lukin, and Theresa Rouse.

We also welcome once again the contributions made by freelance editor Robert L. Marcum, which improved the clarity of ideas and activities presented in this book. His attention to detail and grasp and understanding of the big picture merged to help unify the work of four authors.

We believe that the vision building and strategies for change we describe in this guide can lead any school district to excellence in assessment. We acknowledge the commitment of those who are willing to try.

The Assessment Training Institute Staff
August, 2003

# Contents

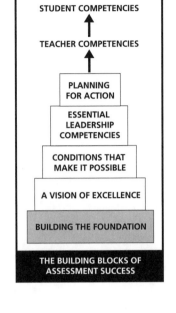

THE BUILDING BLOCKS OF ASSESSMENT SUCCESS

*The attainment of any vision of assessment excellence requires that certain conditions be in place. Those conditions include well-defined learning targets for students, supportive school and district policies, clear communication systems, and probably most important, assessment-literate teachers and administrators.*

*Part One*

# BUILDING THE FOUNDATION

For educational reform efforts to succeed we must be clear about what students need to know and be able to do, and we need to be skillful and intentional in teaching by using proven strategies that best promote student learning. We must also develop balanced assessment systems that not only provide information on how well students have learned, but that also use assessment to promote greater learning. What we teach, how well we teach it, how we assess, and how we use assessment to improve student achievement will all determine the success of our efforts, and ultimately, how we are judged.

In addition, there is strong evidence to suggest that the culture we create in our schools also influences success. Collaborative cultures emphasizing teamwork and learning are able to deliver the necessary professional support for teachers, support aimed at demonstrable results in student achievement.

This action guide is designed to help you as an educational leader achieve your school improvement goals. It provides a structure through which you can review and refine your vision of excellence in assessment for your school or district, examine the skills and knowledge needed to support your vision, and then chart a path by developing a plan of action designed to turn your vision into reality. By using the materials in this guide in leadership study teams collaboratively with other school administrators and teacher leaders, you can design a comprehensive plan for achieving a balanced, instructionally relevant local assessment system in which both classroom assessments *for* learning and standardized assessments *of* learning are used effectively to serve their intended purposes. Both are important. Although we emphasize in this guide what leaders can do to take advantage of the power of assessment *for* learning to improve student achievement, we believe that all uses of assessment can and should help students learn, and therefore assessments *of* learning have a contribution to make in a balanced assessment system. We will explore this distinction in depth later in this guide.

Beyond working at the systems level for achieving assessment balance and quality, this action guide also helps you as a school leader analyze your individual knowledge about assessment and prepares you to plan and initiate your own continuing learning about sound assessment practices. By completing the work outlined in the accompanying activities and resources, you will take the first steps in developing your own assessment literacy. Your team will acquire the tools needed to set your staff on the path to assess accurately, to increase student motivation to learn, and to use assessment to improve learning. The key to completing that journey is sustained support of the collaborative learning process and school culture necessary to turn your vision into everyday reality in the classroom.

## Benefits for Schools, Teachers, and Students

This action guide will allow you and your team to do the following:

- Create your own vision for assessment balance and quality.
- Begin to understand the depth and breadth of classroom assessment and its relationship to student achievement.
- Understand the need to balance the assessment system between large-scale assessment *of* learning and classroom assessment *for* learning.
- Identify assessment needs relevant to your own school or district and prioritize those needs.
- Develop an action plan for realizing your vision of assessment excellence.
- Analyze your own assessment knowledge and leadership skills relative to a set of 10 assessment competencies for school leaders.
- Inspire others to make the same commitment you have made to deepen knowledge of classroom assessment, to help make teaching more efficient, and to improve student achievement.

## Contents of This Guide

The graphic on page 1 shows the building blocks of assessment success. It also maps the reader's journey through this action guide. It begins by establishing the foundation: a clear vision of what assessment can do for any school/district willing to commit to the required scope of work. There are certain conditions that are required for assessment systems to achieve excellence. There also are specific competencies that leaders need to develop and a body of knowledge and set of skills classroom teachers need to develop in order to realize the student success we all desire.

To help you and your leadership team develop a deep understanding of each of the building blocks, we've divided this guide into five parts.

- Part 1 introduces the guide's purpose and goals, describes both its print and media contents, and explains its optimal use in the context of a school or district leadership study team. We encourage the same model of professional development for this action guide that we advocate for teachers to become assessment literate. All it requires is a small group of school leaders willing to meet regularly and invest the time in their own professional growth and in the improvement of their local system. By acquiring certain understandings, considering important issues, and planning for the future as a team, we demonstrate the commitment to learning we seek in all aspects of school culture.

- Part 2 outlines our vision of excellence in assessment and describes the essential ingredients necessary to develop an assessment system rooted in balance, quality, and student involvement. Here we balance assessment *of* and *for* learning.

- The third part asks leadership teams to analyze the current status of their school/district assessment system to see if essential conditions are in place for the vision to be realized. Those conditions include well-defined learning targets for students, supportive school/district policies, clear communication systems, and most important, assessment-literate teachers and administrators.

- In Part 4 we shift emphasis from analyzing organizational and institutional assessment excellence to examining the knowledge and skills that individual leaders must master in order to create and sustain assessment excellence. A further examination of the knowledge and skills needed by classroom teachers is also contained in Part 4, as well as ideas for how school leaders can help teachers gain the skills and support them in their classroom practice.

- In the fifth and final part we help leadership teams understand why and how developing a sound assessment system lays a strong foundation for other local improvement initiatives. We help you create the action plan that will lead to assessment balance and quality.

Each section puts forth specific ideas and suggestions about the use of assessment in schools and districts. From time to time, we will pause and ask your team to discuss and reflect on the ideas and their application in your local context. We have included two different learning aids to help you consider and clarify the ideas, along with suggestions on how to use them to advance your understanding and application of the concepts:

*Thinking About Assessment* pages present activities for your leadership team to complete as part of your processing and understanding the contents of this guide.

*Applying the Skills* pages are resources you can use at any time to advance individual or group knowledge about assessment issues, or help your team prepare for and organize successful implementation of balanced assessment. Some are best suited for use with the leadership team; others can be used as faculty meeting or inservice activities with teachers.

In addition, this guide includes a compact disc (CD-ROM) and digital video disc (DVD) that can be found in plastic sleeves just inside the back cover. On the CD-ROM are PowerPoint presentations used by staff at the Assessment Training Institute when working with educators in professional development settings. The CD-ROM also contains the activities and resources previously described, which are intended to function as tools for leaders to use with other educators when working through the assessment ideas and issues presented here. The table of contents on the CD-ROM shows what sections of this guide correspond to each PowerPoint presentation. We also note those connections elsewhere in this book as appropriate.

The DVD, a key component in one of the first leadership team activities, contains *Assessment for Learning: A Hopeful Vision of the Future,* a 40-minute presentation with a viewer's study guide featuring Rick Stiggins explaining the differences between assessment *of* learning and assessment *for* learning.

# Getting Ready

We think it is important to build your knowledge and understanding of quality assessment and balanced local systems by following the sequence of reading and activities as outlined in this guide. In Part 2 we outline a sharply focused vision for the perfect assessment system. The first two Thinking About Assessment activities will get you started in developing a foundation for understanding excellence in assessment, including understanding a key concept referred to throughout the guide, the difference between assessment *of* and assessment *for* learning.

## Thinking About Assessment

### Activity 1: Building the Foundation for Understanding Quality Assessment

**Purpose:**     This first activity begins your exploration of excellence in assessment by helping you secure a fundamental understanding of the "big ideas" of balance in assessment, assessment quality, the power of student involvement in assessment, and assessment *of* and *for* learning. Throughout this guide our goal is to have you think about a vision of assessment excellence, read papers and/or view videos, consider the concepts and ideas presented, and refine your vision as necessary. We'll ask you to work as a leadership team to progressively shape your vision. Then we'll ask your team to compare the current status of your local assessment system to your vision to see if they line up and identify what you will need to adjust to make them match.

**Time:**     A 2-hour meeting

**Meeting Agenda:**

■   Working as a team, based on your current level of understanding of important assessment issues, outline your vision of a high-quality assessment system. Do this by taking a half hour to brainstorm and refine your team's answers to the following two questions. Take time to think this through pretty thoroughly, as the results will become very important.

1.   What do you want your assessment system to accomplish? What will be its key objectives?

2.   How will your system accomplish these things? What will be its active ingredients, procedures, or components?

■   Next, take about 20 minutes to read "Inside the Black Box," by Paul Black and Dylan Wiliam, pages 10–21. Then take 10 minutes to collect your individual thoughts on the most important lessons and implications of this research. Finally, work as a team to reaffirm, or to rethink and revise as appropriate, your initial vision of excellence in assessment. Refine your vision as needed to reflect any ideas or values learned from Black and Wiliam.

■ Next, again as a team, view the ATI video, *Assessment FOR Learning: A Hopeful Vision of the Future.* This presentation details both the differences in and the need for synergy between assessment *of* and *for* learning and explains why the principles of assessment *for* learning are so powerful. As you prepare to do so, please review the following viewing guidelines.

### *While Viewing:*

■ Consider the ideal balance between standardized and classroom assessment.

■ As the presentation proceeds, make note of the ingredients that distinguish assessment *of* and *for* learning.

■ Look for the power of student involvement in classroom assessment. What can student involvement accomplish?

### *After Viewing:*

■ Read Table 1, pages 22–24, contrasting assessment *of* and *for* learning, discussing the nuances of each and how they compare, as needed. Your purpose in doing so is to be sure everyone on your team understands how they relate.

■ Now go back a third time and review the evolving vision you developed at the start of your meeting and revised after reading the Black and Wiliam article. Using Table 1 and the content of the video presentation, once again make adjustments as needed in your vision of excellence in assessment. What do you want it to do for you and how will it help you accomplish those things? Continue to analyze these things as a team, striving for consensus.

# Inside the Black Box:

## *Raising Standards Through Classroom Assessment*

BY PAUL BLACK AND DYLAN WILIAM

Firm evidence shows that formative assessment is an essential component of classroom work and that its development can raise standards of achievement, Mr. Black and Mr. Wiliam point out. Indeed, they know of no other way of raising standards for which such a strong prima facie case can be made.

RAISING the standards of learning that are achieved through schooling is an important national priority. In recent years, governments throughout the world have been more and more vigorous in making changes in pursuit of this aim. National, state, and district standards; target setting; enhanced programs for the external testing of students' performance; surveys such as NAEP (National Assessment of Educational Progress) and TIMSS (Third International Mathematics and Science Study); initiatives to improve school planning and management; and more frequent and thorough inspection are all means toward the same end. But the sum of all these reforms has not added up to an effective policy because something is missing.

Learning is driven by what teachers and pupils do in classrooms. Teachers have to manage complicated and demanding situations, channeling the personal, emotional, and social pressures of a group of 30 or more youngsters in order to help them learn

PAUL BLACK is professor emeritus in the School of Education, King's College, London, where DYLAN WILIAM is head of school and professor of educational assessment.

immediately and become better learners in the future. Standards can be raised only if teachers can tackle this task more effectively. What is missing from the efforts alluded to above is any direct help with this task. This fact was recognized in the TIMSS video study: "A focus on standards and accountability that ignores the processes of teaching and learning in classrooms will not provide the direction that teachers need in their quest to improve."[1]

In terms of systems engineering, present policies in the U.S. and in many other countries seem to treat the classroom as a black box. Certain *inputs* from the outside—pupils, teachers, other resources, management rules and requirements, parental anxieties, standards, tests with high stakes, and so on—are fed into the box. Some *outputs* are supposed to follow: pupils who are more knowledgeable and competent, better test results, teachers who are reasonably satisfied, and so on. But what is happening inside the box? How can anyone be sure that a particular set of new inputs will produce better outputs if we don't at least study what happens inside? And why is it that most of the reform initiatives mentioned in the first paragraph are not aimed at giving direct help and support to the work of teachers in classrooms?

The answer usually given is that it is up to teachers: they have to make the inside work better. This answer is not good enough, for two reasons. First, it is at least possible that some changes in the inputs may be counterproductive and make it harder for teachers to raise standards. Second, it seems strange, even unfair, to leave the most difficult piece of the standards-raising puzzle entirely to teachers. If there are ways in which policy makers and others can give direct help and support to the everyday

Reprinted from *Phi Delta Kappan*, October 1998, vol. 80, pp. 139–148. Reprinted by permission.

classroom task of achieving better learning, then surely these ways ought to be pursued vigorously.

This article is about the inside of the black box. We focus on one aspect of teaching: formative assessment. But we will show that this feature is at the heart of effective teaching.

## THE ARGUMENT

We start from the self-evident proposition that teaching and learning must be interactive. Teachers need to know about their pupils' progress and difficulties with learning so that they can adapt their own work to meet pupils' needs—needs that are often unpredictable and that vary from one pupil to another. Teachers can find out what they need to know in a variety of ways, including observation and discussion in the classroom and the reading of pupils' written work.

We use the general term *assessment* to refer to all those activities undertaken by teachers—and by their students in assessing themselves—that provide information to be used as feedback to modify teaching and learning activities. Such assessment becomes *formative assessment* when the evidence is actually used to adapt the teaching to meet student needs.[2]

There is nothing new about any of this. All teachers make assessments in every class they teach. But there are three important questions about this process that we seek to answer:

- Is there evidence that improving formative assessment raises standards?
- Is there evidence that there is room for improvement?
- Is there evidence about how to improve formative assessment?

In setting out to answer these questions, we have conducted an extensive survey of the research literature. We have checked through many books and through the past nine years' worth of issues of more than 160 journals, and we have studied earlier reviews of research. This process yielded about 580 articles or chapters to study. We prepared a lengthy review, using material from 250 of these sources, that has been published in a special issue of the

journal *Assessment in Education*, together with comments on our work by leading educational experts from Australia, Switzerland, Hong Kong, Lesotho, and the U.S.[3]

The conclusion we have reached from our research review is that the answer to each of the three questions above is clearly yes. In the three main sections below, we outline the nature and force of the evidence that justifies this conclusion. However, because we are presenting a summary here, our text will appear strong on assertions and weak on the details of their justification. We maintain that these assertions are backed by evidence and that this backing is set out in full detail in the lengthy review on which this article is founded.

We believe that the three sections below establish a strong case that *governments, their agencies, school authorities, and the teaching profession should study very carefully whether they are seriously interested in raising standards in education.* However, we also acknowledge widespread evidence that fundamental change in education can be achieved only slowly—through programs of professional development that build on existing good practice. Thus we do not conclude that formative assessment is yet another "magic bullet" for education. The issues involved are too complex and too closely linked to both the difficulties of classroom practice and the beliefs that drive public policy. In a final section, we confront this complexity and try to sketch out a strategy for acting on our evidence.

## DOES IMPROVING FORMATIVE ASSESSMENT RAISE STANDARDS?

A research review published in 1986, concentrating primarily on classroom assessment work for children with mild handicaps, surveyed a large number of innovations, from which 23 were selected.[4] Those chosen satisfied the condition that quantitative evidence of learning gains was obtained, both for those involved in the innovation and for a similar group not so involved. Since then, many more papers have been published describing similarly careful quantitative experiments. Our own review has selected at least 20 more studies. (The number depends on how rigorous a set of selection criteria are applied.) All these studies show that innovations that include strengthening the practice of formative assessment produce significant and often substantial learning gains. These studies range over age groups from 5-year-olds to university undergraduates, across several school subjects, and over several countries.

For research purposes, learning gains of this type are measured by comparing the average improvements in the test scores of pupils involved in an innovation with the range of scores that are found for typical groups of pupils on these same tests. The ratio of the former divided by the latter is known as the *effect size*. Typical effect sizes of the formative assessment experiments were between 0.4 and 0.7. These effect sizes are larger than most of those found for educational interventions. The following examples illustrate some practical consequences of such large gains.

• An effect size of 0.4 would mean that the average pupil involved in an innovation would record the same achievement as a pupil in the top 35% of those not so involved.

• An effect size gain of 0.7 in the recent international comparative studies in mathematics[5] would have raised the score of a nation in the middle of the pack of 41 countries (e.g., the U.S.) to one of the top five.

Many of these studies arrive at another important conclusion: that improved formative assessment helps low achievers more than other students and so reduces the range of achievement while raising achievement overall. A notable recent example is a study devoted entirely to low-achieving students and students with learning disabilities, which shows that frequent assessment feedback helps both groups enhance their learning.[6] Any gains for such pupils could be particularly important. Furthermore, pupils who come to see themselves as unable to learn usually cease to take school seriously. Many become disruptive; others resort to truancy. Such young people are likely to be alienated from society and to become the sources and the victims of serious social problems.

Thus it seems clear that very significant learning gains lie within our grasp. The fact that such gains have been achieved by a variety of methods that have, as a common feature, enhanced formative assessment suggests that this feature accounts, at least in part, for the successes. However, it does not follow that it would be an easy matter to achieve such gains on a wide scale in normal classrooms. Many of the reports we have studied raise a number of other issues.

• All such work involves new ways to enhance feedback between those taught and the teacher, ways that will require significant changes in classroom practice.

• Underlying the various approaches are assumptions about what makes for effective learning —in particular the assumption that students have to be actively involved.

• For assessment to function formatively, the results have to be used to adjust teaching and learning; thus a significant aspect of any program will be the ways in which teachers make these adjustments.

• The ways in which assessment can affect the motivation and self-esteem of pupils and the benefits of engaging pupils in self-assessment deserve careful attention.

## IS THERE ROOM FOR IMPROVEMENT?

**A poverty of practice.** There is a wealth of research evidence that the everyday practice of assessment in classrooms is beset with problems and shortcomings, as the following selected quotations indicate.

• "Marking is usually conscientious but often fails to offer guidance on how work can be improved. In a significant minority of cases, marking reinforces underachievement and underexpectation by being too generous or unfocused. Information about pupil performance received by the teacher is insufficiently used to inform subsequent work," according to a United Kingdom inspection report on secondary schools.[7]

• "Why is the extent and nature of formative assessment in science so impoverished?" asked a research study on secondary science teachers in the United Kingdom.[8]

● "Indeed they pay lip service to [formative assessment] but consider that its practice is unrealistic in the present educational context," reported a study of Canadian secondary teachers.[9]

● "The assessment practices outlined above are not common, even though these kinds of approaches are now widely promoted in the professional literature," according to a review of assessment practices in U.S. schools.[10]

The most important difficulties with assessment revolve around three issues. The first issue is *effective learning.*

● The tests used by teachers encourage rote and superficial learning even when teachers say they want to develop understanding; many teachers seem unaware of the inconsistency.

● The questions and other methods teachers use are not shared with other teachers in the same school, and they are not critically reviewed in relation to what they actually assess.

● For primary teachers particularly, there is a tendency to emphasize quantity and presentation of work and to neglect its quality in relation to learning.

The second issue is *negative impact.*

● The giving of marks and the grading function are overemphasized, while the giving of useful advice and the learning function are underemphasized.

● Approaches are used in which pupils are compared with one another, the prime purpose of which seems to them to be competition rather than personal improvement; in consequence, assessment feedback teaches low-achieving pupils that they lack "ability," causing them to come to believe that they are not able to learn.

The third issue is the *managerial role* of assessments.

● Teachers' feedback to pupils seems to serve social and managerial functions, often at the expense of the learning function.

● Teachers are often able to predict pupils' results on external tests because their own tests imitate them, but at the same time teachers know too little about their pupils' learning needs.

● The collection of marks to fill in records is given higher priority than the analysis of pupils' work to discern learning needs; furthermore, some teachers pay no attention to the assessment records of their pupils' previous teachers.

Of course, not all these descriptions apply to all classrooms. Indeed, there are many schools and classrooms to which they do not apply at all. Nevertheless, these general conclusions have been drawn by researchers who have collected evidence—through observation, interviews, and questionnaires—from schools in several countries, including the U.S.

**An empty commitment.** The development of national assessment policy in England and Wales over the last decade illustrates the obstacles that stand in the way of developing policy support for formative assessment. The recommendations of a government task force in 1988[11] and all subsequent statements of government policy have emphasized the importance of formative assessment by teachers. However, the body charged with carrying out government policy on assessment had no strategy either to study or to develop the formative assessment of teachers and did no more than devote a tiny fraction of its resources to such work."[12] Most of the available resources and most of the public and political attention were focused on national external tests. While teachers' contributions to these "summative assessments" have been given some formal status, hardly any attention has been paid to their contributions through formative assessment. Moreover, the problems of the relationship between teachers' formative and summative roles have received no attention.

It is possible that many of the commitments were stated in the belief that formative assessment was not problematic, that it already happened all the time and needed no more than formal acknowledgment of its existence. However, it is also clear that the political commitment to external testing in order to promote competition had a central priority, while the commitment to formative assessment was marginal. As researchers the world over have found, high-stakes external tests always dominate teaching and assessment. However, they give teachers poor models for formative assessment because of their limited function of providing overall summaries of achievement rather than helpful diagnosis. Given this fact, it is hardly surprising that numerous research studies of the implementation of the education reforms in the United Kingdom have found that formative assessments is "seriously in need of development."[13] With hindsight, we can see that the failure to perceive the need for substantial support for formative assessment and to take responsibility for developing such support was a serious error.

In the U.S. similar pressures have been felt from political movements characterized by a distrust of teachers and a belief that external testing will, on its own, improve learning. Such fractured relationships between policy makers and the teaching profession are not inevitable—indeed, many countries with enviable educational achievements seem to manage well with policies that show greater respect and support for teachers. While the situation in the U.S. is far more diverse than that in England and Wales, the effects of high-stakes state-mandated testing are very similar to those of the external tests in the United Kingdom. Moreover, the traditional reliance on multiple-choice testing in the U.S.—not shared in the United Kingdom—has exacerbated the negative effects of such policies on the quality of classroom learning.

## HOW CAN WE IMPROVE FORMATIVE ASSESSMENT?

**The self-esteem of pupils.** A report of schools in Switzerland states that "a number of pupils . . . are content to 'get by.' . . . Every teacher who wants to practice formative assessment must reconstruct the teaching contracts so as to counteract the habits acquired by his pupils."[14]

The ultimate user of assessment information that is elicited in order to improve learning is the pupil. There are negative and positive aspects of this fact. The negative aspect is illustrated by the preceding quotation. When the classroom culture focuses on rewards, "gold stars," grades, or class ranking, then pupils look for ways to obtain the best marks rather than to improve their learning. One reported consequence is that, when they have any choice, pupils avoid difficult tasks. They also spend time and energy looking for clues to the "right answer." Indeed, many become reluctant to ask questions out of a fear of failure. Pupils who encounter difficulties are led to believe that they lack ability, and this belief leads them to attribute their difficulties to a defect in themselves about which they cannot do a great deal. Thus they avoid investing effort in learning that can lead only to disappointment, and they try to build up their self-esteem in other ways.

The positive aspect of students' being the primary users of the information gleaned from formative assessments is that negative outcomes —such as an obsessive focus on competition and the attendant fear of failure on the part of low achievers—are not inevitable. What is needed is a culture of success, backed by a belief that all pupils can achieve. In this regard, formative assessment can be a powerful weapon if it is communicated in the right way. While formative assessment can help all pupils, it yields particularly good results with low achievers by concentrating on specific problems with their work and giving them a clear understanding of what is wrong and how to put it right. Pupils can accept and work with such messages, provided that they are not clouded by overtones about ability, competition, and comparison with others. In summary, the message can be stated as follows: *feedback to any pupil should be about the particular qualities of his or her work, with advice on what he or she can do to improve, and should avoid comparisons with other pupils.*

**Self-assessment by pupils.** Many successful innovations have developed self- and peer-assessment by pupils as ways of enhancing formative assessment, and such work has achieved some success with pupils from age 5 upward. This link of formative assessment to self-assessment is not an accident; indeed, it is inevitable.

To explain this last statement, we should first note that the main problem that those who are developing self-assessments encounter is not a problem of reliability and trustworthiness. Pupils are generally honest and reliable in assessing both themselves and one another; they can even be too hard on themselves. The main problem is that pupils can assess themselves only when they have a sufficiently clear picture of the targets that their learning is meant to attain. Surprisingly, and sadly, many pupils do not have such a picture, and they appear to have become accustomed to receiving classroom teaching as an arbitrary sequence of exercises with no overarching rationale. To overcome this pattern of passive reception requires hard and sustained work. When pupils do acquire such an overview, they then become more committed and more effective as learners. Moreover, their own assessments become an object of discussion with their teachers and with one another, and this discussion further promotes the reflection on one's own thinking that is essential to good learning.

Thus self-assessment by pupils, far from being a luxury, is in fact *an essential component of formative assessment.* When anyone is trying to learn, feedback about the effort has three elements: recognition of the *desired goal*, evidence about *present position*, and some understanding of a *way to close the gap* between the two.[15] All three must be understood to some degree by anyone before he or she can take action to improve learning.

Such an argument is consistent with more general ideas established by research into the way people learn. New understandings are not simply swallowed and stored in isolation; they have to be assimilated in relation to preexisting ideas. The new and the old may be inconsistent or even in conflict, and the disparities must be resolved by thoughtful actions on the part of the learner. Realizing that there are new goals for the learning is an essential part of this process of assimilation. Thus we conclude: *if formative assessment is to be productive, pupils should be trained in self-assessment so that they can understand the main purposes of their learning and thereby grasp what they need to do to achieve.*

**The evolution of effective teaching.** The research studies referred to above show very clearly that effective programs of formative assessment involve far more than the addition of a few observations and tests to an existing program. They require careful scrutiny of all the main components of a teaching plan. Indeed, it is clear that instruction and formative assessment are indivisible.

To begin at the beginning, the choice of tasks for classroom work and homework is important. Tasks have to be justified in terms of the learning aims that they serve, and they can work well only if opportunities for pupils to communicate their evolving understanding are built into the planning. Discussion, observation of activities, and marking of written work can all be used to provide those opportunities, but it is then important to look at or listen carefully to the talk, the writing, and the actions through which pupils develop and display the state of their understanding. Thus we maintain that *opportunities for pupils to express their understanding should be designed into any piece of teaching, for this will initiate the interaction through which formative assessment aids learning.*

Discussions in which pupils are led to talk about their understanding in their own ways are important aids to increasing knowledge and improving understanding. Dialogue with the teacher provides the opportunity for the teacher to respond to and reorient a pupil's thinking. However, there are clearly recorded examples of such discussions in which teachers have, quite unconsciously, responded in ways that would inhibit the future learning of a pupil. What the examples have in common is that the teacher is looking for a particular response and lacks the flexibility or the confidence to deal with the unexpected. So the teacher tries to direct the pupil toward giving the expected answer. In manipulating the dialogue in this way, the teacher seals off any unusual, often thoughtful but unorthodox, attempts by pupils to work out their own answers. Over time the pupils get the message: they are not required to think out their own answers. The object of the exercise is to work out—or guess—what answer the teacher expects to see or hear.

A particular feature of the talk between teacher and pupils is the asking of questions by the teacher. This natural and direct way of checking on learning is often unproductive. One common problem is that, following a question, teachers do not wait long enough to allow pupils to think out their answers. When a teacher answers his or her own question after only two or three seconds and when a minute of silence is not tolerable, there is no possibility that a pupil can think out what to say.

There are then two consequences. One is that, because the only questions that can produce answers in such a short time are questions of fact, these predominate. The other is that pupils don't even try to think out a response. Because they know that the answer, followed by another question, will come along in a few seconds, there is no point in trying. It is also generally the case that only a few pupils in a class answer the teacher's questions. The rest then leave it to these few, knowing that they cannot respond as quickly and being unwilling to risk making mistakes in public. So the teacher, by lowering the level of questions and by accepting answers from a few, can keep the lesson going but is actually out of touch with the understanding of most of the class. The question/answer dialogue becomes a ritual, one in which thoughtful involvement suffers.

There are several ways to break this particular cycle. They involve giving pupils time to respond; asking them to discuss their thinking in pairs or in small groups, so that a respondent is speaking on behalf of others; giving pupils a choice between different possible answers and asking them to vote on the options; asking all of them to write down an answer and then reading out a selected few; and so on. What is essential is that any dialogue should evoke thoughtful reflection in which all pupils can be encouraged to take part, for only then can the formative process start to work. In short, the dialogue between pupils and a teacher should be *thoughtful, reflective, focused to evoke and explore understanding, and conducted so that all pupils have an opportunity to think and to express their ideas.*

Tests given in class and tests and other exercises assigned for homework are also important means of promoting feedback. A good test can be an occasion for learning. It is better to have frequent short tests than infrequent long ones. Any new learning should first be tested within about a week of a first encounter, but more frequent tests are counterproductive. The quality of the test items — that is, their relevance to the main learning aims and their clear communication to the pupil — requires scrutiny as well. Good questions are hard to generate, and teachers should collaborate and draw on outside sources to collect such questions.

Given questions of good quality, it is essential to ensure the quality of the feedback. Research studies have shown that, if pupils are given only marks or grades, they do not benefit from the feedback. The worst scenario is one in which some pupils who get low marks this time also got low marks last time and come to expect to get low marks next time. This cycle of repeated failure becomes part of a shared belief between such students and their teacher. Feedback has been shown to improve learning when it gives each pupil specific guidance on strengths and weaknesses, preferably without any overall marks. Thus the way in which test results are reported to pupils so that they can identify their own strengths and weaknesses is critical. Pupils must be given the means and opportunities to work with evidence of their difficulties. For formative purposes, a test at the end of a unit or teaching module is pointless; it is too late to work with the results. We conclude that *the feedback on tests, seatwork, and homework should give each pupil guidance on how to improve, and each pupil must be given help and an opportunity to work on the improvement.*

All these points make clear that there is no one simple way to improve formative assessment. What is common to them is that a teacher's approach should start by being realistic and confronting the question, "Do I really know enough about the understanding of my pupils to be able to help each of them?"

Much of the work teachers must do to make good use of formative assessment can give rise to difficulties. Some pupils will resist attempts to change accustomed routines, for any such change is uncomfortable, and emphasis on the challenge to think for yourself (and not just to work harder) can be threatening to many. Pupils cannot be expected to believe in the value of changes for their learning before they have experienced the benefits of such changes. Moreover, many of the initiatives that are needed take more class time, particularly when a central purpose is to change the outlook on learning and the working methods of pupils. Thus teachers have to take risks in the belief that such investment of time will yield rewards in the future, while "delivery" and "coverage" with poor understanding are pointless and can even be harmful.

Teachers must deal with two basic issues that are the source of many of the problems associated with changing to a system of formative assessment. The first is *the nature of each teacher's beliefs about learning.* If the teacher assumes that knowledge is to be transmitted and learned, that understanding will develop later, and that clarity of exposition accompanied by rewards for patient reception are the essentials of good teaching, then formative assessment is hardly necessary. However, most teachers accept the wealth of evidence that this transmission model does not work, even when judged by its own criteria, and so are willing to make a commitment to teaching through interaction. Formative assessment is an essential component of such instruction. We do not mean to imply that individualized, one-on-one teaching is the only solution; rather we mean that what is needed is a classroom culture of questioning and deep thinking, in which pupils learn from shared discussions with teachers and peers. What emerges very clearly here is the indivisibility of instruction and formative assessment practices.

The other issue that can create problems for teachers who wish to adopt an interactive model of teaching and learning relates to *the beliefs teachers hold about the potential of all their pupils for learning.* To sharpen the contrast by overstating it, there is on the one hand the "fixed I.Q." view—a belief that each pupil has a fixed, inherited intelligence that cannot be altered much by schooling. On the other hand, there is the "untapped potential" view—a belief that starts from the assumption that so-called ability is a complex of skills that can be learned. Here, we argue for the underlying belief that all pupils can learn more effectively if one can clear away, by sensitive handling, the obstacles to learning, be they cognitive failures never diagnosed or damage to personal confidence or a combination of the two. Clearly the truth lies between these two extremes, but the evidence is that *ways of managing formative assessment that work with the assumptions of "untapped potential" do help all pupils to learn and can give particular help to those who have previously struggled.*

## POLICY AND PRACTICE

*Changing the policy perspective.* The assumptions that drive national and state policies for assessment have to be called into question. The promotion of testing as an important component for establishing a competitive market in education can be very harmful. The more recent shifting of emphasis toward setting targets for all, with assessment providing a touchstone to help check pupils' attainments, is a more mature position. However, we would argue that *there is a need now to move further, to focus on the inside of the "black box" and so to explore the potential of assessment to raise standards directly as an integral part of each pupil's learning work.*

It follows from this view that several changes are needed. First, policy ought to start with a recognition that the prime locus for raising standards is the classroom, so that the overarching priority has to be the promotion and support of change within the classroom. Attempts to raise standards by reforming the inputs to and measuring the outputs from the black box of the classroom can be helpful, but they are not adequate on their own. Indeed, their helpfulness can be judged only in light of their effects in classrooms.

The evidence we have presented here establishes that a clearly productive way to start implementing a classroom-focused policy would be to improve formative assessment. This same evidence also establishes that in doing so we would not be concentrating on some minor aspect of the business of teaching and learning. Rather, we would be concentrating on several essential elements: the quality of teacher/pupil interactions, the stimulus and help for pupils to take active responsibility for their own learning, the particular help needed to move pupils out of the trap of "low achievement," and the development of the habits necessary for all students to become lifelong learners. Improvements in formative assessment, which are within the reach of all teachers, can contribute substantially to raising standards in all these ways.

**Four steps to implementation.** If we accept the argument outlined above, what needs to be done? The proposals outlined below do not follow directly from our analysis of assessment research. They are consistent with its main findings, but they also call on more general sources for guidance.[16]

At one extreme, one might call for more research to find out how best to carry out such work; at the other, one might call for an immediate and large-scale program, with new guidelines that all teachers should put into practice. Neither of these alternatives is sensible: while the first is unnecessary because enough is known from the results of research, the second would be unjustified because not enough is known about classroom practicalities in the context of any one country's schools.

Thus the improvement of formative assessment cannot be a simple matter. There is no quick fix that can alter existing practice by promising rapid rewards. On the contrary, if the substantial rewards promised by the research evidence are to be secured, each teacher must find his or her own ways of incorporating the lessons and ideas set out above into his or her own patterns of classroom work and into the cultural norms and expectations of a particular school community.[17] This process is a relatively slow one and takes place through sustained programs of professional development and support. This fact does not weaken the message here; indeed, it should be seen as a sign of its authenticity, for lasting and fundamental improvements in teaching and learning must take place in this way. A recent international study of innovation and change in education, encompassing 23 projects in 13 member countries of the Organisation for Economic Co-operation and Development, has arrived at exactly the same conclusion with regard to effective policies for

change.[18] Such arguments lead us to propose a four-point scheme for teacher development.

*1. Learning from development.* Teachers will not take up ideas that sound attractive, no matter how extensive the research base, if the ideas are presented as general principles that leave the task of translating them into everyday practice entirely up to the teachers. Their classroom lives are too busy and too fragile for all but an outstanding few to undertake such work. What teachers need is a variety of living examples of implementation, as practiced by teachers with whom they can identify and from whom they can derive the confidence that they can do better. They need to see examples of what doing better means in practice.

So changing teachers' practice cannot begin with an extensive program of training for all; that could be justified only if it could be claimed that we have enough "trainers" who know what to do, which is certainly not the case. The essential first step is to set up a small number of local groups of schools—some primary, some secondary, some inner-city, some from outer suburbs, some rural—with each school committed both to a school-based development of formative assessment and to collaboration with other schools in its local group. In such a process, the teachers in their classrooms will be working out the answers to many of the practical questions that the evidence presented here cannot answer. They will be reformulating the issues, perhaps in relation to fundamental insights and certainly in terms that make sense to their peers in other classrooms. It is also essential to carry out such development in a range of subject areas, for the research in mathematics education is significantly different from that in language, which is different again from that in the creative arts.

The schools involved would need extra support in order to give their teachers time to plan the initiative in light of existing evidence, to reflect on their experience as it develops, and to offer advice about training others in the future. In addition, there would be a need for external evaluators to help the teachers with their development work and to collect evidence of its effectiveness. Video studies of classroom work would be essential for disseminating findings to others.

2. *Dissemination.* This dimension of the implementation would be in low gear at the outset—offering schools no more than general encouragement and explanation of some of the relevant evidence that they might consider in light of their existing practices. Dissemination efforts would become more active as results and resources became available from the development program. Then strategies for wider dissemination—for example, earmarking funds for inservice training programs—would have to be pursued.

We must emphasize that this process will inevitably be a slow one. To repeat what we said above, *if the substantial rewards promised by the evidence are to be secured, each teacher must find his or her own ways of incorporating the lessons and ideas that are set out above into his or her own patterns of classroom work.* Even with optimum training and support, such a process will take time.

3. *Reducing obstacles.* All features in the education system that actually obstruct the development of effective formative assessment should be examined to see how their negative effects can be reduced. Consider the conclusions from a study of teachers of English in U.S. secondary schools:

> Most of the teachers in this study were caught in conflicts among belief systems and institutional structures, agendas, and values. The point of friction among these conflicts was assessment, which was associated with very powerful feelings of being overwhelmed, and of insecurity, guilt, frustration, and anger....This study suggests that assessment, as it occurs in schools, is far from a merely technical problem. Rather, it is deeply social and personal.[19]

The chief negative influence here is that of short external tests. Such tests can dominate teachers' work, and, insofar as they encourage drilling to produce right answers to short, out-of-context questions, they can lead teachers to act against their own better judgment about the best ways to develop the learning of their pupils. This is not to argue that all such tests are unhelpful. Indeed, they have an important role to play in securing public confidence in the accountability of schools. For the immediate future, what is needed in any development program for formative assessment is to study the interactions between these external tests and formative assessments to see how the models of assessment that external tests can provide could be made more helpful.

All teachers have to undertake some summative assessment. They must report to parents and produce end-of-year reports as classes are due to move on to new teachers. However, the task of assessing pupils summatively for external purposes is clearly different from the task of assessing ongoing work to monitor and improve progress. Some argue that these two roles are so different that they should be kept apart. We do not see how this can be done, given that teachers must have some share of responsibility for the former and must take the leading responsibility for the latter.[20] However, teachers clearly face difficult problems in reconciling their formative and summative roles, and confusion in teachers' minds between these roles can impede the improvement of practice.

The arguments here could be taken much further to make the case that teachers should play a far greater role in contributing to summative assessments for accountability. One strong reason for giving teachers a greater role is that they have access to the performance of their pupils in a variety of contexts and over extended periods of time.

This is an important advantage because sampling pupils' achievement by means of short exercises taken under the conditions of formal testing is fraught with dangers. It is now clear that performance in any task varies with the context in which it is presented. Thus some pupils who seem incompetent in tackling a problem under test conditions can look quite different in the more realistic conditions of an everyday encounter with an equivalent problem. Indeed, the conditions under which formal tests are taken threaten validity because they are quite unlike those of everyday performance. An outstanding example here is that collaborative work is very important in everyday life but is forbidden by current norms of formal testing.[21] These points open up wider arguments about assessment systems as a whole—arguments that are beyond the scope of this article.

4. *Research.* It is not difficult to set out a list of questions that would justify further research in this area. Although there are many and varied reports of successful innovations, they generally fail to give clear accounts of one or another of the important details. For example, they are often silent about the actual classroom methods used, the motivation and experience of the teachers, the nature of the tests used as measures of success, or the outlooks and expectations of the pupils involved.

However, while there is ample justification for proceeding with carefully formulated projects, we do not suggest that everyone else should wait for their conclusions. Enough is known to provide a basis for active development work, and some of the most important questions can be answered only through a program of practical implementation.

Directions for future research could include a study of the ways in which teachers understand and deal with the relationship between their formative and summative roles or a comparative study of the predictive validity of teachers' summative assessments versus external test results. Many more questions could be formulated, and it is important for future development that some of these problems be tackled by basic research. At the same time, experienced researchers would also have a vital role to play in the evaluation of the development programs we have proposed.

## ARE WE SERIOUS ABOUT RAISING STANDARDS?

The findings summarized above and the program we have outlined have implications for a variety of responsible agencies. However, it is the responsibility of governments to take the lead. It would be premature and out of order for us to try to consider the relative roles in such an effort, although success would clearly depend on cooperation among government agencies, academic researchers, and school-based educators.

The main plank of our argument is that standards can be raised only by changes that are put into direct effect by teachers and pupils in classrooms. There is a body of firm evidence that formative assessment is an essential component of classroom work and that its development can raise standards of achievement. We know of no other way of raising standards for which such a strong prima facie case can be made. Our plea is that national and state policy makers will grasp this opportunity and take the lead in this direction.

1. James W. Stigler and James Hiebert, "Understanding and Improving Classroom Mathematics Instruction: An Overview of the TIMSS Video Study," *Phi Delta Kappan,* September 1997, pp. 19–20.

2. There is no internationally agreed-upon term here. "Classroom evaluation," "classroom assessment," "internal assessment," "instructional assessment," and "student assessment" have been used by different authors, and some of these terms have different meanings in different texts.

3. Paul Black and Dylan Wiliam, "Assessment and Classroom Learning," *Assessment in Education,* March 1998, pp. 7–74.

4. Lynn S. Fuchs and Douglas Fuchs, "Effects of Systematic Formative Evaluation: A Meta-Analysis," *Exceptional Children,* vol. 53, 1986, pp. 199–208.

5. See Albert E. Beaton et al., *Mathematics Achievement in the Middle School Year*s (Boston: Boston College, 1996).

6. Lynn S. Fuchs et al., "Effects of Task-Focused Goals on Low-Achieving Students with and Without Learning Disabilities," *American Educational Research Journal,* vol. 34, 1997, pp. 513–543.

7. OFSTED (Office for Standards in Education), *Subjects and Standards: Issues for School Development Arising from OFSTED Inspection Findings 1994–5: Key Stages 3 and 4 and Post-16* (London: Her Majesty's Stationery Office, 1996), p. 40.

8. Nicholas Daws and Birendra Singh, "Formative Assessment: To What Extent Is Its Potential to Enhance Pupils' Science Being Realized?," *School Science Review,* vol. 77, 1996, p. 99.

9. Clement Dassa, Jes's Vazquez-Abad, and Djavid Ajar, "Formative Assessment in a Classroom Setting: From Practice to Computer Innovations," *Alberta Journal of Educational Research,* vol. 39, 1993, p. 116.

10. D. Monty Neill, "Transforming Student Assessment," *Phi Delta Kappan,* September 1997, pp. 35–36.

11. *Task Group on Assessment and Testing: A Report* (London: Department of Education and Science and the Welsh Office, 1988).

12. Richard Daugherty, *National Curriculum Assessment: A Review of Policy, 1987–1994* (London: Falmer Press, 1995).

13. Terry A. Russell, Anne Qualter, and Linda McGuigan, "Reflections on the Implementation of National Curriculum Science Policy for the 5–14 Age Range: Findings and Interpretations from a National Evaluation Study in England," *International Journal of Science Education*, vol. 17, 1995, pp. 481–492.

14. Phillipe Perrenoud, "Towards a Pragmatic Approach to Formative Evaluation," in Penelope Weston, ed., *Assessment of Pupils' Achievement: Motivation and School Success* (Amsterdam: Swets and Zeitlinger, 1991), p. 92.

15. D. Royce Sadler, "Formative Assessment and the Design of Instructional Systems," *Instructional Science*, vol. 18, 1989, pp. 119–144.

16. Paul J. Black and J. Myron Atkin, *Changing the Subject: Innovations in Science, Mathematics, and Technology Education* (London: Routledge for the Organisation for Economic Co-operation and Development, 1996); and Michael G. Fullan, with Suzanne Stiegelbauer, *The New Meaning of Educational Change* (London: Cassell, 1991).

17. See Stigler and Hiebert, pp. 19–20.

18. Black and Atkin, op. cit.

19. Peter Johnston et al., "Assessment of Teaching and Learning in Literature-Based Classrooms," *Teaching and Teacher Education*, vol. 11, 1995, p. 359.

20. Dylan Wiliam and Paul Black, "Meanings and Consequences: A Basis for Distinguishing Formative and Summative Functions of Assessment," *British Educational Research Journal*, vol. 22, 1996, pp. 537–548.

21. These points are developed in some detail in Sam Wineburg, "T. S. Eliot, Collaboration, and the Quandaries of Assessment in a Rapidly Changing World," *Phi Delta Kappan*, September 1997, pp. 59–65.

**Table 1**

# Comparing Assessment OF and FOR Learning

### Overview of Key Differences

|  | *Assessment OF Learning* | *Assessment FOR Learning* |
|---|---|---|
| *Reasons for Assessing* | Document individual or group achievement or mastery of standards; measure achievement status at a point in time for purposes of reporting | Promote increases in achievement to help students meet more standards; support ongoing student growth |
| *To Inform* | Others about students | Students about themselves |
| *Focus of Assessment* | Achievement standards for which schools, teachers, and students are held accountable | Specific achievement targets selected by teachers that enable students to build toward standards |
| *Driving Priority* | Accountability | Improvement |
| *Place in Time* | Event after learning | Process during learning |
| *Unique Characteristics* | Secure test often externally scored; test items and scoring procedures standardized for all students | Exercises and scoring criteria are written in student-friendly terms and frequently scored in the classroom; procedures may not be standardized |

*Source:* Adapted from *Understanding School Assessment* (Tables 1.5 and 1.6, pp. 17 and 18), by J. Chappuis and S. Chappuis, 2002, Portland, OR: Assessment Training Institute. Adapted by permission.

## Differences in Assessment Context

| | *Assessment OF Learning* | *Assessment FOR Learning* |
|---|---|---|
| *Primary Users* | Policy makers, program planners, supervisors, teachers | Students, teachers |
| *Typical Uses* | Certify competence or sort students according to achievement for public relations, gatekeeper decisions, grading, graduation, or advancement | Provide students with insight as to how to improve achievement; help teachers diagnose and respond to student needs; help parents see progress over time |
| *Primary Motivator* | Threat of punishment, promise of rewards | Belief that success in learning is achievable |
| *Teacher's Role* | Administer the test carefully to ensure accuracy and comparability of results; use results to help students meet standards; interpret results for parents; teachers also build assessments for report card grading | Transform standards into classroom targets; inform students of targets; build assessments; provide feedback to students; adjust instruction based on results; involve students in assessment |
| *Student's Role* | Study to meet standards; take the test; strive for the highest possible score; avoid failure | Help in setting goals; learn to self-assess; act on classroom assessment results to be able to do better next time |
| *Potential Problems* | Test might not cover curriculum; students can give up in hopelessness; standardized test may narrow taught curriculum | Teacher who has no time, skill, or desire to assess dependably or involve students |

## Differences in Assessment Procedures

| | *Assessment OF Learning* | *Assessment FOR Learning* |
|---|---|---|
| *Timing of Assessment* | Conducted at the end of teaching to gather evidence of learning | Conducted during teaching to influence learning |
| *Frequency of Assessment* | Periodic, often once per year in large-scale testing | Continuous throughout learning |
| *Origin of Assessment* | Test typically developed by a test or text publisher; teachers often develop those used for grading | Typically developed by the teacher and with students involved |
| *Assessment Formats* | Typically rely on selected response or essay formats; some performance assessments used in classroom | Include the full range of methods: selected response, essay, performance assessment, personal communication |
| *Administration* | Standard for all students; typically timed | Variable across students; typically not timed |
| *Scoring* | Teacher or external scoring service | Student and teacher may score in collaboration |
| *Reporting* | Feedback typically delayed, takes the form of a grade or score—a summary judgment | Feedback describes performance as it relates to the assigned task; is immediate; is informative about strengths and how to improve |

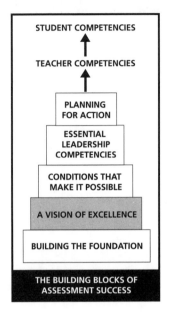

THE BUILDING BLOCKS OF
ASSESSMENT SUCCESS

*A balanced assessment system takes advantage of assessment **of** learning and assessment **for** learning; each can make essential contributions. When both are present in the system, assessment becomes more than just an index of school success. It also serves as the cause of that success.*

*Part Two*

# A VISION OF THE PERFECT ASSESSMENT SYSTEM

American education has been embroiled in a pitched battle with standardized testing since the middle of the twentieth century. We have had immense difficulty agreeing on what to assess, why to assess it, how to assess it, and how to use the results productively to assist learning. It is testimony to our failure to come to terms with the relationship between assessment and effective schools that, in the year 2003, we are unable to present convincing evidence that 60 years of standardized testing has contributed to the improvement of our educational system. This, in spite of the fact that we have spent billions of dollars over the past six decades developing and administering college admissions, district, state, national, and international assessments. Yet, even given this disturbing history, we rush headlong into our first-ever national every-pupil examination system with the implementation of the unprecedented testing requirements of the No Child Left Behind Act.

The time has come to analyze our assessment problems once and for all, figure out the roadblocks to our effective use of assessment, and implement programs that verifiably help educators help students learn.

The purpose of this section of the guide is to orient school leaders to the active ingredients in a truly effective assessment system. Here we provide a unique and powerful vision of excellence in assessment. With this vision in mind, educators can determine where they are now, develop a roadmap to excellence in assessment, and make their journey to a sound, balanced, and instructionally supportive total assessment system.

## Excellence Defined

One challenge we face in this endeavor is defining the standards by which we gauge excellence in assessment. By what criteria does one determine perfection in this domain? What are or should be the attributes of a truly effective assessment system? As it turns out, different judges might provide different answers to these questions.

For example, business leaders and politicians want assessments that tell them if students are learning or not. They pay the bills and want schools held accountable for learning. They intend to reward high test scores and to impose sanctions for low scores. This, they believe, will force school improvement. Thus, by wielding the power of high-stakes tests, they hope to create better schools.

School leaders tend to hold a different view of excellence in assessment. They feel the need to be in compliance with political leaders' demands for high test scores. So they desire an assessment system that permits them to manage their own destiny. For them, perfection is an assessment system where the standards—the focus of the tests—are sufficiently clear that educators can build instructional programs that help students learn more.

Teachers lobby for their own unique features in the perfect assessment system: "Don't take too much instructional time administering tests that are useless to me. I need information that is specific and timely enough to help me diagnose needs and figure out what to do next. Assessment needs to be focused on targets that are clear to me, and it needs to be frequent enough to help me track and support student progress."

The measurement community—those who design and develop assessments for a living—has tended to define excellence in assessment in terms of that which produces the most accurate scores at the lowest possible cost. Test score dependability and assessment efficiency rule. Thus, the perfect system provides these stakeholders with the dependable, low-cost information they need to do their jobs.

Given these different values, it becomes clear that different assessment users need different kinds of information about student achievement in different forms and at different times to do their jobs. No single assessment can meet all of these information needs. For this reason, in this guide, *a high-quality assessment system relies on a variety of assessments to provide timely and understandable information to all who need it, so they can make the instructional decisions that maximize student success.* In this sense, the concept of a "total system" attends carefully to the following:

- Defining the achievement expectations to be assessed
- Understanding who is to use assessment results and how
- Deciding when and how achievement will be assessed
- Communicating results effectively to intended users

In an organization that functions as a system, we know that the system is viewed as a whole, with all component parts connected, each working toward a common purpose. Those component parts affect each other over time, and so actions taken in the system consider all components rather than function as isolated decisions with a narrow focus. We contend that, because of the diverse information needs of instructional decision makers, the only assessment system that can work effectively is one that balances the effective use of periodic standardized tests with the effective use of day-to-day classroom assessment. Either level of assessment by itself will be insufficient because it cannot meet all relevant information needs. We will examine how to balance classroom and standardized assessments in the service of excellence by detailing (1) what they must share if we are to blend them into an integrated system and (2) how their differences can be effectively managed to permit them to work in harmony. But first, we must understand why synergy between classroom and standardized assessments, as depicted in Figure 1, is so critical to promoting the well-being of students. Both levels of assessment serve functionally different purposes in different ways. For either to work we must know what needs to be assessed and how to assess accurately.

## Figure 1

## Assessment Synergy

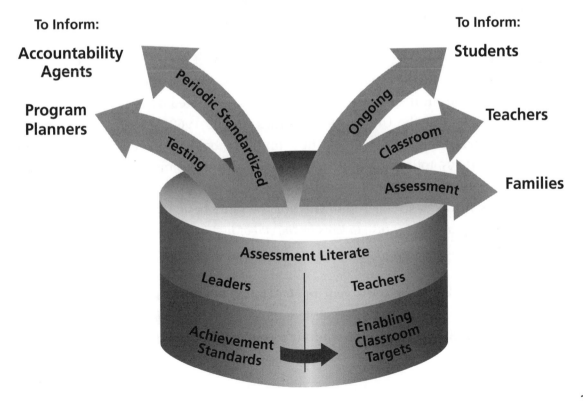

# Why Aspire to Excellence in Assessment?

The evolution of assessment in the United States over the past five decades has led to the strongly held view that school improvement requires the following:

■ Articulation of higher achievement *standards*

■ Transformation of those expectations into accurate *assessments*

■ Expectation that educators will be held *accountable* for student achievement as reflected in test scores

Achievement standards frame accepted or valued definitions of academic success. Assessment provides the evidence of student success. Accountability compels attention to these standards as educators plan and deliver instruction in the classroom.

To drive school improvement forward, policy makers and school leaders have "raised the bar" by setting world-class standards for student achievement. In this context, we rely on high-stakes assessments *of* learning to inform accountability decisions. These tests tell us how much students have learned, whether standards are being met, and if educators have done the job they are hired to do.

## *Historical Perspectives on Excellence in Assessment*

We have been evolving toward this concept of standards-based education for decades. The idea that all students might be held to the same expectations has its origins in the mastery learning models originated by Professor Bloom and his associates at the University of Chicago in the 1960s. The first sweeping application of this thinking took the form of the behavioral objectives movement of the 1970s, followed by the minimum competencies movement of the 1980s and the development of outcomes-based education in the 1990s. Each new iteration has yielded a stronger following for the same basic concepts: *effective schools do more than merely rank students by the end of high school—they maximize the achievement of all students.*

The evolution of assessment in the United States tracks along similar lines. We began with standardized college admissions testing in the early decades of the twentieth century, which continues essentially unchanged today. But these tests are not used merely for college selection. For decades, we have ranked states based on average College Board and ACT scores, based on the contention that these tests can be used to judge school quality. In the 1950s and 1960s, in further response to demands for accountability in public schools, local educators launched districtwide standardized testing programs that also remain in place today. In the 1970s, we began to implement statewide testing programs, which have spread into every state. Also in the 1970s and extending into the 1980s, we added a national assessment program that continues today. During the 1990s, we added criterion-referenced tests aligned to state standards. In addition, we saw growing attention to the results of international assessment programs. Across the nation, across the various levels, and over the decades we have invested billions of dollars to develop, administer, and ensure the accuracy of the scores on these assessments.

In 2001 President Bush signed the No Child Left Behind Act into law, a school reform measure requiring standardized testing of every pupil in the United States in mathematics and reading every year in grades three through eight, once again revealing our faith in assessment *of* learning as a school improvement tool.

Clearly, we have seen scores on standardized tests used as the indicators of school quality. It is testimony to our societal belief in the power of these assessments that we would permit all of these layers of testing to remain in place at the same time and at astronomical costs. Without question, over the decades, policy makers and school leaders have believed that, by demanding universal achievement standards, passing laws requiring demonstration of student mastery as reflected in test scores, checking achievement status with standardized tests, and reporting the results to the public, they can apply the pressure needed to intensify and thus speed school improvement. And as an added benefit, they can provide policy makers and practicing educators with evidence of the level of student learning that can inform the critically important school improvement decisions at district, state, and federal levels.

## The Flaws in the Vision

The evolving assessment environment we have described is a direct manifestation of a set of beliefs about what role assessment ought to play in promoting excellence in American schools. For example, we have believed that assessment should serve two purposes: to inform instructional decisions and to motivate students to learn.

With respect to the former, we have built our assessment systems around the belief that the most important instructional decisions are made by those program planners and policy makers whose decisions span the broadest range of classrooms and students. The broader the reach of the decision makers (such as across an entire school, district, or state), the more imperative it has been that we provide for their information needs first and foremost. Their far-reaching programmatic decisions require evidence of student achievement that is comparable across classrooms and schools, yielding test scores that can be aggregated across schools, districts, and states. This is the foundation of our strong belief in the power of standardized tests. These are the levels of assessment in which we have invested almost exclusively.

With respect to the use of assessment to motivate, we all grew up in classrooms guided by the belief that the way to maximize learning is to maximize anxiety, and assessment has always been the great intimidator. Because of their own very successful personal experiences in ascending to positions of political leadership and authority, many policy makers and school leaders hold the worldview that "when the going gets tough, the tough get going." They learned that the way to succeed when confronted with a tougher challenge is to redouble your efforts—work harder, work smarter—that's how you win! And so, they contend, the way to cause students to learn more, and thus the way to improve schools, is to confront them with a tougher challenge. This will cause them to redouble their efforts, they will learn more, test scores will go up, and schools will become more effective. They can motivate greater effort, they believe, by "setting higher academic standards," "raising the bar," or implementing ever more intense "high-stakes" testing. The foundation of our belief in the power of accountability-oriented standardized tests to drive school improvement is our belief in a particular relationship among challenge, effort, and success.

In point of fact, when confronted with the prospect of tougher standards and the challenge of high-stakes testing, some students do redouble their efforts and they do learn more as a result of this added incentive. For them, the accountability movement and the implementation of high-stakes testing of very high standards works as desired. But please note that this only happens for *some students*.

The critically important point missed by many at the highest levels of educational policy and leadership in the United States: There is another huge segment of our student population who, when confronted with academic standards even tougher than those they have been failing at before, will not redouble their efforts. They will see "raise the bar" standards and high-stakes testing as yet another occasion in which they will be blasted with public evidence of their failure, they will see the standards as personally unattainable, and *they will give up in hopelessness.*

Because of their personal experiences of achieving success in life, many political and school leaders have never experienced the painful, embarrassing, and discouraging effect of chronic and public academic failure. As a result, they have no way to understand how a high-stakes testing program, whether local or state, could lead, not to success, but to even greater failure for large numbers of students. For those students, our attempt to tap the intimidation power of the standardized tests for public accountability has exactly the opposite effect on their success as we intend or desire: it causes them to learn even less.

Thus, it is folly to build our assessment environments on the assumption that standardized testing will have a desirable, or even the same, effect on all students. It will not. Some students approach the tests with a strong personal academic history and an expectation of success. Others approach with a personal history and expectation of ongoing and very painful failure. Some come to slay the dragon, while others expect to be devoured by it. As a result, high-stakes assessment will work to enhance the learning of some while discouraging others and causing them to give up. Yet, as they attempt to weave assessment into the school improvement equation, federal, state, and local policy makers seem unable to understand or to accommodate this critically important difference.

The policy question we must ask is, What is our responsibility with respect to those students who are giving up in hopelessness? Shall we merely write them off as collateral damage or might we consider a different kind of assessment environment that brings them hope? In the schools that educated most of us, our graduating classes included a valedictorian at the top, a salutatorian next, everyone had a rank in class, and our parents would judge the system to have "worked again." This result was consistent with the assigned mission of school in society: sort students into the various segments of our social and economic system.

Please understand that, given that mission, if some of our classmates gave up in hopelessness, that was regarded as acceptable because they would finish low in the rank order. In our high schools, there were the winners and the devil take the hindmost. We didn't grow up in schools designed to "leave no child behind." In fact, we grew up in just the opposite environment.

But now we have a new assignment: help every student become a competent reader, writer, and math problem solver. Help all students meet standards. Given that mission, if we have some students giving up hopelessness, they and we are in trouble. Now we must rely on assessment, not merely to produce a dependable sorting of students, but to foster their success. This requires a fundamental re-evaluation of the role of assessment in learning. The vision of excellence in assessment depicted in this guide describes that new role.

## Consider a More Powerful Vision

There is a way in which assessment can contribute to the development of effective schools that has been largely ignored in the evolution of the standards, assessment, and accountability scenario described here. We combine our high-stakes standardized assessments *of* learning with other assessments to be used *for* learning (Assessment Reform Group, 1999). Whereas assessment *of* learning as described provides an index of school success, assessment *for* learning serves to help students learn more. Assessment becomes more than an index of school success, it becomes a cause of school success. The crucial distinction is between *assessment to determine the status of learning* and *assessment to promote greater learning*.

A truly high-quality assessment system takes advantage of both assessment *of* and *for* learning, as both can make essential contributions. Since, in general, we have our standardized tests in place, to balance the two we must make a much stronger investment in assessment *for* learning in the United States.

Compelling research evidence, presented in the following section, reveals that we can realize unprecedented gains in student achievement if we take advantage of day-to-day classroom assessment as the powerful tool for learning that it can be. We know that schools will be held accountable for raising test scores. Now we must provide teachers with the assessment tools needed to do the job.

## What Is "Assessment for Learning"?

It is tempting to equate this concept with our more common term, *formative assessment.* But they are not the same. Assessment *for* learning is about far more than testing more frequently or providing teachers with evidence so they can revise instruction, although these are part of it. In addition, we now understand that assessment *for* learning must actively involve students.

When they assess *for* learning, teachers use classroom assessment and the continuous flow of information about student achievement that it provides to advance, not merely check on, student learning. They accomplish this by doing the following:

- Understanding and articulating *in advance of teaching* the achievement targets that their students are to hit.
- Informing their students about those learning goals *in terms that students understand* from the very beginning.
- Becoming assessment literate so they can transform those expectations into assessment exercises and scoring procedures that *accurately reflect student achievement.*
- Using classroom assessments *to build student confidence* in themselves as learners, helping them take responsibility for their own learning so as to lay a foundation for lifelong learning.
- Translating classroom assessment results into *frequent, descriptive (versus judgmental) feedback* for students, providing them with specific insights regarding their strengths as well as how to improve.
- Continuously *adjusting instruction* based on the results of classroom assessments.
- Engaging students in *regular self-assessment* with standards held constant so they can watch themselves grow over time and thus learn to become in charge of their own success.
- Actively *involving students in communicating* with their teachers and their families about their achievement status and improvement.
- Making sure that students understand *how the achievement targets* that they strive to hit now *relate to those that will come after.*

In short, the effect of assessment *for* learning as it plays out in the classroom is that students succeed, and they remain confident that they can continue to learn at productive levels if they keep trying. They don't give up in frustration. They persist because it's working.

## Teachers Are Not Prepared to Assess for Learning

Few teachers are prepared to face the challenges of classroom assessment, because they have not been given the opportunity to learn to do so. It is currently the case that only a few states explicitly require competence in assessment as a condition to be licensed to teach. There is not a licensing examination currently in place at the state or federal level in the United States that verifies competence in classroom assessment. Since teacher preparation programs are designed to prepare candidates for certification in these terms, the vast majority of programs fail to provide the assessment literacy required to fulfill the tenets listed previously. It has been so for decades.

Further, lest we believe that teachers can turn to their principals for help, it is currently the case that almost no states require competence in assessment to be licensed to be a principal or school administrator at any level. As a result, assessment training is almost nonexistent in administrator training programs. Again, it has been so for decades.

As a result, we remain a national faculty unschooled in the principles of sound assessment, whether *of* or *for* learning. To date, as a nation, we have invested almost nothing in assessment *for* learning. Teachers rarely have the opportunity to learn how to use assessment as a teaching and learning tool. And our vigorous assessment *of* learning in the context of our various layers of standardized tests cannot overcome the effects of information missing through a lack of assessment *for* learning.

As a result, we face the danger that student progress may be mismeasured, day to day, in classrooms across the nation. The critically important day-to-day instructional decisions made by students, teachers, and parents may be based on misinformation about student achievement. The result will be the misdiagnosis of student needs, student misunderstanding of their own ability to learn, miscommunication to parents and others about student progress, and virtually no effective assessment *for* learning in classrooms. The harmful consequences for student learning are obvious.

# The Great Promise of Balanced Assessment Systems

The critical school improvement question is this: What would happen to standardized test scores if we brought classroom assessment *for* learning online as a full partner in support of school improvement? Several published reviews of research reveal the very encouraging answer.

## Research Results

In 1984, Bloom provided a summary of research on the impact of mastery learning models comparing standard whole-class instruction (the control condition) with two experimental interventions, a mastery learning environment and one-on-one tutoring of individual students. One hallmark of both experimental conditions was extensive use of classroom assessment *for* learning as a key part of instruction. The analyses revealed differences ranging from one to two standard deviations in student achievement favoring the assessment *for* learning experimental conditions.

You will recall the 1998 research review presented in Part 1. Black and Wiliam examined the research literature on assessment worldwide, asking if there is evidence that improving the quality and effectiveness of use of formative (classroom) assessments raises student achievement as reflected in summative assessments. If so, they asked, what kinds of improvements in classroom assessment practice are likely to yield the greatest gains in achievement?

They uncovered and then synthesized over 250 articles that addressed these issues. Of these, several dozen directly addressed the question of impact on student learning with sufficient scientific rigor and experimental control to permit firm conclusions. Pooling the information on the estimated effects of improved formative assessment on summative test scores, they discovered unprecedented positive effects on student achievement. They report effect sizes of a half to a full standard deviation. Further, Black and Wiliam (1998) report that "improved formative assessment helps low achievers more than other students and so reduces the range of achievement while raising achievement overall." *This result has direct implications for districts seeking to reduce achievement gaps between minorities and other students.* We know of no other school improvement innovation that can claim effects of this nature or this size.

This research reveals that these achievement gains are maximized in contexts where educators do the following:

■ Increase the accuracy of classroom assessments

■ Provide students with frequent informative feedback (versus judgmental feedback)

■ Involve students deeply in classroom assessment, record keeping, and communication, especially low-achieving students

In short, students learn a lot more when teachers apply the principles of assessment *for* learning as a matter of routine in their classrooms.

## Anticipating the Benefits of Balance

Students benefit from balancing assessment *of* learning with assessment *for* learning in several critical ways. First, they become more confident learners because they get to watch themselves succeeding. This permits them to take the risk of continuing to try to learn. The result will be greater achievement for all students—especially low achievers, thus yielding a reduction in the achievement gap that has separated middle and low socioeconomic–status students. Further, they come to understand what it means to be in charge of their own learning—to monitor their own success and make decisions that bring greater success—the foundation of lifelong learning.

Teachers benefit because their students become more highly motivated to learn. Further, their instructional decisions are informed by more accurate information about student achievement, increasing the power or impact of those assessments. Teachers benefit from the time savings that result from their ability to develop and use classroom assessments with increased efficiency.

Parents benefit in seeing greater enthusiasm for learning in their children, seeing greater achievement, and understanding that their children are learning to manage themselves as learners.

School administrators and instructional leaders benefit from the reality of meeting accountability standards and the public recognition of doing so.

Political officials benefit in the same way. Schools work more effectively and they are recognized as contributing to that outcome.

In other words, everyone wins! There are no losers. There are no compelling arguments against balance. But the price that we must pay to achieve such benefits is an investment in teachers and their classroom assessment practices in balance with our ongoing investment in standardized testing. Only then can we achieve the perfect assessment system.

# The Foundations and Structure of a Quality Assessment System

To build and implement the perfect assessment system, with its classroom and standardized assessment components working in harmony, several issues must be addressed. The systems development and ongoing implementation must be guided by a set of three fundamental beliefs about the role of assessment in student learning. Four active ingredients must become operational. Several necessary conditions must be satisfied.

## A Foundation of Strong Beliefs

All assessment events that take place within a truly effective assessment system must arise from the following three beliefs about schools, assessment, and learners. These three beliefs must drive all dimensions of the system. If any are disregarded, the system will remain ineffective.

1. *The mission of school is to promote maximum student success—it is not merely to produce a rank order of students.*

The educator's purpose must be to bring as many students as possible to their highest possible level of achievement. This was not the purpose or mission of the schools in which most adults today grew up. We were reared in schools in which the quality of our schools and our teachers was judged by their ability to produce a dependable rank order of students by the end of high school. Since these were schools specifically designed to leave some students behind, they are no longer acceptable in today's society. We aspire to schools that leave no child behind. The perfect assessment system assists in the completion of this mission by translating clear and appropriate achievement targets into accurate assessments that are used to inform instructional decisions and to keep students striving for success.

2. *All students can learn—but they will not all start at the same place, learn at the same rate, or ascend to the same ultimate level of achievement.*

It will never be the case that all students' will learn the same things at the same rate to the same level of mastery. In other words, because we will never attain equity of academic ability, we will never attain equity of academic achievement. But this does not mean that we permit students or ourselves to give up in hopelessness. Rather, based on the belief that all students can learn at a rate and to a level appropriate for them, we aspire to equity of motivation. The perfect assessment system keeps students, their teachers, and others informed of their growth, as that growth varies across individuals. In addition, it uses assessment to keep students believing that they can keep learning if they keep trying.

3. *Learning doesn't happen merely because adults demand it—rather, learners must want to learn, feel able to learn, see learning as worth the effort needed to achieve it.*

Instituting accountability for learning, by itself, cannot create good schools. Decades of evaluating its sufficiency in district, state, national, and international assessment programs should have told us this by now. Merely instructing educators and students that annual test scores must go up and then threatening dire consequences if they do not, does little by itself to improve the quality of schools. As the saying goes, you don't fatten the hog merely by weighing it. Rather, we must intervene in the system to cause change to happen. We didn't put men on the moon by building a great telescope through which to watch them land. We built, tested, and implemented systems to put them there, continually evaluating and adjusting their progress. Doctors don't cure patients just by checking lab tests. They intervene with pharmacological treatments and use the lab tests to see if the treatments are working. Schools will not maximize learning merely by testing it once a year. We get good schools by intervening in the classroom to promote greater achievement. In the perfect system, we use assessment to check for achievement, to be sure. But in addition, we use assessment to promote learning.

## A System of Active Ingredients

The development of the perfect assessment system requires the careful assembly of four active ingredients coordinated to function together.

*1. Proper academic achievement standards must guide all assessment.*

Primary among the ingredients is a fundamental vision of the meaning of academic success—a set of achievement standards detailing a local vision of academic success understood and embraced by all.

This vision must focus on standardized and classroom assessment. We cannot assess (or teach!) achievement that we have not defined. To reach the goal of establishing clear and appropriate achievement expectations, a school district must establish competencies for high school graduation, create a K–12 curriculum map leading to those competencies, and verify that every teacher is, in fact, a master of the achievement targets his or her students are expected to hit.

### Differences in Treatment of Standards

Although classroom and standardized assessments must arise from the same set of academic achievement standards, they must treat those standards in fundamentally different ways. State assessments, for example, consist of exercises and rely on scoring schemes that ask students to demonstrate that they actually have met state standards. They lead to conclusions regarding student mastery of those standards. They lead to decisions about competence and school effectiveness in bringing students to competence.

However, that should *not* be the focus of classroom assessment. The teacher's classroom assessment job is not to create mini-versions of the state assessment, nor is it to practice old state assessments. Rather, the teacher's classroom assessment job is to evaluate student mastery of the classroom-level achievement targets that underpin student success in working up to a place where they are ready to demonstrate that they have met the state standard. To do this, district curriculum must be developed that is linked to state standards and addresses the following four questions:

- What do our students need to *know and understand* to be ready to demonstrate that they have met the standards when the time comes to do so? In other words, what are the knowledge foundations of students' success here?

- What *patterns of reasoning*, if any, must our students be in control of to be successful when the time comes to demonstrate mastery of this competence?

- What *performance skills*, if any, must our students have mastered prior to the time when they must demonstrate that they have met this standard?

- What *product development capabilities*, if any, must our students be ready to bring into play when they are assessed on mastery of this standard?

These should be the focus of classroom instruction and assessments *for* learning. They represent the building blocks that lead up to competence, the scaffolding students climb over time to ascend to competence. Students never come instantaneously to mastery of a standard. Rather, they build toward it over time. Day-to-day classroom assessment must take them along the journey to a standardized-test demonstration of competence. This is the synergy we seek in a perfect system.

*2. The information needs of all users must be honored.*

If the purpose of assessment is to gather information about student achievement, then it is always relevant to ask precisely what information is needed by whom to inform what decision(s). Without an answer, it is impossible to devise an assessment system that will yield all or even most of what is needed.

In fact, a variety of different people use assessment results to serve a variety of fairly important uses. No single assessment can meet everyone's information needs. There are policy-level users, instructional-support users, and classroom-level users. As a universal foundation of excellence, the perfect assessment system must be responsive to the information needs of all users.

### Differences in Intended Users

Within this foundation, however, once again we find important differences between classroom and standardized assessment. The users are different, but they must work in harmony.

For example, when standardized tests are administered, they typically are intended to provide information to various decision makers about student achievement. Those include policy and instructional-support decisions. Often the results are used to inform parents and the larger community about student achievement. Typically, students are not on the list of active users. Rather, we seek to inform others about students.

When evidence of achievement is gathered and used in the context of classroom assessment *for* learning, we intend to inform students about themselves. In this case, we seek to inform students about the continuous changes in their achievement to permit them to feel in control of that growth.

Both purposes are important. We strive to use the student's sense of being personally responsible for hitting the target (accountability) together with the student's confident sense that she or he can, in fact, master the required material to underpin ultimate success. We document growth over time with an eye toward demonstrating competence periodically. Synergy.

Thus, among these different users, we must remain keenly aware of student uses of assessment. We almost never think of students as assessment users, let alone as instructional decision makers. Most often, we think of them as the objects (or victims) of assessment. They decide whether to try to learn based on their beliefs about their chances of success in learning if they do try. They determine that probability based on their prior record of success; that is, based on the assessment evidence that they receive from their teachers about their achievement. In other words, they decide whether they are capable of learning. And, based on their judgment, they decide whether to take the risk of trying to learn. Everything about school effectiveness turns on our ability to keep students confident enough to keep trying. That makes students the most important assessment users.

*3. Accurate assessments are essential.*

If decision makers are to fulfill the various roles spelled out previously, then all of them must have access to dependable information about student achievement. Quality assessments are a must in the perfect assessment system—both for standardized and classroom assessments. We can develop and use high-quality assessments only if we formulate and apply rigorous standards of quality. To apply those standards consistently within their contexts, teachers and administrators must have the opportunity to learn about and practice using them. In short, they must become *assessment literate*.

This means they need to be ready to apply five assessment quality control standards, used to judge accuracy, which are outlined in more detail in Part 4. They take the form of the five questions that one can ask about any assessment. Are we clear about *what* we want to assess? Do we know *why* we're assessing? Are we sure about *how* to assess? Have we gathered *enough* evidence? Have we controlled for *bias* in results? Answers to these questions help us judge and maximize the quality of our classroom and standardized assessments, and thus, student well-being (Stiggins, 2001).

*4. Effective communication is required.*

The mission of schools is to help all students progress toward mastery of state achievement standards. If teachers and schools are to track student progress using classroom assessments along with periodic standardized tests, our academic record-keeping strategies must be able to store, summarize, and report information about student mastery of specific standards. Merely communicating by means of A, B, C, etc., letter grades connected to very broad course titles will not accomplish this.

Further, if we want students to track and communicate about their own improvement as learners, we need to implement information management and communication systems that students can use. Historically, our communication systems have not included a role for students. In the future they must because of the critically important instructional decisions students make.

To be effective at any of this, whether sharing classroom or standardized assessment information, our district and classroom communication systems must arise from a communication environment in which the following are true:

- Message sender and message receiver must share a common understanding of the achievement target.
- The assessments used to gather information about achievement must be accurate.

- Message sender and message receiver must understand the symbols used to convey information (e.g., scores or grades) to mean the same thing.
- Message receivers must be open to hearing and understanding the information being shared.

### Differences in the Nature and Communication of Results

In compiling and sharing information about student achievement, once again, we uncover differences between classroom and standardized assessment. For instance, evidence of learning gathered via standardized tests is specifically intended for summary across student groups so as to inform decisions about group performance. For this reason, results must be comparable. So all students respond to the same exercises under the same conditions. All student papers are scored in exactly the same manner. The resulting scores have the same meaning across all students and groups of students. This is necessitated by the intended use of results.

However, this standard of comparability need not apply in the classroom. Instead, classroom assessments may rely on exercises and conditions of administration that are unique to an individual student or a particular group of students. As long as the evidence is accurate (i.e., comes from a high-quality assessment) and has clear and important meaning to student and teacher, then effective assessment is at hand. As long as those results suggest proper action on the part of both—action that will result in greater achievement—sound practice is in place.

In addition, there is another sense of difference in the nature of results. Standardized tests *of* learning are intended to serve as a dipstick into student achievement at a particular point in time. The experience of taking the assessment does not change achievement. However, when we speak of classroom assessment *for* learning, our goal is to use the very process to change student achievement. By involving them in assessment, record keeping, and communication, we help students learn more as a result of that involvement.

# The Necessary Conditions

Considering the fundamental beliefs that must permeate the system and the key ingredients that will make it work, we can identify conditions that must be satisfied for the balanced system to come into existence and flourish.

*1. The system must confront and resolve teacher qualifications.*

The perfect assessment system is achievable only if we acknowledge and address two long-standing realities about teacher and administrator preparedness to assess well.

- *Some teachers are assigned teaching responsibilities in academic domains for which they are not prepared.*

When this happens they don't understand the achievement targets that their students are expected to hit. They cannot connect their instruction or classroom assessments to relevant state standards because they don't see a vision of ultimate success for their students, nor do they see the path there. When this is true, they are incapable of dependably assessing the achievement of their students.

To illustrate why this issue must be addressed, consider the results of research reported by Ingersoll (1999). He investigated the faculties of 2000 high schools across the United States and reported that 20 percent of those assigned teaching responsibilities in social studies completed neither a major nor a minor in this field during training. This also was true for 20 percent of science teachers, 25 percent of English teachers, and 33 percent of mathematics teachers. One cannot and should not conclude from this that all of these teachers are ineffective. Some may have mastered the material on their own. But nevertheless, these data do suggest that some students may be working in classrooms where their achievement is being mismeasured because of the state of their teacher's preparation.

Thus there is the danger that some students are trapped in classrooms in which their achievement may be systematically mismeasured because their teacher does not understand that which is to be assessed.

■ *Educators (teachers and administrators at all levels) generally have not been given the opportunity to become assessment literate.*

In the year 2003, as mentioned previously, it is still the case that few states require competence in assessment as a condition to be licensed to teach, and almost no states require competence in assessment for administrator licensure. Teacher and administrator preparation programs to date have not been able to deliver into the profession educators prepared to fulfill their critically important assessment responsibilities. This represents the most prominent barrier to the creation of a perfect assessment system. Quality remains out of reach to those unable to recognize, let alone aim for it.

*2. Every assessment must build student confidence and teacher efficacy.*

Every assessment event, whether classroom or standardized assessment, must leave every student believing that she or he is a capable learner. This can be accomplished when the evidence produced reveals improvement. In addition, each assessment must leave teachers believing that they can contribute productively to student success. If students or teachers come out of any assessment feeling hopeless, they will stop trying. Those who stop trying stop learning.

Some of the specific circumstances that can *lead to hopelessness for students* are these:
■ A lack of understanding of precisely what is expected by way of achievement
■ A sense that they have no opportunity to learn the expected material
■ A record of failure over time that leads to a sense of futility
■ A sense of being doomed to fail from the start because of a lack of mastery of prerequisites
■ A sense that effort invested to learn does not pay off with assessment success
■ A sense that their real achievement has been mismeasured
■ The feeling that failure resulted, not from a lack of learning, but from other personal factors or conflicts

Some of the circumstances that can *rob teachers of their sense of self-efficacy* in the classroom are these:
■ A lack of understanding of precisely what is expected by way of achievement
■ A lack of resources needed to promote learning

- A lack of helpful, growth-producing supervision, particularly during early years of teaching
- A record of student failure to learn that leads to a sense of futility
- The sense that students lack the prerequisites needed to succeed, so success is beyond reach
- An apparent inability to get students to want to learn or to try
- The feeling that competence as a teacher is being incorrectly evaluated by a supervisor
- The sense that effort invested in teaching is not paying off with student success

While the perfect assessment system cannot counter all potential sources of students' and teachers' feelings of not being in control of their own destiny, the thoughtful use of high-quality classroom and standardized assessments can make major contributions to everyone's sense of self-efficacy. For example, by developing and publicly communicating clear and appropriate achievement expectations, schools make clear for all involved the definition of success. All guesswork is removed, allowing students and teachers to understand and aspire to the same vision of academic excellence.

Or, by mapping and publicizing a grade-to-grade curriculum as the foundation for continuous assessment, and by accommodating the differences in the pace of student learning along the journey to becoming an effective reader or writer, schools permit student and teacher to achieve continuous success. The hopelessness of being left behind is held at bay as both students and teachers see the energy invested paying off with success.

By making sure a solid foundation of assessment literacy is in place throughout the system, we reduce the possibility of mismeasuring either student or teacher performance and maximize the probability of appropriate decision making, and thus increase the chances of learning success.

In these and other ways, the perfect assessment system permits both students and teachers to retain the hope that, if they continue to take the risk of trying to succeed, learning will result.

*3. Every assessment must accommodate differences among students.*

One of the realities mentioned is that, while all students can learn, they will not all start at the same place, learn at the same rate, or ascend to the same ultimate level of proficiency. This is because of differences in academic ability, interests, and commitments. The perfect assessment system will accommodate these by providing a continuous-progress curriculum and then by relying on assessment, record-keeping, and communication processes that provide accurate information in a timely manner that adjusts to student needs.

This need to accommodate certainly manifests itself with those students who bring special needs to the classroom. Those with learning challenges are entitled to special accommodations in assessment procedures that are consistent with the stipulations of their individual educational plans. This represents an entitlement granted to them as a matter of law. But in a perfect assessment system, there is more.

For example, in a perfect system, students with learning disabilities are never held accountable for meeting standards that they have no hope of achieving. Specifically, that means that they are never given a test consisting of exercises on which they are doomed to fail. For instance, when they are given test exercises that they cannot even read, let alone respond to, hopelessness results. When the test is written in a language that they don't speak, discouragement and then hopelessness result. The effect of doing these kinds of things can be devastating to their confidence in themselves as learners. Hopelessness brings an end to their willingness to risk trying to learn. To counter this, in a perfect system, these students complete standardized tests when everyone is sure they are ready to demonstrate competence. Thus, the assessment is intended to corroborate what is already known about the student's achievement.

Accommodations also are needed for those who bring diverse cultural or linguistic backgrounds to the classroom. In assessment contexts, the danger of bias is strong. Accurate assessment is only possible if exercises and scoring procedures are developed and applied in ways that ensure the collection of dependable information.

For all students, from those most academically challenged to the most gifted, the perfect assessment system accommodates their rate of achievement, always presenting opportunities to demonstrate success at learning when that success is achieved—not before or long after.

*4. Assessments must reveal trends in student achievement over time.*

In a perfect assessment system, periodic standardized assessments *of* learning and continuous classroom assessments *for* learning, each reflective of enabling achievement targets or standards, feed information about the achievement of individual students into an information management system that shows where each student is at any point in time in making the journey through the continuous-progress curriculum. This reservoir of information is used in calculated ways—in its entirety or in summary form—to help decision makers keep all students believing that they can keep learning if they keep trying—regardless of the pace of their development or how other students are progressing. In all cases, student, teacher, and family remain in touch with the student's improvement over time.

Periodically, evidence of achievement is aggregated across students to reflect group performance for public reporting. That evidence can be presented in both criterion- and norm-referenced ways and will influence important programmatic decisions. But once again, the evidence is interpreted in terms of how performance today compares to performance at a previous time. Only then can the public see viable evidence of school effectiveness.

*5.  Communities must understand and support sound assessment practices.*

In the perfect assessment system, those stakeholders in school quality who are not professional educators, such as parents, taxpayers, and politicians, also know and understand sound assessment practice. While they are not able to apply those practices as teachers and administrators can and must, they understand that assessments gather evidence of student learning for purposes of instructional planning—not just to assign grades and raise annual test scores (although those will be among the effects of implementing sound practices). It is only with this kind of understanding that community members will sign off on implementing sound practices in ways that permit their use in the classroom and school.

This requires community education. The schools that most parents and taxpayers grew up in aspired to a sort and select mission. Some students were destined to be left behind. Teachers were evaluated in terms of their ability to spread students along a normal distribution of achievement—a few high grades, a few low, and lots in the middle. Assessment fed a grading system that served to sort, with rewards going to the uppermost and punishments to the hindmost. Giving too many high grades was considered to be grade inflation, and was deemed problematic because it violated the mission of schooling.

Today, however, we aspire to a different mission, as described. We seek to compress the normal distribution toward the high end of achievement. We no longer aspire to a normal distribution of grades. Higher grades over time become the desired end. We want all students to become competent readers, writers, math problem solvers, users of science, and the like. Community members must come to understand this change in mission. They need to understand that the new mission places a huge premium on accurate, continuous day-to-day classroom assessment—something in which we have not yet invested.

Therefore, those in positions of instructional leadership must have the capacity to understand, interpret, and communicate effectively about both classroom and standardized assessment. They need to understand the strengths and limitations of each. Only then can they bring the community along. But again, we have not invested in developing in administrators the foundation of assessment literacy they must have to fulfill this important community relations role. Communities need to know this. They need to be educated about the current state of assessment affairs. They need to become supporters of immediate professional development in this arena.

In short, in the perfect assessment system, communities are not stuck in a bygone era of assessment. They understand the advances in our understanding of sound assessment practice that have occurred over the past decade and they support the resulting changes in evidence gathering, information management, and effective communication.

## *Relevant Policy Statements*

The need to include classroom assessment as a school improvement practice has received widespread support but less concrete action. For example, during the 1990s, virtually every professional association that had anything to do with teaching adopted standards of professional competence for teachers that included an assessment component. This group includes the American Federation of Teachers (AFT), the National Education Association (NEA), the Council of Chief State School Officers (CCSSO), the National Board for Professional Teaching Standards (NBPTS), and the National Council on Measurement in Education (NCME).

The documents issued included a joint statement of assessment competencies for teachers developed by a committee representing AFT, NEA, and NCME (1990). In addition to other standards, this joint statement expects teachers to be trained to choose and develop proper assessment methods; to administer, score, and interpret assessment results; to connect those results to specific decisions; to assign grades appropriately; and to communicate effectively about student achievement. It is troubling to realize that these standards are more than a decade old and still have had little impact on the professional preparation of teachers and administrators.

In its 2001 report (Pellegrino, Chudowsky, and Glaser, 2001), the Committee on the Foundations of Assessment of the National Research Council advanced recommendations for the development of assessment in American schools that included the following:

> *Recommendation #9: Instruction in how students learn and how learning can be assessed should be a major component of teacher preservice and professional development programs.* This training should be linked to actual experience in classrooms in assessing and interpreting the development of student competence. To ensure that this occurs, state and national standards for teacher licensure and program accreditation should include specific requirements focused on the proper integration of learning and assessment in teachers' educational experience.

> *Recommendation #11: The balance of mandates and resources should be shifted from an emphasis on external forms of assessment to an increased emphasis on classroom formative assessment designed to assist learning.*

Similarly, the Commission on Instructionally Supportive Assessment (2001) convened by the American Association of School Administrators, the National Association of Elementary School Principals, the National Association of Secondary School Principals, the NEA, and the National Middle School Association included the following in its list of nine requirements for state-mandated accountability tests:

> *Requirement #8: A state must ensure that educators receive professional development focused on how to optimize children's learning based on the results of instructionally supportive assessment.*

In 2003, the NEA, in collaboration with the Assessment Training Institute, published *Balanced Assessment: The Key to Accountability and Improving Student Learning.* In it the NEA calls for balanced assessment systems that meet the needs of multiple stakeholders, and explains the role of classroom assessment in a balanced system and how it can be used to improve student learning.

We understand what teachers need to know and the proficiencies that they need to develop to be able to establish and maintain productive assessment environments. The challenge we face is to provide the opportunity for teachers to master those essential classroom assessment competencies. The depth of this challenge becomes clear when we realize that we must provide learning opportunities for both teachers new to the profession to gain the competencies before they enter the classroom and for experienced teachers who had no chance to master them during their training.

## Summary: How to Leave Lots of Students Behind

It is a lofty goal to aspire to excellence in assessment systems. But is it realistic? Can the perfect system be achieved in fact? Perhaps we could aspire to a "good" system, or perhaps even a "very good" or "excellent" system on our way to perfect. To understand how essential *perfect* is to student well-being, consider how counterproductive an assessment system that violates any of the preceding criteria would be in a standards-driven educational environment. It is virtually certain that we will leave lots of students behind if we continue to develop and implement systems that do any or all of the following:

1.  Arise from mistaken fundamental beliefs, such as
    - Serving a mission of merely ranking students versus maximizing their competence
    - Assuming that all students are alike and must be assessed in exactly the same manner
    - Believing that the way to maximize learning is to maximize intimidation and anxiety
2.  Disregard the four important ingredients in a sound assessment system, such as by
    - Focusing on unclear or inappropriate achievement standards
    - Failing to meet the information needs of important assessment users, thus leading to poor-quality instructional decision making
    - Relying on inaccurate information about student achievement due to inept assessment
    - Communicating about student achievement in an ineffective manner
3.  Fail to have in place key necessary conditions, such as by
    - Counting on teachers who are not masters of the targets that their students are expected to hit or who are not assessment literate
    - Using assessment practices that have the effect of destroying student confidence in themselves as learners or that rob teachers of their sense of self-efficacy
    - Failing to accommodate differences in the assessment needs of students
4.  Fail to track and clearly report progress or improvement in learning, whether short or long term
5.  Lack community understanding of and support for sound assessment practices

## Time for Action

We cannot cite a single context in the United States or Canada in which such a perfect assessment system exists today. But we can see it very clearly and we are confident that it can be created. To accomplish this would *require* the following:

- A responsible community of professional educators ready to learn and grow
- Academic achievement expectations (standards and enabling achievement targets) clearly articulated and embraced by all
- An assessment-literate faculty and leadership team

The *costs* of designing and developing such as system include the following:
■ Time for grade-to-grade curriculum development
■ Time and materials for collaborative professional development in
  1. Content-area expertise for teachers who need it
  2. Sound assessment practices for all
■ Resources for purchasing or developing and installing an information management system and training for system use
■ Resources for standardized testing
■ Time to develop community understanding of and commitment to sound assessment practices

The *benefits* to expect from such a system are legion. We begin with greater teacher efficacy and satisfaction, leading to stability on the job. This supports retention of quality faculty in times of teacher shortage. In addition, students benefit from enhanced quality of instructional decision making at all levels. The result will be greater productivity. But perhaps the greatest benefits are greater student confidence, motivation, and effort, leading directly to unprecedented gains in student achievement—for all students, but especially for low achievers, helping to close achievement gaps. This in turn leads to everyone's goal: accountable schools that demonstrate they are improving.

To ensure victory in all of these arenas, school districts must find their balance by conducting an *institutional self-study,* to determine where they are now in relation to a balanced vision of excellence in assessment:
1. Do we understand and embrace the appropriate foundational beliefs? What are our beliefs about assessment's role in school improvement?
2. Is our achievement standards house in order as a foundation for dependable assessment?
3. Do we understand and serve the information needs of all assessment users?
4. As we assessment literate? Are our assessments accurate?
5. Do we communicate effectively about student achievement, delivering information in a timely and understandable form to all users?
6. Do our policies support and demand the effective use of high-quality assessment throughout the system?
7. Are we prepared to get teachers and administrators the assessment literacy they need?
8. Do we use assessment and its results to build student and teacher confidence or to destroy it?

9. Do we accommodate differences in the starting place, rate, and upper limits of student learning?
10. Are we tuned in to trends in student achievement over time, both day to day in the classroom and annually with our standardized tests?
11. Could we educate our community in the essentials of the perfect assessment system and gain support for its development?

Each of the standards for excellence in assessment systems framed here must be regarded as essential. They cannot be regarded as negotiable. If any is missing the system cannot work effectively and students may harmed. Most systems in place today violate at least some, if not many, of these standards. Our collective mission as leaders of school improvement is to gather the will and the resources needed to instill a new vision.

Ultimately, the bottom-line question must be, Can we achieve the synergy that must exist between classroom and standardized assessment? We must build an answer in the affirmative, so no child *will* be left behind. The time has come to set policies that guide sound practice and to support the professional development needed to achieve excellence in assessment.

The DVD that accompanies this guide (found inside the back cover) contains a presentation entitled *Assessment* **for** *Learning: A Hopeful Vision of the Future.* In addition, the accompanying CD-ROM, also found inside the back cover, includes a PowerPoint presentation titled *A Vision of The Perfect Assessment System.* You may use both of these resources to extend your own understanding of the ideas and concepts presented in these pages, and to help others understand them as well.

## Thinking About Assessment

### Activity 2: Examining Your Assessment Beliefs

**Purpose:** This activity is designed to help leadership team members continue to construct their own vision of assessment excellence by understanding the reasons why assessment has played the roles it has in American education over the past century.

**Time:** 30 minutes of team brainstorming and discussion after reading Part 2.

**Directions:** As a team, reflect on the evolution of assessment depicted in the historical perspective described in Part 2:

1940s College admissions testing

1950s Commercial test batteries become prominent in the marketplace

1960s Birth of accountability for test scores and explosion of districtwide testing

1970s Proliferation of statewide testing programs

1980s National assessment

1990s Standards-based assessments and international assessment

2000s National every-pupil testing for NCLB

- What does this progression say about what role society believes assessment should play in the development of effective schools? Historically, what does it say about what we have wanted assessment to do for us? Brainstorm a list of those fundamental beliefs.

- Now think about the balanced system described in Part 2. Think also about the evolving mission of school from a place that sorts students based on achievement to an institution intended to maximize the achievement of all students. Given that mission, what beliefs do you think ought to be driving the development of assessment systems today? Brainstorm a list of those new beliefs.

- Compare the two lists of beliefs. What are the differences? What are the implications of those differences for the future of assessment in our schools?

■ Now think about the motivational aspects of assessment. How do we currently use assessments, including grades, to motivate our students to want to learn? Do these methods work for all students? If not, for whom do they work? For whom do they not work? In what ways might we supplement our current motivational strategies with those that involve students in assessment?

■ Finally, review the initial vision your team created at the end of Part 1. Based on the study experience just completed in Part 2, revise your vision of excellence in assessment as needed, and save your revised vision for later use.

## Thinking About Assessment

### Activity 3: "Emily's Story"

**Purpose:**   To illustrate high-quality assessment in action in the lives of real students, teachers, administrators, and policy makers.

**Time:**   40 minutes after reading and discussing Part 2 of this guide.

**Directions:**   Read the story of Emily, reflecting on the keys to success: What conditions needed to be in place for Emily and her classmates, Ms. Weathersby and her colleagues, school leaders, and the community to facilitate this success?

Then brainstorm lists of those necessary conditions by answering the following questions:

- What conditions needed to be in place in Ms. W's classroom?
- What conditions needed to be in place in the English Department and the high school?
- What contribution did the district need to make for this success to happen?
- What contribution did the school board and community need to make?

As a leadership team, then, address the following questions:

- To what extent are these conditions satisfied in your classrooms, schools, district, and community?
- Do you need to change or add to your team's vision of assessment excellence as a result of reading this story?

A STORY OF CLASSROOM SUCCESS

# Emily's Story

## *A Vision of Success*

**V**isualize yourself at a particularly important meeting of the school board in the district where you teach. This is the once-a-year meeting at which the district presents the annual report of standardized test scores to the board and the media. Every year it's the same: Will scores be up or down? How will you compare to national norms? How will your district compare to others in the area?

What most present don't realize as the meeting begins is that, this year, they are in for a big surprise with respect to both the achievement information to be presented and the manner of the presentation.

The audience includes a young woman named Emily, a junior at the high school, sitting in the back of the room with her parents. She knows she will be a big part of the surprise. She's only a little nervous. She understands how important her role is. It has been quite a year for her, unlike any she has ever experienced in school before. She also knows her parents and teacher are as proud of her as she is of herself.

The assistant superintendent begins by reminding the board and the rest of the audience that the district uses standardized tests that sample broad domains of achievement with just a few multiple-choice test items. Much that we value, she points out, must be assessed using other methods. She promises to provide an example later in the presentation. Emily's dad nudges her and they both smile.

Having set the stage, the assistant superintendent turns to carefully prepared charts depicting average student performance in each important achievement category tested. Results are summarized by grade and building, concluding with a clear description of how district results had changed from the year before and from previous years. As she proceeds, board members ask questions and receive clarification. Some scores are down slightly; some are up. Participants discuss possible reasons. This is a routine annual presentation that proceeds as expected.

Next comes the break from routine. Having completed the first part of the presentation, the assistant superintendent explains how the district has gathered some new information about one important aspect of student achievement. As the board knows, she points out, the district has implemented a new writing program in the high school to address the issue of poor writing skills among graduates. As part of their preparation for this program, the English faculty attended a summer institute on assessing writing proficiency and integrating such assessments into the teaching and learning process. The English department was confident that this kind of professional development and program revision would produce much higher levels of writing proficiency.

For the second half of the evening's assessment presentation, the high school English department faculty shares the results of their evaluation of the new writing program.

As the very first step in this presentation, the English chair, Ms. Weatherby, who also happens to be Emily's English teacher, distributes a sample of student writing to the board members (with the student's name removed), asking them to read and evaluate this writing. They do so, expressing their dismay aloud as they go. They are indignant in their commentary on these samples of student work. One board member reports in exasperation that, if these represent the results of that new writing program, the community has been had. The board member is right. These are, in fact, pretty weak pieces of work.

*Source:* Reprinted from *Student-Involved Classroom Assessment,* 3d ed. (pp. 7–10, 11–16), by R. J. Stiggins, 2001, Englewood Cliffs, NJ: Merrill/Prentice Hall. Reprinted by permission.

Emily's mom puts her arm around her daughter's shoulder and hugs her.

But Ms. Weatherby urges patience and asks the board members to be very specific in stating what they don't like about this work. As the board registers its complaints, the faculty records the criticisms on chart paper for all to see. The list is long, including everything from repetitiveness to disorganization to short, choppy sentences and disconnected ideas.

Next, the teacher distributes another sample of student writing, asking the board to read and evaluate it. Ah, this, they report, is more like it! This work is much better! But be specific, the chair demands. What do you like about this work? They list positive aspects: good choice of words, sound sentence structure, clever ideas, and so on. Emily is ready to burst! She squeezes her mom's hand.

The reason she's so full of pride at this moment is that this has been a special year for her and her classmates. For the first time ever, they became partners with their English teachers in managing their own improvement as writers. Early in the year, Ms. Weatherby (Ms. W, they all call her) made it crystal clear to Emily that she was, in fact, not a very good writer and that just trying hard to get better was not going to be enough. She expected Emily to *be* better—nothing else would suffice.

Ms. W started the year by working with students to set high writing standards, including understanding quality performance in word choice, sentence structure, organization, and voice, and sharing some new "analytical scoring guides" written just for students. Each explained the differences between good and poor-quality writing in understandable ways. When Emily and her teacher evaluated her first two pieces of writing using these standards, she received very low ratings. Not very good. . . .

But she also began to study samples of writing her teacher supplied that Emily could see were very good. Slowly, she began to understand *why* they were good. The differences between these and her work started to become clear. Ms. W began to share examples and strategies that would help her writing improve one step at a time. As she practiced with

these and time passed, Emily and her classmates kept samples of their old writing to compare to their new writing, and they began to build portfolios. Thus, she literally began to watch her own writing skills improve before her very eyes. At midyear, her parents were invited in for a conference at which Emily, not Ms. Weatherby, shared the contents of her portfolio and discussed her emerging writing skills. Emily remembers sharing thoughts about some aspects of her writing that had become very strong and some examples of things she still needed to work on. Now, the year was at an end and here she sat waiting for her turn to speak to the school board about all of this. What a year!

Now, having set the board up by having them analyze, evaluate, and compare these two samples of student work, Ms. W springs the surprise: The two pieces of writing they had just evaluated, one of less sophistication and one of outstanding quality, were produced by the same writer at the beginning and at the end of the school year! This, she reports, is evidence of the kind of impact the new writing program is having on student writing proficiency.

Needless to say, all are impressed. However, one board member wonders aloud, "Have all your students improved in this way?" Having anticipated the question, the rest of the English faculty joins the presentation and produces carefully prepared charts depicting dramatic changes in typical student performance over time on rating scales for each of six clearly articulated dimensions of good writing. They accompany their description of student performance on each scale with actual samples of student work illustrating various levels of proficiency.

Further, Ms. W informs the board that the student whose improvement has been so dramatically illustrated with the work they have just analyzed is present at this school board meeting, along with her parents. This student is ready to talk with the board about the nature of her learning experience. Emily, you're on!

Interest among the board members runs high. Emily talks about how she has come to understand the truly important differences between good and bad writing. She refers to differences she had not understood before, how she has learned to assess her own writing and to fix it when it doesn't "work well," and how she and her classmates have learned to talk with her teacher and each other about what it means to write well. Ms. W talks about the improved focus of writing instruction, increase in student motivation, and important positive changes in the very nature of the student–teacher relationship.

A board member asks Emily if she likes to write. She reports, "I do now!" This board member turns to Emily's parents and asks their impression of all of this. They report with pride that they had never seen so much evidence before of Emily's achievement and most of it came from Emily herself. Emily had never been called on to lead the parent-teacher conference before. They had no idea she was so articulate. They loved it. Their daughter's pride in and accountability for achievement had skyrocketed in the past year.

As the meeting ends, it is clear to all in attendance that evening that this two part assessment presentation—one part from standardized test scores and one from students, teachers, and the classroom—reveals that assessment is in balance in this district. The test scores cover part of the picture and classroom assessment evidence completes the achievement picture. There are good feelings all around. The accountability needs of the community are being satisfied and the new writing program is working to improve student achievement. Obviously, this story has a happy ending.

Can you visualize yourself walking out of the boardroom at the end of the evening, hearing parents wish they had had such an experience in high school? I sure can. Can't you just anticipate the wording of the memo of congratulations the superintendent will soon write to the English department? How about the story that will appear in the newspaper tomorrow, right next to the report of test scores? *Everyone involved here, from Emily to her classmates to parents to teachers to assessment director to (at the end) school board members, understood how to use assessment to promote student success and effective schools.*

## Success from the Student's Point of View

The day after the board meeting, I interviewed Emily about the evening's events. As you read, think about how our conversation centers on what really works for Emily.

RICK: You did a nice job at the school board meeting last night, Emily.

EMILY: Thanks. What pleases me most is that, last year, I could never have done it.

RICK: What's changed from last year?

EMILY: I guess I'm more confident. I knew what had happened for me in English class and I wanted to tell them my story.

RICK: You became a confident writer.

EMILY: Yeah, but that's not what I mean. Last night at the board meeting I was more than a good writer. I felt good talking about my writing and how I'd improved. It's like, I understand what I've learned and I have a way to describe it.

RICK: Let's talk about Emily the confident writer. What were you thinking last night when the board members were reacting to your initial writing sample—the one that wasn't very good? Still confident?

EMILY: Mom helped. She squeezed my hand and I remember she whispered in my ear, "You'll show 'em!" That helped me handle it. It's funny, I was listening to their comments to see if they knew anything about good writing. I wondered if they understood as much about it as I do—like, maybe they needed to take Ms. Weatherby's class.

RICK: How did they do?

EMILY: Pretty well, actually. They found the problems in my early work and described them pretty well. When I first started last fall, I wouldn't have been able to do that. I was a terrible writer.

RICK: How do you know that?

EMILY: I understand where I was, how little I could do. No organization. I didn't even know my own voice. No one had ever taken the time to show me the secrets. I'd never learned to analyze my writing. I wouldn't have known what to look for or how to describe it. That's part of what Ms. Weatherby taught us.

RICK: Say more about what she taught you.

EMILY: To begin with, she taught us to do what the board members did last night: analyze other people's writing. We looked at newspaper editorials, passages from books we were reading, letters friends had sent us. She wanted us to see what made those pieces work or not work.

RICK: Why do you suppose she started you there?

EMILY: Well, she would read a piece to us and then we'd brainstorm what made it good or bad. Pretty soon, we began to see patterns —things that worked or didn't work. She wanted us to begin to see and hear stuff as she read out loud.

RICK: Like what?

EMILY: Well, look, here's my early piece from the meeting last night. See, just read it!

## Time for Reflection

*Please take time to read Emily's beginning of the year writing sample before you read on.*

---

*BEGINNING OF THE YEAR Writing Sample*

Computers are a thing of the future. They help us in thousands of ways. Computers are a help to our lives. They make things easier. They help us to keep track of information.

Computers are simple to use. Anyone can learn how. You do not have to be a computer expert to operate a computer. You just need to know a few basic things.

Computers can be robots that will change our lives. Robots are really computers! Robots do a lot of the work that humans used to do. This makes our lives much easier. Robots build cars and do many other tasks that humans used to do. When robots learn to do more, they will take over most of our work. This will free humans to do other kinds of things. You can also communicate on computers. It is much faster than mail! You can look up information, too. You can find information on anything at all on a computer.

Computers are changing the work and changing the way we work and communicate. In many ways, computers are changing our lives and making our lives better and easier.

*END OF THE YEAR Writing Sample*

So there I was, my face aglow with the reflection on my computer screen, trying to come up with the next line for my essay. Writing it was akin to Chinese water torture, as I could never seem to end it. It dragged on and on, a never-ending babble of stuff.

Suddenly, unexpectedly—I felt an ending coming on. I could wrap this thing up in four or five sentences, and this dreadful assignment would be over. I'd be free.

I had not saved yet, and decided I would do so now. I clasped the slick, white mouse in my hand, slid it over the mouse pad, and watched as the black arrow progressed toward the "File" menu. By accident, I clicked the mouse button just to the left of paragraph 66. I saw a flash and the next thing I knew, I was back to square one. I stared at the blank screen for a moment in disbelief. Where was my essay? My ten-billion-page masterpiece? Gone?! No—that couldn't be! Not after all the work I had done! Would a computer be that unforgiving? That unfeeling? Didn't it care about me at all?

I decided not to give up hope just yet. The secret was to remain calm. After all, my file had to be *somewhere*—right? That's what all the manuals say—"It's in there somewhere." I went back to the "File" menu, much more carefully this time. First, I tried a friendly sounding category called "Find

File." No luck there; I hadn't given the file a name.

Ah, then I had a brainstorm. I could simply go up to "Undo." Yes, that would be my savior! A simple click of a button and my problem would be solved! I went to Undo, but it looked a bit fuzzy. Not a good sign. That means there is nothing to undo. Don't panic ... don't panic ...

I decided to try to exit the program, not really knowing what I would accomplish by this but feeling more than a little desperate. Next, I clicked on the icon that would allow me back in to word processing. A small sign appeared, telling me that my program was being used by another user. Another user? What's it talking about? I'm the only user, you idiot! Or at least I'm trying to be a user! Give me my paper back! Right now!

I clicked on the icon again and again—to no avail. Click ... click ...clickclickclickCLICKCLICKCLICK!!!! Without warning, a thin cloud of smoke began to rise from the back of the computer. I didn't know whether to laugh or cry. Sighing, I opened my desk drawer, and pulled out a tablet and pen. It was going to be a long day.

*Source: Personal writing by Nikki Spandel. Reprinted by permission.*

EMILY: It's correct—no mistakes. But these short, choppy sentences don't work. And it doesn't say anything or go anywhere. It's just disconnected thoughts. It doesn't grab you and hold your attention. Then it just stops. See, we needed to learn how to fix these things in our own writing. Now look at my other piece. Let me read it to you, so you can hear the rhythm of these sentences (She reads aloud). Ms. W taught us to read our writing out loud to hear how to fix it.

## Time for Reflection

*Please take time to read Emily' end of the year writing sample before you read on.*

EMILY: In this one, I tried to tell about the feelings of frustration that happen when humans use machines. See, I think the voice in this piece comes from the feeling that "We've all been there." Everyone who works with computers has had this experience—or something close to it. A tiny writer's problem (not being able to find a good ending) turns into a major problem (losing the whole document). This idea makes the piece clear and organized. I think the reader can picture this poor, frustrated writer at her computer, wanting, trying to communicate in a human way—but finding that the computer is just as frustrated with her!

RICK: You sound just like you did last night.

EMILY: I'm always like this about my writing now. I know what works. Sentences are important. So is voice. So are organization and word choice—all that stuff. If you do it right, it works and you know it.

RICK: What else did your teacher do to help you?

EMILY: When we were first getting started, Ms. Weatherby gave us a big stack of student papers she'd collected over the years—some good, some bad, and everything in between. Our assignment was to sort them into four stacks based on quality, from real good to real bad. When we were done, we compared who put what papers in which piles and then we talked about why—we argued, really. Soon, we began to describe what the differences were among the piles. From here, Ms. W helped us develop the six five-point rating scales that we used for the rest of the year to analyze, evaluate, and improve our writing.

RICK: When did you begin to write and then evaluate your own work?

EMILY: As soon as we finished the rating scales.

RICK: Your own and each other's work?

EMILY: Only our own to begin with. Ms. W said she didn't want anyone being embarrassed. We all had a lot to learn. It was supposed to be private until we began to trust our own judgments. She kept saying, "Trust me. You'll get better at this and then you can share."

RICK: Did you ever move on to evaluating each other's work?

EMILY: You bet. When we began to trust ourselves and each other, we were free to ask classmates for opinions. But Ms. Weatherby was very clear about saying that we could only give opinions in the form of ratings, with specific descriptions of what we saw in the work we evaluated. No blanket judgments, like this is good or bad. And we were always supposed to be honest. If we couldn't see how to help someone improve a piece, we were supposed to say so.

RICK: Then what?

EMILY: Lots of practice—all year. I've still got my writing portfolio full of practice, see? It starts out pretty bad back in the fall and slowly gets pretty good toward spring. This is where the two pieces came from that the board read last night. I picked them. I talk about the changes in my writing in the self-reflections in here. My portfolio tells the whole story. Want to look through it?

RICK: I sure do. What do you think Ms. Weatherby did right?

EMILY: Nobody had ever been so clear with me before about what it took to be really good at school stuff. It's like, there's no mystery —no need to psych her out. She said, "I won't ever surprise you, trust me. I'll show you what I want and I don't want any excuses. But you've got to deliver good writing in this class. You don't deliver, you don't succeed."

RICK: What else did she do right?

EMILY: A bunch of us were talking about this the other day. She trusted us. Every so often, she would give us something she had written, so we could evaluate her work. She listened to our comments and said it really helped her. We were her teachers! That was so cool!

RICK: Anything else?

EMILY: You know, she was the first teacher ever to tell me that it was okay to fail. But just at first, like, when you're trying to do something new. But we couldn't keep failing. We had to get a little better each time. If we didn't, it was our own fault. She didn't want us to give up on ourselves. If we kept improving, over time, we could learn to write well. I wish every teacher would do that. She would say, "There's no shortage of success around here. You learn to write well, you get an 'A.' My goal is to have everyone learn to write well and deserve an 'A.'"

RICK: Thank you for filling in the details, Em.

EMILY: Thank you for asking!

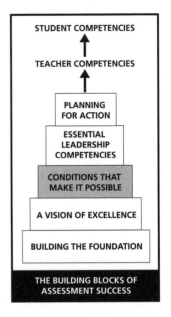

## 3

*Leadership in the pursuit of excellence in assessment begins with a guiding vision, clearly showing how assessment fits into effective instruction. All school leaders must understand the importance of quality assessment at all levels, and must put forth the standards that will guide assessment practices in every classroom.*

## *Part Three*

# THE PATH:

# FIVE DOORS
# TO EXCELLENCE
# IN ASSESSMENT

**U**p to this point we've examined a vision of balance, quality, and student involvement in local assessment systems. We emphasized these big ideas because they form the core of effective assessment systems. Should any of these pieces be missing, leaders run the risk of not just having systems that are out of balance, but of assessing inaccurately, misrepresenting student achievement, and missing the learning opportunities presented to us through the principles of assessment *for* learning. We'll describe those more in Part 4.

At the end of Part 2, Activity 3, "Emily's Story," closed by asking your team to consider what conditions would have been necessary in the district, school, and classroom in order to have achieved that level of student success. We introduced those conditions briefly in the latter part of Part 2. Here in Part 3, we will explain in detail the conditions we believe are necessary for your vision to take hold. To some extent, these conditions may already be in place, or you may discover work needs to be done in some areas but not in others. Whatever the case, it is a function of leadership to either establish or maintain the necessary conditions; without that leadership, little is likely to change in the name of quality assessment.

## The Need for District Leadership in Assessment

In this third part we offer a roadmap, a path school district leaders can follow to tap a powerful synergy between standardized and classroom assessment, culminating in the design of a balanced system. However, implementing this plan may take considerable time and effort. The journey may take years to complete, and will require contributions from all who have a stake in the quality of schools. But schools need not wait years to see the benefits of the development of balanced assessment systems. Indeed, benefits begin to accrue almost immediately for those who set about completing the scope of work outlined here. *The key is to start the journey, and that requires leadership.* Although largely focused on the classroom, the most important roles in accomplishing this work are to be played initially by the superintendent, school board, principals, and the district leadership team.

This leadership requires the following:

- Having a vision of excellence in assessment that is in balance in terms of understanding and meeting the assessment needs of *all* users, from students and teachers to board members and legislators.

- Understanding the conditions, including the assessment competencies of administrators, that must be in place for a balanced vision to be attained; that is, knowing the path that will take you from where the district is now to an assessment system that is in balance.

- Understanding the research on classroom assessment, recognizing that assessment quality and accuracy, descriptive feedback, and student involvement in assessment are essentials in realizing the gains available to schools when principles of assessment *for* learning are routinely applied in the classroom.

- Leading the school or district team to excellence in assessment by securing and allocating the resources needed to remove barriers to completing the journey.

## Overview of the Path to the Perfect Assessment System

To reach this goal of integrating assessment into the instructional program, we ask districts and schools to journey through five doors to excellence in assessment. Behind each door is a set of tasks to be completed and suggestions for how to complete them. As the district accomplishes each task, it removes barriers and moves closer to its desired destination of a perfect assessment system. This is a challenging program of improvement: no district or school will be able to move forward on all five fronts at once. Each organization must establish its own priorities, its own starting places, and its own sequence for completing the work.

**Door 1** calls for developing a *clearly articulated and appropriate set of achievement standards for each student* as the foundation for quality assessment. We can assess accurately only those achievement targets we have defined. Even with academic content standards now defined in every state, this is still far easier said than done.

**Door 2** requires a commitment to providing *accurate, understandable, and usable information about student achievement to all key decision makers*. Many users of assessment data use them in the service of student success. Therefore, we will consider how to plan to meet those many needs.

**Door 3** demands an *assessment-literate school culture.* All concerned with the quality of schools must understand the differences between sound and unsound assessment practices as well as the implications of both. We will outline standards for quality assessment and suggest efficient ways to be sure that all educators are assessment literate. We'll also introduce a set of nine Principles of Assessment *for* Learning.

**Door 4** leads us to reconsider how best to *collect, store, manage, and communicate information about student achievement.* All stakeholders in the educational system deserve information that is timely, accurate, understandable, and can lead to continued improvement.

**Door 5** directs us to lay a *foundation of assessment policy that demands and supports quality practices.* Some policies must be set at the state level. But most are put in place at the district and school levels. Sound assessment policy guides sound assessment practice. We will consider what that means, and which policies are most likely to lead to an educational environment supportive of quality, balanced assessment.

Here in Part 3 we'll pose a series of questions about a school's or school district's preparedness to take maximum advantage of assessment as a school improvement tool, with the intent of encouraging personal and organizational reflection, self-evaluation, and growth.

At the end of this part is a series of templates against which the leadership of any school or school district can gauge the current state of their assessment system, permitting an organization to profile itself in terms of standards of assessment excellence. If that evaluation leads to the conclusion that your district's assessment house is completely in order, kudos to the teachers, administrators, and communities who made that happen. But sometimes such appraisals also point to needed improvements. In those cases, we offer possible solutions.

# DOOR 1

## Focusing on Achievement Expectations

To assess student achievement accurately, teachers and administrators must know and understand the achievement standards that their students are to meet. Again, we cannot assess (or teach!) achievement that we have not defined. To reach the goal of establishing clear and appropriate achievement expectations, a school district must take three critical steps.

First, the community must agree on the meaning of academic success within its schools by asking, What do we expect successful graduates of our local educational system to know and be able to do? The answer should take the form of high school graduation requirements stated in competency terms, not in credit hours or grade-point averages.

Second, district curriculum directors and faculty members for all grade levels must meet to decide how that general vision of success can be realized within the local curriculum. The result of their work must be a curriculum, articulated grade to grade and aligned to state standards, that specifies how students move along a path to competence—how they progress from kindergarten through high school.

Third, leaders must conduct a careful audit to be sure all teachers are confident, competent masters of the achievement standards assigned as their instructional responsibility. For reasons framed here, neither school districts nor communities should assume that all teachers are prepared to deliver their part of the big learning picture.

Let's examine how these three pieces come together.

### The Evolving Mission of Schools

Members of a school community do not always agree on the definition of an "effective school." For some, an effective school is a safe place to house children while their families fulfill their adult responsibilities. Thus, effective schools serve a custodial function. For others, the mission of schools is to rank students from the highest to the lowest achiever. In this case, schools serve a sorting function. And for still others, schools serve the purpose of producing competent students. So the most effective schools are those that help the largest proportion of students attain their highest levels of achievement.

These purposes for schooling need not be mutually exclusive. As parents, we demand safe schools because the law demands that we place our children there. Further, in a competitive society where resources for postsecondary education and job opportunities are limited, society asks that students be ranked. But ultimately, an increasingly complex, technically sophisticated society demands that graduates master the academic competencies needed to be productive contributors.

*For this reason, we assume that effective schools maximize the achievement of the largest possible number of students.* They are standards-driven institutions. The more students that succeed in reaching their potential, the better the school. The higher, more sophisticated the achievement standards they meet, the better the school.

To be standards driven, schools must work with their communities to define their local vision of academic success. The place to start is with the articulation of achievement expectations for high school graduation. We face divergent opinions about what those expectations should be. In almost every state, academic standards have been established that seem on the surface to define what it is that teachers should teach and students should learn. Some are specific, yet many others are very broad and do not provide the scaffolding needed for teachers or students to make immediate sense of them in the class-room. Others stop short of defining learning expectations for the end of high school. Regardless of the nature of the standards in your state, to fully succeed, districts/schools must continue the work begun by the state and find strategies for blending the views of at least four segments of the community with that delivered by the state.

Curriculum standards that have been designed at the state level clearly play a major role in the development of a locally established curriculum. But without question, schools should solicit the opinions of the "family community"—the parents who entrust their children to schools and the taxpayers who support the social institution. In addition, educators must get input from the "business community"—future employers of those successful graduates. Still other advice can come from the "higher education community"—the other destination for our successful graduates. And finally, careful consideration should be given to the opinions of those in the "school community"—the teachers who are masters of the disciplines students are to learn.

In tapping segments of community opinion, schools bring a range of background and experience to bear on the question of essential learning expectations for students. For instance, the family community may bring input regarding values. The business community will bring a sense of the future development of a technological society. The higher education community will balance that with a sense of our intellectual foundations. And the school community will bring the best current thinking about academic standards from national organizations within their particular disciplines as well as any state-level academic standards that must be woven into the mix. The result will be a statement of specific *achievement destinations* for students.

The process most school districts use to achieve this synthesis of community values is a combination of community meetings or forums and community surveys of public opinion. Often several iterations of each are needed to reach a consensus on the sense of the community—to work through strongly held differences of opinion. We can offer no advice as to how to make this process easy; we can say only that it is critically important in producing rigorous and relevant curriculum that reflects the needs of adult work and life in the twenty-first century and includes the values and priorities of the local community.

Many school districts have succeeded in assembling these diverse sets of educational objectives into composite portraits of their successful graduates. In doing so they have generated the "characteristics of the learner" they desire upon exit from a K–12 system that are the result of the combined power of the "characteristics of the learning," or, the academic standards in the written curriculum.

## Creating an Effective Curriculum

Once the school/community vision of ultimate success is completed, the professional education community must take over to add the next ingredient. They must work collaboratively across grade levels to back those end-of-high-school achievement standards into the grade-level curriculum so as to map out the routes that students will take from kindergarten to grade twelve to succeed. The result of this work must be a carefully planned, specifically detailed, and completely integrated curriculum, linked grade to grade, that begins with a vision of what desired student performance looks like after K–12 schooling. That means teachers from primary grades, elementary grades, middle schools or junior high, and high schools within the district must meet and assume and assign responsibility for helping students progress through higher levels of academic attainment. It means that teachers must interact with one another and plan for the contributions to be made by each K–12 team member. It means that a level of specificity not contained in the standards is fully described in writing, guiding the teacher in preparing daily lessons. The result will be a clear set of *roadmaps* for students to follow on their journey to mastery of the standards.

To illustrate, if students are to become competent writers, educators must specify what writing foundations primary grade teachers will need to help their students master. How will elementary teachers then build on that foundation? What forms of writing competence will middle school or junior high teachers contribute? And how will high school teachers complete writing competence that launches confident, effective writers into work or college? Not only must each question be thoughtfully answered, each teacher must know how his or her contribution fits into this big picture, and what comes before and after his or her own contribution.

This same planning must be carried out in science, math, reading, social studies, and other disciplines. We must plan for student mastery of content knowledge, specific patterns of reasoning, performance skills, and product development capabilities as they play out within and across disciplines. Planning teams must decide who will take what responsibility for which forms of student academic growth.

Many districts have found it useful to meet and work in cross-grade-level or vertical teams on a regular basis.  These articulation planning teams tap into state standards and grade-level benchmarks to assist in finding appropriate divisions of content.  They can also consult, along with the state standards,  the standards developed by national teams working within the professional associations, such as the National Council of Teachers of Mathematics, the International Reading Association, and the National Council of Teachers of English.

A locally developed, high-quality curriculum, aligned to state and national standards where appropriate, sufficiently specific, and consistently formatted across subjects and grade levels for easy use, is the foundation of quality assessment, because it tells us what we should be assessing to track student progress. And when made public in a variety of ways and forms, it becomes a guide for all stakeholders to use in helping students learn.

The development of this high-quality curriculum can be challenging for several reasons. Teaching has historically been something teachers do alone. Within general curricular guidelines, they select their own educational objectives and design instruction to achieve those objectives. Given this history, the concept of collaborative planning around teaching a common set of learning expectations can be intimidating and therefore difficult to complete.

In addition, as educators, we haven't established an outstanding track record over the years reflecting mutual respect across grade levels. Given this history, it can be difficult to blend into a team.

Additionally, our history of academic freedom has entitled teachers to tailor their own instructional priorities to topics that interest them or that represent their strengths. Those with well-established personal priorities may be reluctant to align their instruction to the district curriculum, a necessary part of the collaboration that leads to a fully implemented, integrated curriculum. For all these reasons, many districts find it productive to precede curriculum-building activities with organizational development in the form of team-building activities.

Another reason curriculum development can be tricky is that it can pose some challenging community relations problems. Many who view education from the community assume that we already have a curriculum that is connected across grade levels. After all, the grade-level numbers run in consecutive order and each subject is identified as important in each grade. We hear and make common reference to subsets of this curriculum—"third-grade math," "a sixth-grade reading level," "eighth-grade science," and the like. Parents naturally assume that these labels must mean that a well-planned and articulated sequence of instruction (and therefore assessment) has been laid out for their children, with the intended learning in each grade building thoughtfully on the learning that preceded it. Unless the community understands that such a curriculum has *not* been fully developed, they won't know or understand what resources are needed to accomplish the task.

And once established, special and ongoing care must be taken to ensure the curriculum is not shelved on the back bookcase. Implementing the curriculum in every classroom so the learning expectations are common for students from one school to the next and one classroom to the next is a leadership challenge and should be planned for in advance. Both what we teach our students and how well we teach them will be reflected in local or state assessments, and all students deserve exposure to the same high-quality curriculum in order to truly show us what they know and can do. Providing teachers the time to work together to learn the curriculum, plan lessons and assessments, and continue their own learning in the academic disciplines they teach is essential (Schmoker, 2002).

## Teacher Mastery of Student Standards

With the development of a vision of academic success and an articulated K–12 curriculum supporting state standards, as outlined here, we establish our academic expectations for students. But obviously, the key to student success in meeting those standards is in the instruction provided by their teachers. In that regard, one necessary condition for success in the classroom is that teachers use the written curriculum as their guide for lesson development and delivery. And a further condition must be that they are masters of the achievement targets their students are expected to hit. In other words, if students are to make it to their achievement destinations by following the curriculum roadmaps, then their *guides* must understand the ground to be covered. This is the third part of the scope of work to be completed behind Door 1.

Teachers can neither teach nor accurately assess learning that they themselves have not mastered. A school district cannot afford even one classroom where this condition is not satisfied. If just one teacher is incapable of helping students master essential achievement targets, that teacher becomes a weak link in a continuous chain that will cause some students to fail later because they will not have mastered prerequisites.

Consequently, once achievement standards are clearly identified at all grade levels in all subjects, school districts must be sure teachers are prepared to help students meet them. One challenging part of this is helping teachers conduct the open and honest internal self-reflection needed to evaluate their own preparedness. Most of us did not grow up in an environment where it was safe to admit our inadequacies, nor has the evaluative relationship that often characterizes teacher–supervisor relations made it easy for teachers to be frank about their need for improvement.

Given this history, it is essential that we strive to establish supervisory and professional development environments devoted to the pursuit of excellence—not just minimum competence—in teaching. This takes a kind of collaboration, trust, and confidence that will permit teachers to go to their supervisors in the spirit of professional growth, ask for support in gaining greater mastery of their academic discipline(s), and get that help, without being penalized at the next evaluation. This kind of environment is essential in helping teachers gain the knowledge and skills they need to be confident, competent classroom assessors. As important, supervisors and districts must be prepared to deliver the professional development teachers may need in acquiring the required content knowledge, and also must continuously help teachers understand the state standards and the district curriculum in ways that help them turn the objectives into everyday lessons. Special attention should be given to those teachers new to the profession by providing them with sample lessons, specialized content training to better understand the standards, and the time needed to plan lessons aligned to the curriculum.

## Summary

An effective school is one that maximizes the achievement of the largest possible proportion of its student population. The school believes, and shows in its policies and practices, that all students are capable of learning well. It is prepared to take supportive action when students do not perform as expected. In an effective, standards-driven school, both students and their teachers are judged in terms of the amount of learning accomplished.

Door 1 to excellence in assessment requires that we define what students must learn to be considered academically successful. Schools cannot work effectively unless students and teachers understand what it means to succeed academically. So teachers must both have and be able to share their vision of the learning targets we have established for their students.

Ultimately, this planning must be completed at the district level in order to provide equally high-quality educational opportunities across buildings. But preliminary work can also be done within school buildings, grade levels, and even classrooms. Teachers can examine their educational priorities by auditing their classroom curriculum (what they actually teach) against the written curriculum and adjust their teaching as needed, always focusing on what needs to be learned for students to be able to demonstrate proficiency, either in the classroom or on state-level assessments of learning for accountability purposes (see Activity 16).

In laying the foundation for quality assessments, we must agree on what is to be measured by answering three questions:

- What does the community want its students to know and be able to do when they complete high school? The destinations must be clear, understandable, balanced, assessable, and made public for all to see.

- How can the curriculum be planned to take them there? The road must be carefully, clearly, and completely mapped out, and then improved/revised as needed.

- How can we be sure their teachers are ready to help them succeed? The guides must be prepared to advise, with ongoing district support in content training, lesson planning, and curriculum implementation.

These three ingredients pave the first part of the path to excellence in assessment.

# DOOR 2
## Serving ALL Assessment Users

By definition, assessment results reflect a particular student's attainment of a specified set of achievement standards at a single point in time. Standardized test results provide achievement data summarized across large numbers of students on multiple targets broadly defined for a particular grade level at one point during the school year. These tests, assessments *of* learning, are most useful in providing periodic status reports for the program planning level of decision making, and can also provide information about the overall health of the system.

As we have already established, classroom assessments *for* learning are focused on each individual student's ongoing attainment of far more narrowly defined achievement targets during a particular course of study. Because teachers can use frequent assessments over time, each reflective of the achievement of individual students, they can see and manage the evolution of that achievement.

Educational decision makers who need only periodic access to achievement information reflecting group performance can use standardized test results effectively to satisfy those needs. Teachers, students, and parents who need continuous access to the high-resolution portraits of individual student achievement receive that information through *classroom* assessments.

Let us restate a critical point: because decision makers at these different levels have such diverse information needs, no single assessment can meet all their needs. In today's testing for accountability environment, we have asked (and in some cases believed) that standardized tests serve double and even triple duty: reporting large group scores, serving diagnostic purposes for individual students, and being an instrument for high-stakes decisions all at once. If we are to administer and use assessments with maximum effectiveness and efficiency, we must plan carefully for their use, understand what information is actually needed, and know whether the assessment can provide the information required for the intended purpose.

## Understanding Who the Users Are

In schools, there are three levels of assessment users: classroom, instructional support, and policy. The first column in Table 2 describes these categories. Columns two and three identify key questions to be answered and the information needed to help each user. A school district committed to meeting the needs of all assessment users must develop plans for conducting the assessments needed to provide the required information—at all levels.

If you study the information needs of the first category of users—instructional staff—it will become obvious that they will obtain the information they need from the teacher's day-to-day classroom assessments. User needs at the other two levels will be served by standardized assessments.

The essential planning question is, *How can we be sure all users receive relevant student achievement information in a timely and understandable form?* At the classroom level, each individual teacher must develop a plan for answering this question. At instructional support and policy levels, we need a district plan.

## Planning for Classroom Assessment

To monitor student achievement effectively and efficiently, all classroom teachers must begin each unit of instruction or course of study with a clear vision of the specific achievement targets their students are to hit. Beginning with the foundational instructional targets, teachers must understand how their students will progress over time to higher levels of academic proficiency. In what order will they master more refined structures of content knowledge? How will they come to use that knowledge productively to reason and solve problems? What performance skills will they master, and in what sequence? What kinds of achievement products will they be called on to create? As we described in Door 1, at the classroom level this requires a grade-by-grade curriculum made visible and shared with parents and students in an understandable format.

With this in mind, then, teachers must start their instruction with a predetermined plan for assessing whether, or to what extent, each student has reached the intended learning. In Door 3, we explore the range of assessment methods available to teachers for this purpose. But for now, we should be able to ask any teacher at any time for her or his written plan of targets, written plan for the sequence of assessments intended to track student progress, and where students are now in relation to both plans.

Further, teachers need to weave into their plans a description of how the results will be made meaningful to students and parents (that is, how results connect to specific targets) so they may make timely, informed decisions. Since students, like teachers, make decisions of the sorts identified in Table 2 on a continuous basis, the feedback plan should also reflect ways to keep students in touch with their own progress all along the way. This classroom assessment planning completed by each teacher at the beginning of each program of study asks, *What targets will be assessed, when they will be assessed, and how will the results be used?*

## Table 2

### Users and Uses of Assessment Results

| Users | Key Question(s) to Be Answered | Information Needed |
|---|---|---|
| *Classroom Level* | | |
| Student | Am I meeting the teacher's standards? What help do I need to succeed? Are the results worth my investment of energy? | Continuous information about individual student attainment of specific instructional requirements |
| Teacher | Which students need what help? Who among my students should work together? What grade should appear on the report card? | Continuous information about individual student achievement |
| | Did my teaching strategies work? How do I become a better teacher? | Continuous assessment of group performance |
| Parent | Is my child succeeding in school? What does my child need to succeed? Is my child's teacher(s) doing a good job? Is this district doing a good job? | Continuous feedback on the student's mastery of required material |

| Users | Key Question(s) to Be Answered | Information Needed |
|---|---|---|
| *Instructional Support Level* | | |
| Principal/ Vice Principal | Is instruction in particular areas producing results? Is this teacher effective? What kinds of professional development will help? How shall we spend building resources to be effective? | Periodic assessment of group achievement |
| Lead/Mentor Teacher | What does this teacher need to do the job? | Periodic assessment of group achievement |
| Counselor/ Psychologist | Who needs (can have access to) special support services such as remedial programs? What students should be assigned to which teachers to optimize results? | Periodic assessment of individual achievement |
| Curriculum Director | Is our program of instruction effective? | Periodic assessment of group achievement |
| *Policy Level* | | |
| Superintendent | Are programs producing student learning? Is the building principal producing results? Which programs need/ deserve more resources? | Periodic assessment of group mastery of district curriculum |
| School Board | Are students in the district learning? Is the superintendent producing results? | Periodic assessment of group achievement |
| State Dept. of Education | Are programs across the state producing results? | Periodic assessment of group mastery of state curriculum |
| Citizen/ Legislator (state or national) | Are students in our schools achieving in ways that will allow them to be effective citizens? | Periodic assessment of group mastery of valued targets |

## Planning for Standardized Testing

This essential question, *How can we be sure all users receive relevant student achievement information in a timely and understandable form?*, must guide the administration and use of standardized tests at instructional support and policy levels. By compiling a complete inventory of ALL of the standardized tests students take during the course of a year, we take a critical step in knowing if the needs of all users are being met. This analysis will also reveal if there are overlaps or duplications in the testing program, if some valued learning targets are going unassessed, and how much time the administration of all of the tests takes. *What standardized tests are to be administered at what grade levels, reflecting what standards and/or achievement targets at what point in time?* State tests and district tests are the most obvious, but often there are school tests and grade-level or department tests also administered that should be included to achieve a full and accurate picture. Further, *what specific assessment users are to be served by the results? What decisions will be made on their basis?* This analysis should reveal which achievement targets are being assessed and which are not, as well as whose information needs are being met by these tests and whose are not.

For example, if the district administers an annual districtwide standardized achievement battery for public reporting, what targets are assessed for what students, when are the assessments administered, and what specific information/ decision-making needs are served? If standardized tests are used for selection of students for special services, which targets are assessed, when are they assessed, and precisely how are the results being used? In the statewide assessment, what are the targets tested, at what levels, and for whose purposes? What kinds of decisions are they designed to inform? Are the tested targets the same or different from those on the district assessment? Are the methods similar or different?

Each assessment fills in part of the district's big assessment picture. Mapping that picture reveals both overlaps and gaps in the standardized assessment program. This plan (also explained with additional examples in Resource 7) can take the form of a table with these column headings:

- Name and form of the standardized test (list each test in a battery separately)
- Amount of time required for administering the test

- Students tested (grade level and time of year)
- Specific achievement targets assessed (content knowledge, specific patterns of reasoning, performance skills, product development capabilities or some combination of these?)
- Specific state/district standards assessed through those test items
- Specific assessment method(s) used
- How the results will be reported
- Intended users of results and decisions made based on those results
- Procedures for communication of results for all relevant users and ways to verify that the results were understood, interpreted, and used correctly

The big picture of standardized testing that emerges from this analysis will reveal how the results connect to users. Each test will be connected to its place in the grade-by-grade curriculum. It will also become clear which valued targets are covered at strategic times and which are not. It will become clear what additional assessments might be needed to meet information needs, and which assessments are redundant or without specific purpose and can be eliminated. And, it will help connect a state assessment system to a local one so there can be synergy between the two.

Further, this analysis will show how each set of test results fits into the record of each individual student's mastery of achievement expectations—how each contributes to the evolving picture of the growing learner. Here again, assessments that are redundant, fail to align properly with the curriculum, or fail to contribute needed information can be eliminated. It may also become clear that managing the amount of data generated, if it is to be put to optimum use for programmatic improvement and also be communicated to users to help students become better learners, may require specialized software. Districts that have taken advantage of technology to compile, store, manipulate, and report student assessment data both systematically and systemically are able to meet the needs of all users in timely and efficient ways.

This planning, conducted at the classroom, school, and district levels, can contribute to both the efficiency and effectiveness of districts' assessment systems and allow them to operationalize their commitment to all assessment users.

*Summary*

Door 2 helps school leaders lay an essential part of the foundation of balanced assessment systems by preparing to build their system around the thoughtfully analyzed needs of real assessment users. It calls for developing a keen awareness of who those users are and what specific information needs they bring to the table. Periodic standardized tests will meet some of those needs; classroom assessments will meet others. Both are essential. If either is not delivering accurate information or is misunderstood by intended users, students are at risk. Schools and districts progress on their journey to excellence in assessment as they discover how to blend the two levels of assessment according to the information needs of those who work to help students learn.

# DOOR 3
# Developing Assessment Literacy

If decision makers are to fulfill the various roles spelled out previously, they must have access to dependable information about student achievement. Quality assessments are a must. We can develop and use high-quality assessments only if we formulate and apply rigorous standards of quality. To apply those standards consistently, within known contexts, teachers and administrators must have the opportunity to learn about and practice using them. In short, they must become assessment literate.

A set of assessment quality standards is outlined here, along with several road-blocks to their implementation and specific strategies for removing those obstacles.

## Standards of Assessment Quality

We can frame the key attributes of sound assessments in the form of five standards (Stiggins, 2001). They can take the form of the five questions that appear inside the bubbles in Figure 2. Are we clear about *what* we want to assess? Do we know *why* we're assessing? Are we sure about *how* to assess? Have we gathered *enough* evidence? Have we controlled for *bias* in results? Answers to these questions help us judge the quality of our classroom and standardized assessments.

**Standard 1.** *Quality assessments arise from and accurately reflect clearly specified and appropriate achievement expectations for students.*

Knowing precisely what we are asking students to master is important because different achievement targets require the application of different assessment methods. This takes the need for clear achievement expectations, described in Door 1, a step further. Behind Door 1, we asked for a general statement of expectations in the form of standards, or competencies that students need to master. This first assessment quality standard relates directly to Door 1, but it asks a more precise question: What are the specific classroom level achievement targets that underpin success in meeting the overarching state or local achievement standard? These must be the focus of the teacher's classroom assessments. In any classroom assessment context, we must begin assessment development by defining the precise vision of what it means to succeed. As you will see, we can select proper assessment methods only when we know what kind of achievement needs to be assessed. Do we expect our students to

- Master subject matter content, meaning to *know and understand*?

    Does this mean they must know it outright?

    Or does it mean they must know where and how to find it, using references?

- Use knowledge to *reason* and solve problems?

## Figure 2
## Standards of Assessment Quality

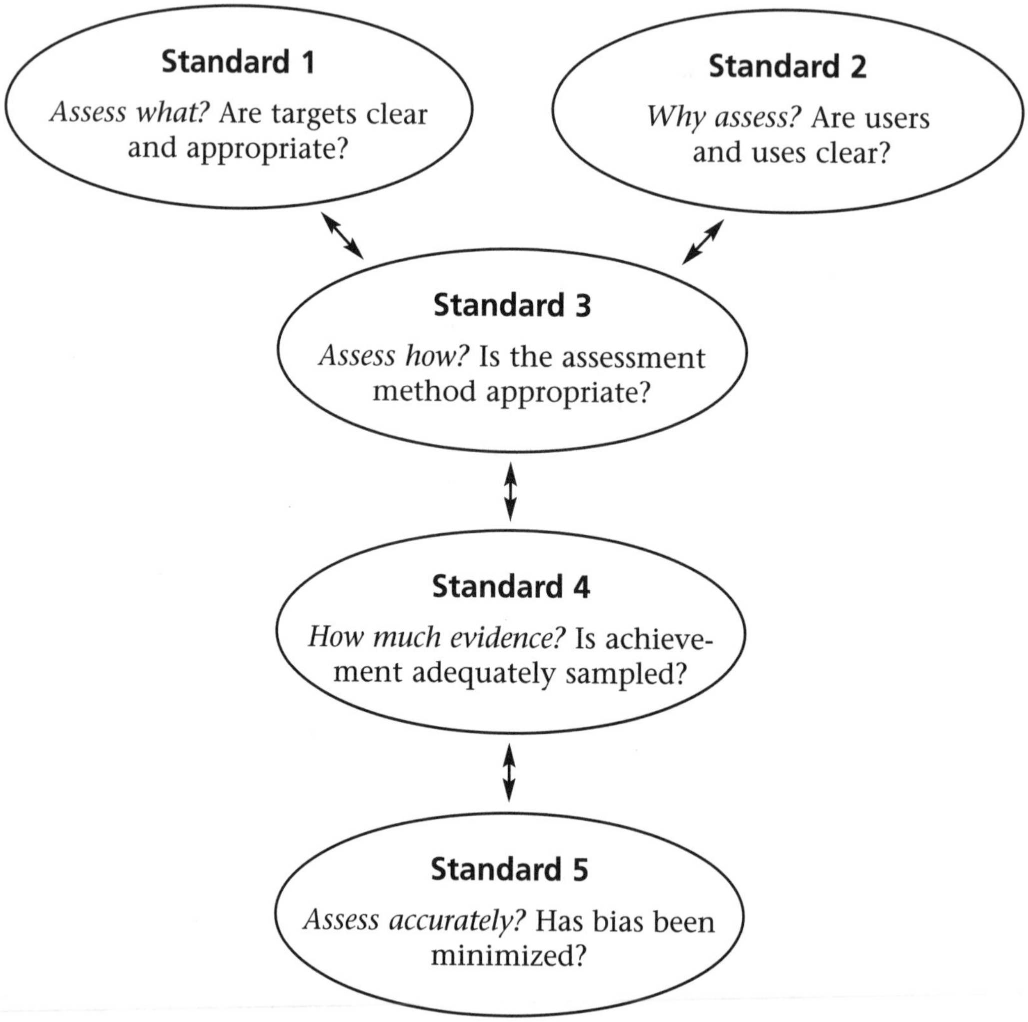

**Standard 1**

*Assess what?* Are targets clear and appropriate?

**Standard 2**

*Why assess?* Are users and uses clear?

**Standard 3**

*Assess how?* Is the assessment method appropriate?

**Standard 4**

*How much evidence?* Is achievement adequately sampled?

**Standard 5**

*Assess accurately?* Has bias been minimized?

*Source:* Adapted from *Student-Involved Classroom Assessment*, 3d ed. (p. 20), by R. J. Stiggins, 2001, Englewood Cliffs, NJ: Merrill/Prentice Hall. Reprinted by permission of Pearson Education, Inc., Upper Saddle River, NJ.

- Demonstrate mastery of specific *performance skills,* where it's the doing that is important?
- Use their knowledge, reasoning, and skills to create *products* that meet standards of quality?

Because there is no single assessment method capable of assessing all these various forms of achievement, one cannot select a proper method without a clear focus on which of these expectations is to be assessed. Our quality-control challenge is to be sure the target is clear before we begin to devise assessment tasks and scoring procedures to measure it.

**Standard 2.** *Sound assessments are specifically designed to serve particular purposes.*

This standard obviously relates to Door 2, which demands a commitment to meeting the information needs of all users. But this quality standard takes that generalized demand a step further. It asks us to build each assessment in light of specific information about its intended users: What purposes will *this* assessment serve? We cannot design sound assessments without asking who will use the results and how. Recall that Table 2 lists the important users of assessment in schools, each of whom needs different information at different times to answer different questions. Providing quality information that will meet people's needs requires that we analyze their needs. For instance, if students are to be involved in assessment by using its results to make important decisions about their own learning, we must conduct the assessment and provide the results in a manner that will make the results useful to them. Their needs might be distinctly differ-ent from the information needs of a teacher, parent, or principal. Thus in this case, the developer of any assessment should be able to provide evidence of having examined the needs of the intended user of that assessment and having conducted that assessment in a manner consistent with that purpose. Otherwise the assessment is without purpose. The quality-control challenge is to develop and administer an assessment only after we have determined precisely who will use its results and how.

Within this standard of quality, we believe that special emphasis needs to be given to one particular assessment user, the student. It has been our habit to think of the student as the subject of the assessment. The fact is that the deci-sions students make on the basis of the evidence of their success that they get from their teachers drive their ultimate success in school. It is essential that they remain in touch with and feel in control of their own improvement over time. For this reason, we advocate deep student involvement in classroom assessment, record keeping, and communication. We believe that the most powerful way to meld assessment and instruction is through student involvement in classroom assessment. (See also Competency 1 for school leaders in Part 4.) Thus, the second standard of classroom assessment quality asks how students are being involved in their own assessment—not every time, but as a matter of routine over time.

**Standard 3.** *Quality assessments rely on assessment methods (exercises and scoring procedures) that accurately reflect the intended target.*

Since we have several different kinds of achievement to assess (see Standard 1), and since no single assessment method can reflect them all, we must rely on a variety of methods. The options available to the classroom teacher include *selected response* (multiple choice, true/false, matching, and fill-in), *essays, performance assessments* (based on observation and judgment), and direct *personal communication* with the student. Our assessment task is to match a method with an intended target (see Table 3). Our quality-control challenge is to be sure all concerned with ensuring quality assessment know and understand how the various pieces of this puzzle fit together.

**Standard 4.** *Quality assessments provide a representative sample of student performance that is sufficient in its scope to permit confident conclusions about achievement.*

All assessments rely on a relatively small number of exercises to permit the user to draw inferences about a student's mastery of larger domains of achievement. A sound assessment offers a representative sample of all those possibilities that is large enough to yield dependable inferences about how the respondent would have done if given all possible exercises. Each assessment context places its own special constraints on our sampling procedures. Our quality-control challenge is to know how to adjust the sampling strategies to produce results of maximum quality at minimum cost in time and effort.

**Table 3**

**Aligning Achievement Targets to Assessment Methods**

| *TARGET TO BE ASSESSED* | *ASSESSMENT METHOD* | | | |
|---|---|---|---|---|
| | SELECTED RESPONSE | ESSAY | PERFORMANCE ASSESSMENT | PERSONAL COMMUNICATION |
| KNOWLEDGE MASTERY | Multiple choice, true/false, matching, and fill-in can sample mastery of elements of knowledge | Essay exercises can tap understanding of relationships among elements of knowledge | Not a good choice for this target | Can ask questions, evaluate answers and infer mastery—but a time-consuming option |
| REASONING PROFICIENCY | Can assess understanding of basic patterns of reasoning | Written descriptions of complex problem solutions can provide a window into reasoning proficiency | Can watch students solve some problems and infer about reasoning proficiency | Can ask student to "think aloud" or can ask followup questions to probe reasoning |
| PERFORMANCE SKILLS | Can assess mastery of the prerequisites of skillful performance, but cannot tap the skill itself—not a good choice for this target | Can assess mastery of the prerequisites of skillful performance, but cannot tap the skill itself—not a good choice for this target | Can observe and evaluate skills as they are being performed | Strong match when skill is oral communication proficiency; also can assess mastery of knowledge prerequisite to skillful performance |
| ABILITY TO CREATE PRODUCTS | Can assess mastery of knowledge prerequisite to the ability to create quality products, but cannot assess the quality of products themselves—not a good choice | Can assess mastery of knowledge prerequisite to the ability to create quality products, but cannot assess the quality of products themselves—not a good choice | A strong match; we can assess: (a) proficiency in carrying out steps in product development, and (b) attributes of the product itself | Can probe procedural knowledge and knowledge of attributes of quality products—but not product quality |

*Source:* Adapted from *Student-Involved Classroom Assessment, 3d ed.* (p. 93), by R. J. Stiggins, 2001, Englewood Cliffs, NJ: Merrill/Prentce Hall. Reprinted by permission of Pearson Education, Inc., Upper Saddle River, NJ.

***Standard 5.*** *Sound assessments are designed, developed, and used in such a manner as to eliminate sources of bias or distortion that interfere with the accuracy of results.*

Even if we devise clear achievement targets, transform them into proper assessment methods, and sample student performance appropriately, there are still factors that can cause a student's score on a test to misrepresent his or her real achievement. Problems can arise from the test, the student, or the environment where the test is administered.

For example, tests can consist of poorly worded questions, place reading or writing demands on respondents that are confounded with mastery of the material being tested, have more than one correct response, be incorrectly scored, or contain racial or ethnic bias. The student can experience extreme evaluation anxiety or interpret test items differently from the author's intent, as well as cheat, guess, or lack motivation. Any of these could give rise to inaccurate assessment results. Or the assessment environment could be uncomfortable, poorly lighted, noisy, or otherwise distracting.

Part of the quality-control challenge is to be aware of the potential sources of bias and to know how to devise assessments, prepare students, and plan assessment environments to deflect these problems before they ever affect results.

## Barriers to Accurate Assessment

Even though these five quality standards are straightforward and relatively easy to understand, they can be very difficult to meet. As it turns out, we face an imposing array of personal, community, and institutional barriers to quality assessment. Let's explore four such roadblocks, along with a strategy for their removal.

### A Personal Barrier to Quality Assessment

So far in this guide, we've asked educators to be clear about targets, assess them well, and be public about results. But what if teachers administer rigorous assessments and the results reveal that students did not hit the target? And what if that failure was due to factors beyond the teacher's control—for example students who failed to fulfill their responsibilities? If this happens, teachers or administrators may be unjustly blamed for students' lack of learning.

Under these circumstances, it may seem safer, from their point of view, to remain vague about achievement expectations and to couch assessment results in such technically complex test scores and complicated gradebook manipulations that no one could ever determine how much learning really took place in classrooms or schools. Such procedures appear to address accountability for student learning without risking real personal accountability.

But the question we must ask is this: If we preserve our own safety in these ways, what are the implications of our behavior for student learning? Clearly, the implications will be far from positive. In this way, an individual teacher's sense of personal vulnerability about being evaluated can lead to distinctly unsound practices. But how do we overcome this pervasive fear? We do so by helping all educators become assessment literate. We will explore more about that.

### The Institutional Barrier: A Lack of Time to Assess Well

Without doubt, the most prominent barrier to quality assessment from the teacher's point of view is the lack of time to assess well.  If teachers feel they don't have time to meet the standards of assessment quality, they won't act to do so. Several specific time issues trouble teachers deeply.

One concern is the broadening curriculum, which means teachers must teach and assess an ever-expanding array of student achievement goals. The curriculum is growing to include more achievement targets such as important technology and health-related topics, more complexity within the "established" targets (for instance, an enhanced understanding of what it means to be a proficient reader or writer), more learning targets classified as problem solving or reasoning, and more complex ways of integrating the curriculum across disciplines. How can teachers assess even more when they already have too little time to assess current targets?

There is only one answer: Learn to assess smarter, not harder. One way to narrow the curriculum and therefore focus on assessments more sharply is to differentiate between (1) core content knowledge students must know outright to function within a discipline, and (2) content we can teach them to retrieve when they need it through the use of reference materials. If we assess mastery of the core and the students' skill in retrieving the rest, we focus the assessment challenge.

A second solution, defined in Door 1, is to start with a vision of twelfth-grade achievement and trace that vision back down through the K–12 curriculum so as to develop a smooth and complete transition from beginning student to competent student. In this way, we can remove redundant and irrelevant material and promote efficient instruction and assessment. Finding what is currently taught and assessed that doesn't relate to or support the attainment of the content standards and then eliminating that from the classroom curriculum would add value and time to any classroom teacher's instruction. Both of these strategies make the teacher's assessment job easier to define and complete.

Here is another time problem: Many teachers contend that some assessment methods are too labor intensive. The message many administrators and teachers are receiving is that performance assessment methodology—"authentic" exercises leading to observations and judgments of students—is the best way to assess student achievement. Advocates cite the richness of results they can derive from detailed observations of performance and judgment based on complex performance standards. Hidden between the lines for many teachers is the subliminal message, "lots of hard work!" Some respond by digging in their heels. Few educators are actively looking for more work to do.

Again, the solution is to learn to assess smarter, not harder. An over-obsession with performance assessment can throw the picture out of balance. Performance assessment is not always the best way. In fact, sometimes it isn't even an acceptable way to assess. In certain instances, and with certain achievement targets, other methods such as multiple-choice or true/false tests are better choices. When they fit, these options are always more efficient. And even when we *do* turn to performance assessment, it can also be a powerful source of instruction, with scoring guides being turned into teaching tools and students being taught to self-assess using the rubrics. But a rich knowledge of how to use performance assessments efficiently is required. Consequently, to tap assessment options with maximum efficiency, we must be assessment literate.

A third time problem is that for many districts the only acceptable way to store and communicate information about student achievement, according to the district policy manual, is the gradebook and report card grades. That process eats huge amounts of time all by itself, leaving neither time nor opportunity to consider alternatives.

If we conceive of record keeping as a teacher-centered activity relying on turn-of-the-century gradebook methodology, the time demands far outstrip anything a teacher or administrator can manage. Again, the solution to this problem lies in breaking an outdated mold. Information-processing technology of the 1920s will not—indeed cannot—meet today's twenty-first century needs. We must start with a sharply focused vision of achievement targets, thoroughly developed assessment plans, highly efficient assessment methods, and strategies for record keeping that rely on information management software. But to tap this technology, we need access to it and sufficient assessment literacy to use it wisely.

## A Community Barrier to Quality

It is not uncommon for parents to define sound assessment practices in terms of their own personal experience when they were in school. The standard they set is this: "Anything you do to my child by way of assessment that I didn't experience in school is unsound practice." If the practices they experienced were sound and appropriate, parents are right to compel us to use them. But the problem arises when the practices they demand are, in fact, unsound. Then, this parental resistance or advocacy becomes a barrier to quality.

The only way past this roadblock is for educators to be sufficiently assessment literate to be able to describe their assessment practices in nondefensive and convincing terms to those who question them.

## The Ultimate Barrier to Quality

The bottom line: We cannot meet standards of quality if we don't know what those standards are or how to meet them. A lack of assessment literacy is the ultimate barrier to quality. After reflecting on the first three barriers to quality—our emotions, a lack of time, and community beliefs—it should be clear that removal of this fourth barrier sets up the removal of the other three. Here's why. The reason educators fear assessment and evaluation is that many don't understand it and therefore cannot gain control over it. But as we gain assessment wisdom we gain that control, and anxiety dissipates. Removal of barrier number four—a lack of assessment know-how—is the key to removing personal barriers to quality.

We have difficulty finding time to assess well because we lack knowledge of assessment strategies that can make our teaching job faster, easier, and better. With assessment literacy comes the time to do the assessment job we are hired to do within the time allotted. Removal of barrier four is the key. The reason many local educators have difficulty dealing with assessment concerns in their communities is that they lack the understanding and confidence to address these issues in a forthright manner. So they negotiate a treaty to do what was always done in testing, or grading and reporting student progress, regardless of its appropriateness. But the more we know about assessment, the easier it is to help our communities understand what assessment practices are sound. So again, the development of assessment literacy is the key to removing this barrier.

## A Plan for Removing the Barriers

Assessment-literate educators are masters of the standards of quality assessment. They know and understand the five standards. But more importantly, they are able to routinely apply them in their schools and classrooms.

The vast majority of educators practicing today have not been given the opportunity to learn about the standards or their application. High-quality professional development programs are needed to provide that foundation—especially given our long history of failing to train teachers and administrators in assessment. The objectives of a practitioner-centered professional development program in classroom assessment, along with highly efficient training strategies, are outlined on the following pages.

Teachers and administrators are prepared to fulfill their ongoing assessment responsibilities when they

- Understand essential differences between sound and unsound assessment practices and commit to meeting key quality standards.
- Know how to meet standards of quality in all classroom, school, and district assessment contexts.
- Know how to apply the nine principles of assessment *for* learning that follow, using the classroom assessment process as a teaching tool to motivate students to strive for higher levels of learning.

### *The Nine Principles of Assessment* **for** *Learning*

1. Teachers understand and can articulate in advance of teaching the achievement targets students are to hit.

2. Students are informed regularly about those targets in terms they can understand, in part through the study of the criteria by which their work will be evaluated and samples of high-quality work.

3. Students can describe what targets they are to hit and what comes next in their learning.

4. Classroom teachers can transform those targets into dependable assessments that yield accurate information.

5. Classroom assessment information is used by both the teacher and the student to revise and guide teaching and learning.

6. Feedback given to students is descriptive, constructive, frequent, and immediate, helping students know how to plan and improve.

7. Students are actively, consistently, and effectively involved in assessment, including learning to manage their own learning through the skills of self-assessment.

8. Students actively, consistently, and effectively communicate with others about their achievement status and improvement.

9. Teachers understand the relationship between assessment and student motivation and use assessment to build student success and confidence rather than failure and defeat.

### *Assumptions Regarding Effective Professional Development Practice*

Achieving these objectives requires designing, developing, and implementing professional development strategies that

- Provide practical new assessment ideas and teaching strategies in an efficient manner.

- Support practice in applying those new strategies in the classroom.
- Give participants responsibility for managing their own learning and development, and promote the sense of professionalism that comes from pursuit of excellence.
- Provide collegial support in a flexible framework, where educators learn by sharing the lessons they have learned individually.
- Deliver benefits very quickly to those who apply lessons learned to their classroom.
- Encourage a healthy concern for quality assessment by emphasizing the research findings about formative assessment done well, and the implications for student learning and well-being, and teacher effectiveness.

### *Organizing Learning Teams for Professional Development*

To satisfy these requirements, we recommend a professional development program that relies heavily on a blend of *learning teams* (also referred to as study groups or study teams) and *individual study* and practice by teachers as the basis of interaction and growth. In these teams, a small group of teachers and administrators agree to meet regularly to share responsibility for their mutual professional development.

Between meetings, each team member commits to completing assignments designed to advance his or her assessment literacy. They might, for example, study the same piece of professional literature and try the same assessment strategies, and then bring the lessons they have learned from that experience to share and discuss in the group meeting. Or team members might complete different assignments, learn different lessons, and meet to share a more diverse array of insights to the benefit of all.

Learning teams can be configured in any of a variety of ways. Groups might be formed on the basis of grade level (within or across levels) or within or across disciplines (math, science, arts, etc.). Learning teams might come into existence as opportunities arise; when, for example, an ad hoc committee is assembled to evaluate and consider revising report card grading or when a curriculum-development team decides to deal with some underlying assessment issues. All such instances represent opportunities for developing effective assessment strategies.

We believe that collaborative learning teams represent the future of professional development in American schools (see Activity 19). Their effectiveness has been proven over time by hundreds of successful learning teams in schools across the country. They are especially effective in schools embracing a professional learning community approach to school improvement. In the learning team model, teachers are drawn to the promise of time to concentrate on one important topic long enough to internalize some new and useful ideas. This, combined with time to talk with and learn from colleagues (both rare commodities for too many educators), makes this model of professional development attractive. Participants in assessment literacy learning teams often recognize and welcome the "permission" to focus on quality classroom assessment rather than prepping for the state test through the endless use of mini-versions of that test.

In a learning team participants can build a portfolio of evidence of their own improvement as classroom assessors, including a journal of self-reflection illustrating evolving assessment competence, and examples of assessments collected over time, with written commentary on their increasing quality. Periodically, team members might also conduct "student-led conferences" detailing to the rest of the team their evidence of progress as classroom assessors.

To support our commitment to this methodology, we have developed a full complement of training materials and step-by-step instructions on creating and facilitating learning teams. These materials, when used by learning teams, will result in effective classroom assessment practices that will involve and motivate students to reach their own academic potential. Resource 6 in Part 4 goes into more detail on this topic, and describes what principals can do to support learning teams.

## Summary

Instruction is most effective when it includes the use of quality assessments. Such assessments are built around users' needs, arise from clearly articulated achievement targets, rely on proper methods, sample student achievement appropriately, and avoid sources of bias and distortion that can lead to inaccurate results.

However, fear of accountability, a lack of time and other resources needed to assess well, an educational environment dominated by having students perform well on large-scale accountability measures, and community or parent expectations can present imposing barriers to quality. The removal of these potential roadblocks requires the development of an assessment-literate school culture.

We have offered a plan for developing that foundation of assessment literacy that places control of professional development in the hands of each practitioner. It calls for an individual commitment to learning about excellence in assessment but supports that effort with a collaborative team. If schools and school districts can support the teamwork part of that process, motivated educators will ante up the rest.

# DOOR 4
## Communicating Effectively About Student Achievement

If schools are to help all students progress toward higher levels of academic proficiency as measured by state standards and locally developed curriculum expectations, and if teachers are to track the progress and development of their students using classroom assessments, our academic record-keeping strategies will have to evolve rapidly. We must communicate effectively about student achievement relative to the written standards to all who need dependable information. We can take advantage of information management software for generating, storing, retrieving, and delivering information about student achievement.

In other words, a grade on a report card every nine weeks based on a summary of handwritten and often uninterpretable gradebook notations cannot tell the student, teacher, or parent precisely where the student is at any point in time on the path to becoming competent. Moreover, students charged with tracking and communicating their own improvement need ongoing access to far greater detail about their own achievement than such records can provide. Teachers receiving new students at the beginning of the year or students coming from a different school, and who are expected to take students from where they are to new levels of competence, also require greater detail. A C+ on a transcript or report card does nothing to inform a new teacher what the student has and has not learned. Likewise, parents who desire and expect to see specific information about the progress of their children are not served by grades on a report card every nine weeks. Further, the time required to enter, retrieve, and summarize records by hand, as teachers do with gradebooks, will soon prove too cumbersome to be practical in a standards-based curriculum.

For these reasons, among others, school districts must commit to developing effective information management and communication systems. To be effective, such systems must adhere to the following basic principles:

- Both message sender and message receiver must understand the achievement target being communicated about. If they don't share a common language and meaning of expectations, then sharing success information will be difficult.
- The assessments used to gather information about achievement must be accurate. If they are not, misinformation will be fed into the communication system.

- Both message sender and message receiver must understand the symbols used to convey information to mean the same thing. If they think the grades, scores, words, pictures, and so on being used mean different things, then miscommunication is assured.
- And finally, message receivers must be open to hearing and understanding the information being shared. If they are not, that is, if the door is closed, then the message will not get through. For this reason, effective communication systems contain a built-in feedback mechanism for verifying that the message was heard and understood.

To develop such communication systems in standards-driven schools where students are progressing through an articulated curriculum, we recommend that school districts take advantage of information management software systems. These systems can assist teachers and districts with essential assessment activities in a number of efficient and effective ways, including the following:

- Organize the goals and objectives that comprise the curriculum.
- Provide standards-based report card formats.
- Generate assessments using a variety of exercise formats.
- Assist teachers in collecting classroom observational data.
- Print assessments for use in the classroom or permit their administration online.
- Permit instant scanning and scoring of selected response assessments.
- Allow direct scanning of virtually any form of record desired, such as actual samples of student writing or videotapes of student performance.
- Provide long-term dependable and efficient storage of that information and instant retrieval and summary as needed.
- Facilitate immediate access to summative assessment records online by anyone authorized to see them, permitting teachers or parents to obtain instant information about the status of any student or any group of students for conferencing or planning purposes.

The time savings and communication advantages available to assessment literate teachers and administrators through the use of these information management systems can be considerable. We believe every school district should form an ad hoc committee of teachers, administrators, and technology staff to review and evaluate the options. The leadership role in this case is that of supporting professional development so teachers can understand the advantages that can come with these systems, and to help them understand how to involve students in the use of such information management systems to their benefit.

# DOOR 5
## Creating a Supportive Policy Environment

Another important part of a quality assessment program is a statement of commitment to quality from school and district leaders. This can take the form of school or district policy, and should make the standards of sound assessment practice clear and understandable. While sound assessment policies don't ensure sound practices, they can contribute by reaffirming a commitment to quality.

To develop such a policy at the district level, the superintendent should draft for school board review and approval an assessment philosophy that articulates the assessment responsibilities for all who contribute to the effectiveness of schools. A few sample entries for such a policy are discussed in this section, and others are included in Activity 20. The final policy statement within any district must be tailored to local needs and should anticipate the need for professional development in assessment.

It has been our experience that district leadership teams do the best job of analyzing and revising assessment policy after they have completed a professional development program in assessment literacy themselves—after they have completed the work of Door 3.

### A Sample District Assessment Policy

A district assessment policy should establish the standards by which quality assessment will be judged (as described previously). Further, it should assert an expectation that staff will apply standards of quality in all assessment contexts. This kind of policy might be worded as follows:

*Because effective instruction depends on high-quality assessment, this district expects all assessments to provide accurate information about student achievement. Each assessment must meet five standards of quality. It must arise from a clearly articulated set of achievement expectations, serve an instructionally relevant purpose, rely on a proper method, sample student achievement in an appropriate manner, and control for all relevant sources of bias and distortion that can lead to inaccurate assessment. Any assessments not meeting these standards are to be discarded.*

Since the quality standards specified previously hold that assessments must serve clear purposes, reflect clear targets, and rely on proper methods, the district policy might outline the full range of appropriate purposes, kinds of targets, and acceptable methods as follows:

*It is the expectation of this school district that all assessments will be directly linked to specific instructional uses and thus to student academic well-being. Two types of use are considered appropriate: (1) assessment as a source of information for decision making and (2) assessment for the purpose of promoting higher levels of student achievement.*

*With respect to the former, several levels of decision making and decision makers are considered important to student academic well-being: classroom level (students, teachers, and parents), instructional support level (principals, curriculum specialists, support teachers, and guidance personnel) and policy level (superintendent, school board, citizens, and taxpayers). The district will allocate assessment resources and devise assessment, evaluation, and communication programs to meet the information needs of all these users.*

*With respect to the use of assessment in promoting high student achievement, the district acknowledges that assessment can serve as a powerful teaching tool. By involving students in the assessment and evaluation of their own achievement under direct supervision, teachers can use assessment to help students understand the meaning of academic success and meet the highest achievement expectations.*

*Any assessments that cannot be linked specifically to student academic well-being through effective decision making or instruction should be discarded. District staff will devise an articulated curriculum from kindergarten through high school designed to divide responsibility for helping students make continuous progress toward state standards. Further, the district will create an assessment and communication system that permits continuous and thorough tracking of student progress.*

*A variety of assessment forms are considered appropriate for use within this district, including*

■  *Selected response (multiple choice, true/false, matching, and fill-in)*

■  *Essay assessments*

- *Performance assessments (based on observation and judgment)*
- *Direct personal communication with the student*

*All staff are expected to understand all of these options and know how and when to rely on each within their context. In addition, each staff member must know how to use each method to sample student achievement appropriately and how to avoid bias and distortion of assessment results when developing and implementing each method. Given these understandings, staff are encouraged to apply these methods in the development of ever more accurate assessments of student achievement.*

Again, in this sample policy statement we see an explicit expectation of assessment competence that is grounded in comprehensive professional development.

## Personnel Policy and Excellence in Assessment

Several dimensions of personnel policy may be in need of revision to ensure the long-term development of an assessment-literate staff. Beginning at the most general level, state licensing requirements should include explicit expectations of assessment competence as a condition for certification in a teacher or administrator role. Only 14 of the 50 states currently impose this licensing standard for teachers and only 3 states are explicit in expecting assessment literacy in administrators who are certified to practice.

Similarly, teacher and administrator training programs in higher education institutions should be encouraged to offer coursework that includes relevant assessment training. Over the decades, higher education has not delivered in this area of professional training.

Admittedly, neither certification standards nor college course offerings are the responsibility of district superintendents or building principals. But the quality of teaching is. And administrators cannot assure their communities of high quality until these aspects of personnel policy change. If we keep pumping new teachers into the system who lack the needed competence, the requirement for local professional development in assessment—often an expensive proposition—will never go away. For these practical reasons, district superintendents might work through their professional associations to lobby state legislatures and higher education to fulfill their responsibilities regarding matters of assessment competence.

Other personnel policy matters hit closer to home. The criteria that districts apply when screening and selecting new teachers and administrators should be adjusted to reflect an expectation of competence in assessment. The criteria used to evaluate ongoing teacher and administrator performance on the job might be adjusted to include evaluation of the quality of assessments and their use. (Refer to Activity 15 and Activity 17 in Part 4.) District staff-development policy might be adjusted—at least on an interim basis—to reflect the strength of the need for assessment training, and assessment and professional development resources might be channeled in this direction.

In short, leadership is needed in creating a local personnel environment that expects and supports competence in assessment, as well as the effective application of that competence in the service of student academic well-being.

## Rethinking Other Relevant Policies

In addition to personnel policy, there are other policy areas that may be in need of reevaluation in pursuing excellence in assessment. These might include policies on curriculum, homework, graduation requirements, promotion/retention, communicating about student achievement (including grading), and policy related to expenditure of assessment resources.

For example, a school district might specify in policy and regulation its commitment to a standards-based curriculum and to communicating clearly about student achievement. It is not uncommon for district policy manuals to be limited to procedures for report card grading and for conducting parent–teacher conferences. These policy statements might be revamped to reflect the expectation that standards of effective communication be observed. These standards might hold practitioners accountable for formulating clear, accurate messages about student achievement that are consistent across classrooms, delivering those messages to students and teachers in understandable terms, and verifying that the messages got through. Further, communication policy may need to be expanded to permit the sharing of information about student achievement via portfolios and various student-involved conference formats. In Part 4 we offer a variety of example policies, some good and some not so good, for review and consideration in terms of how policies can support productive assessment.

It is not uncommon in school district budgets to find just one entry related to assessment: the allocation of funds for the standardized testing program. Since we now understand that assessment happens at many other levels for many other purposes, resources also need to be allocated for all purposes, including professional development to ensure the quality of classroom assessment *for* learning. Other resources might be needed to create and then maintain an information management system for student achievement data.

## Summary

Effective leaders develop their own vision of excellence to guide the efforts of their organization. In schools and especially school districts, that vision takes the form of policies and regulations that guide everyday practice and support balance, quality, and student involvement. Every school district needs a vision of excellence in assessment to guide its practices, and this calls for a carefully worded district assessment philosophy, approved as policy.

We recommend that districts transform into policy a vision of excellence in assessment that calls for the effective use and balance of high-quality standardized and classroom assessments. This policy should make standards of quality clear and explicit, and should *be clear in the expectation that all teachers and administrators consistently meet those standards.*

School districts need to reevaluate and revise personnel, curriculum, reporting, and assessment resource allocation policies to be sure they provide a solid foundation for the development of high-quality assessment programs that can improve student achievement.

# Summarizing the Path to Excellence in Assessment

For decades we have been searching for ways to use the power of assessment to achieve truly effective schools—schools that help all students learn well. Our success in reaching this goal remains contingent on the ability of school and district leaders to see and embrace a vision that includes and extends far beyond our assessment traditions.

We take advantage of what assessment can do productively when we use it to provide evidence of student achievement for public accountability and information for internal programmatic decision making. But we promote student growth and tap the true power of assessment as a tool beyond measurement when we provide information for students, teachers, and parents to inform classroom-level decisions.

We can take advantage of these only if both our classroom assessments and standardized tests are of the highest quality. Our assessments must arise from clear purposes and clearly articulated achievement targets, rely on appropriate assessment methods, sample student achievement appropriately, and minimize bias and distortion in assessment results.

As we have seen, the barriers to quality assessment, and therefore the barriers to tapping the power of assessment *for* learning in the service of effective schools, are significant. But they can be removed if we can become an assessment-literate school culture. Those in school leadership positions can open the doors to excellence in assessment by having their leadership teams and faculties profile their school or district by using the self-analysis profiling activity that follows to ask and answer these questions:

1. Developing a Clear Vision of Achievement Expectations
   A. Have our district and community established a set of expectations for successful graduates—are our achievement destinations clear?
   B. Has our faculty worked as a team to take that vision to the classroom in an articulated, well-defined, and rigorous curriculum—are our roadmaps to achievement success in place?
   C. Are we sure all teachers have mastered the achievement targets they expect their students are to master—are our guides ready to direct their student travelers?

2. Committing to Quality Assessment Information for All Users
   A. What is our plan for meeting the information needs of students, teachers, and parents using classroom assessment?
   B. What is our plan for meeting the information needs of building and district administrators and the community with standardized tests?

3. Building an Assessment-Literate School Culture
   A. What is our plan for evaluating and then building the assessment literacy of school/district faculty and staff?
   B. What is our plan for developing assessment literacy within our community (parents, taxpayers, school board members)?

4. Communicating Effectively About Student Achievement
   A. Has the school/district committed to communicating effectively and accurately about student achievement?
   B. What technology do we need to collect, store, retrieve, and report information about student achievement effectively and efficiently?

5. Developing a Supportive Assessment Policy Environment
   A. What is our plan for evaluating existing policies and for identifying new policy areas not currently addressed that will support and encourage the use of quality assessment?

The answers to these questions help us develop high-performing schools through excellence in assessment, where excellence is defined as the balanced and effective use of both high-quality classroom assessments *for* learning and standardized assessments *of* learning to promote student success.

Leadership in the pursuit of excellence in assessment begins with a guiding vision, clearly showing how assessment fits into effective instruction. All school leaders must understand the importance of quality assessment at all levels and must put forth the standards that will guide assessment practices in every classroom. This vision of quality is committed to paper in the form of a plan that guides district practice. In addition, leaders must ensure an assessment-literate staff, both in the classroom and in the principal's office. The school board must establish the districtwide policy environment that will underpin the pursuit of that vision in every classroom and school within the district. Curriculum directors must contribute clear visions of achievement expectations, holding the entire team together to function as a unit across grade levels and disciplines, and ensuring that state, district, and building assessments are used in a coordinated, aligned fashion in support of student achievement. And principals must be prepared to use assessment to show the community how effective their schools are, while at the same time assisting teachers in developing the assessment literacy needed to create and use high-quality assessments day to day with students in the classroom. By applying the principles of assessment *for* learning, teachers will follow clear research findings about raising student achievement through the use of classroom assessment. These are essential keys to providing leadership for excellence in assessment and for building more effective schools.

On the CD-ROM, found inside the back cover of this book, is a PowerPoint presentation entitled *Five Doors to Excellence in Assessment.* You may use this resource to extend your own understanding of the ideas and concepts presented in these pages, and to help others understand them as well.

## Thinking About Assessment

### Activity 4: Creating an Assessment Profile for Your School/District

**Purpose:**     This activity is critical to your success in charting a path toward your assessment vision. When completed, your assessment profile will show you what work has already been accomplished and what work lies ahead of you. In effect, it helps identify priorities and by doing so, maps the course for achieving balance and quality.

**Time:**     Variable; likely to be 2–5 hours.

**Directions:**     Read through the items in the self-analysis grids correlated to the five doors described in Part 3. Discuss each item with your team and come to agreement about where you would place your school/district along the 5-point continuum. Consider the following as you move through the activity:

- The larger, more diverse a team you can assemble that is representative of your school/district, the more accurate your profile is likely to be. Expanding participation in this activity to others in your system not part of your leadership study team is beneficial. Or your team can do the profiling activity first and then repeat the activity with a larger group to create more understanding of the issues and have a larger representation of opinion.

- If a larger district or school team is assembled, coming to consensus about each item may be more difficult because people will bring not just different perspectives but also very different realities. For example, one person's school may deserve a high rating on one item while another school in the district hasn't even considered that scope of work and therefore admittedly gets a lower mark. How can that be reconciled to reflect the work the district needs to accomplish? Or, the district may be doing well overall in one area but that work has not filtered into the schools. How should the team rate the district overall? In this process there is likely to be rich, revealing discussion about many of the issues raised in the profile; staying focused on the status of the level of analysis (school or district) is essential.

- What we know and don't know at the time we're asked to make judgments or evaluations influences our answers to questions. In this activity and in many others in this guide, the responses from participants are directly related to their level of assessment literacy.

**Closure:** As we noted at the start of this guide, our intention is to help you in two areas: (1) at an organizational/institutional (school or district) level, and (2) at a personal/professional level, one that considers the necessary knowledge and skills for leading assessment reform. We think it is helpful for teams to revisit this self-analysis profile after reading and doing many of the activities in Part 4. Doing the analysis before going on to Part 4 will help clarify and increase understanding of the 10 competencies for leaders you will encounter there. Coming back after reading Part 4 and reviewing the profile in light of these 10 competencies will produce a deeper, more complete analysis.

# SCHOOL/DISTRICT ASSESSMENT SELF-ANALYSIS

**Instructions:** Rate your local assessment system on each of the performance scales provided.

## Door 1: Achievement Standards

Check Appropriate Rating

| | | |
|---|---|---|
| Everyone acknowledges the need to have clearly identified achievement standards. | —  —  —  —  —  —  — | Standards are considered unnecessary or unattainable. |
| Achievement standards have been designed with a clear vision of desired student performance at the end of K–12 schooling. | —  —  —  —  —  —  — | They have not. |
| Those standards are clearly written, contain the appropriate level of rigor, and reflect the needs of adult work/life in the 21st century. | —  —  —  —  —  —  — | They are unclear, etc. |
| If needed, time and resources have been allocated to make the necessary improvements. | —  —  —  —  —  —  — | It has not. |
| The community is/was involved in developing achievement standards. | —  —  —  —  —  —  — | It was not. |
| Achievement standards are published for all to see, reviewed regularly, and revised as needed. | —  —  —  —  —  —  — | They are not. |
| Local achievement standards have been aligned to state standards. | —  —  —  —  —  —  — | They have not been aligned to state standards. |
| Those standards have been further clarified as grade-level curriculum in every subject and every grade. | —  —  —  —  —  —  — | Each teacher develops his/her own curriculum. |
| The written curriculum has been audited/ reviewed to ensure it contains a balance of knowledge, reasoning, skill, and product targets. | —  —  —  —  —  —  — | The curriculum has not been audited for this balance. |

| Positive | Rating Scale | Negative |
|---|---|---|
| A curriculum implementation plan has been written describing roles and responsibilities that ensures standards-based instruction is achieved through use of the adopted curriculum. | \| — \| — \| — \| — \| | There is no plan to ensure standards-based instruction. |
| There is consistency in achievement expectations across teachers. | \| — \| — \| — \| — \| | Each teacher has unique expectations. |
| Teachers are held accountable for teaching the adopted curriculum. | \| — \| — \| — \| — \| | There is no monitoring of what is taught. |
| Staff training and support in curriculum implementation is ongoing in all subjects. | \| — \| — \| — \| — \| | There is little inservice training for staff on teaching to the standards. |
| New teachers in particular are given specialized assistance understanding and teaching to the standards. | \| — \| — \| — \| — \| | Mentoring new teachers in the use of the written curriculum is absent. |
| Teachers are given time to collaboratively plan lessons aimed at accomplishing grade-level expectations. | \| — \| — \| — \| — \| | Time is not dedicated for this purpose. |
| Teachers are trained in strategies such as the use of curriculum mapping or vertical teaming as tools for adding clarity and focus to what is taught. | \| — \| — \| — \| — \| | No training in this area. |
| Achievement standards are held high for all students. | \| — \| — \| — \| — \| | Expectations vary depending upon the student. |
| Model lessons linked to the content standards are available and used for professional development. | \| — \| — \| — \| — \| | No examples are provided. |
| Each teacher's mastery of her/his assigned content has been verified. Those needing support in developing content area knowledge are provided that support. | \| — \| — \| — \| — \| | Little is known about this. |

## Door 2: Commitment to ALL Assessment Users

Check appropriate rating

| | | Educators understand the need to provide information to all users of assessment data. | We have little awareness of the different information interests in the range of users. |
|---|---|---|---|
| | | The information needs of all users are systematically planned for, differentiating and balancing assessments *of* and *for* learning. | Important needs are overlooked; we are not in balance. |
| | | We have a specific plan for how we attend to user needs at these levels: | |
| | | Classroom | This level of users has been neglected. |
| | | Instructional Support (program evaluation/effectiveness, instructional materials, etc.) | This level of users has been neglected. |
| | | Policy (board, legislature, etc.) | This level of users has been neglected. |
| | | A technology-based information management system accessible to all users is in place. | We have no way to manage or communicate assessment data from the various levels. |
| | | Assessment results for all uses are related back to the content standards. | We assess items not in our written curriculum. |

## Door 3: Developing Assessment Literacy

Check appropriate rating

| | | Educators are aware of the consequences of inaccurate measurement. | Most are unaware of this or don't believe it is a problem. |
|---|---|---|---|
| | | We have defined appropriate quality standards for assessments, both *of* and *for* learning. | We have no standards of assessment quality. |
| | | Educators are receptive to improving their assessment competence, as needed. | There is disinterest or resistance to doing so. |
| | | Teachers understand what assessment methods to use when and how to use them. | Matching the assessment method to the type of learning target is not practiced. |

116

Check appropriate rating

| | | | | |
|---|---|---|---|---|
| Teachers understand and apply the principles of sound grading practices, assigning report card grades that are accurate, fair, and representative of current achievement status. | \| | \| | \| | No opportunities have been offered to learn these practices. |
| Assessment is systematically woven into instruction using student involvement and is used formatively to inform teaching and learning. | \| | \| | \| | It is not clear how assessment can be good teaching. |
| Sufficient resources as needed are allocated for learning team–based professional development training in classroom assessment. | \| | \| | \| | No resources have been allocated. |
| Professional development in subject-area content is part of our professional development program. | \| | \| | \| | Nothing is offered in subject-area content. |
| The 9 principles of assessment *for* learning are understood and known and integrated by all into daily classroom instruction. | \| | \| | \| | These principles are not known or applied. |
| Educators all understand that the strengths and limitations of assessment data from various levels of assessment can guide curriculum and instruction. | \| | \| | \| | There is not a clear sense in the ways data can and cannot be used from various assessments. |

### Door 4: Effective Communication

| | | | | |
|---|---|---|---|---|
| Communication to parents focuses on student progress toward the defined learning expectations in the written curriculum and the criteria used to assess that progress. | \| | \| | \| | This does not routinely happen. |
| The district has committed to communicating effectively about student achievement. | \| | \| | \| | No priority has been attached to effective communication. |
| Shared understanding of learning targets, including "student-friendly" and "parent-friendly" versions of the curriculum, is a communication priority. | \| | \| | \| | This has been neglected. |

117

| Accurate assessments of student mastery of the standards is at the heart of the communication plan. | — | — | — | — | This has been neglected. |
| The district uses a data management system for collecting, storing, retrieving, and communicating achievement data. | — | — | — | — | Is neither investigating or implementing such use. |
| The school/district verifies receipt of the message. | — | — | — | — | This has been neglected. |
| Schools report multiple types of data to parents in meaningful and timely ways. | — | — | — | — | They do not. |
| Students are involved in communicating about their own progress and achievement status. | — | — | — | — | Students play no role in this. |
| The communication of standardized test results to parents is in clear, understandable terms. | — | — | — | — | We have no plan or procedures for this. |
| There is agreed meaning of symbols used in communicating student learning. | — | — | — | — | This has been neglected. |

## Door 5: Creating Supportive Policies Based on Assessment Beliefs
Check appropriate rating

| The district has adopted a guiding assessment philosophy, a mission, and beliefs regarding student assessment. | — | — | — | — | Has not adopted assessment philosophy. |
| Our view of policy is one of opportunity to achieve the vision and to positively impact professional practice rather than one of compliance and regulation. | — | — | — | — | Our policy perspective is mostly one of rules and regulations. |
| Personnel policies reflect an expectation of assessment competence. | — | — | — | — | Policies do not reflect an expectation of assessment competence. |

| | | | | | |
|---|---|---|---|---|---|
| Hiring policies and procedures require it. | — | — | — | — | — | Policies and procedures do not require it. |
| Ongoing staff evaluations require it. | — | — | — | — | — | Evaluations do not require it. |
| District professional development policies reflect it. | — | — | — | — | — | Professional development policies do not reflect it. |
| Budget allocations assure the quality of both classroom *for* learning and standardized assessment *of* learning. | — | — | — | — | — | Resources are not allocated for both. |
| We have identified those policies at the school/district level that contribute to productive assessment practice. | — | — | — | — | — | We have not. |
| Our approach to developing and coordinating policies relating to assessment is systemic. | — | — | — | — | — | It is a random approach. |
| We routinely evaluate the impact of assessment policies and practices. | — | — | — | — | — | We do not routinely evaluate them. |

119

## Leadership for Assessment Reform

Check appropriate rating

| | | |
|---|---|---|
| We are committed to academic excellence and this is communicated through a clear vision for the instructional program. | \| \| \| \| \| | Are committed to minimum competence. |
| This vision defines how assessment fits into effective teaching and learning. | \| \| \| \| \| | It does not. |
| We define success as high achievement for all learners, not sorting into winners and losers. | \| \| \| \| \| | Define success in terms other than high achievement. |
| Leaders are assessment literate themselves and are committed to assessment literacy for all. | \| \| \| \| \| | Are not schooled in sound assessment practices and are unaware of or negative about the need for staff literacy throughout. |
| We are willing to risk changing assessment priorities and practices to achieve excellence and balance. | \| \| \| \| \| | Prefer maintaining the status quo. |
| The district has developed a written comprehensive assessment action plan. | \| \| \| \| \| | A plan has not been written. |
| An assessment planning team with representatives from all key stakeholder groups has been established and meets regularly. | \| \| \| \| \| | No planning group exists. |
| A schedule of assessments given has been established displaying grade level, time of year, type of assessment, subject area, standards assessed, and use of results. | \| \| \| \| \| | This information has not been compiled. |
| A plan has been developed that coordinates state, district, and building level tests. | \| \| \| \| \| | No written plan exists. |

120

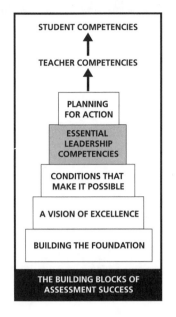

STUDENT COMPETENCIES

TEACHER COMPETENCIES

PLANNING FOR ACTION

ESSENTIAL LEADERSHIP COMPETENCIES

CONDITIONS THAT MAKE IT POSSIBLE

A VISION OF EXCELLENCE

BUILDING THE FOUNDATION

THE BUILDING BLOCKS OF ASSESSMENT SUCCESS

4

*Political turmoil and public debate will undoubtedly surround the No Child Left Behind legislation in the foreseeable future. While that plays out, most of America's students will come to school every day wanting to learn, trusting their teachers and schools to prepare them effectively for success. Meeting the challenge requires school leaders know and do what's right in the area of student assessment. The school leader's assessment responsibilities can be met through the application of a set of 10 assessment competencies.*

*Part Four*

# THE REQUIRED SKILLS FOR ASSESSMENT BALANCE AND QUALITY
## TEN COMPETENCIES FOR EDUCATIONAL LEADERS

So far, we've developed a vision for a balanced, quality assessment system, considered the essential components for such a system, and examined the foundation that needs to be in place for that system to raise student achievement. In Part 4 we turn our attention to the specific competencies school leaders need to develop in order to create local systems that prosper. The 10 competencies we'll describe help ensure that all assessments are used for their intended purposes and that assessment and its results benefit student learning.

As principals and other educational leaders work to understand and comply with the requirements of the No Child Left Behind Act (NCLB), the once-a-year standardized tests that serve as the core of that legislation continue to be called into question. Some cite the current state of testing technology as not being up to the task of accurate and reliable tracking of adequate yearly progress (Center on Education Policy, 2003). Others point to the long-term disadvantages and harmful effects of high-stakes tests on student learning, citing few achievement gains on independent measures and higher overall dropout rates as an outcome when tests are connected to high stakes (Amrein and Berliner, 2003). Political turmoil and public debate will undoubtedly surround this legislation in the foreseeable future.

While that plays out, most of America's students will come to school every day wanting to learn, trusting their teachers and schools to prepare them effectively for success. Meeting that challenge requires knowing and doing what's right in the area of student assessment (Stiggins, 2002). Part of knowing what we're doing from an assessment perspective means having the skill to use assessment in ways never envisioned by NCLB. It means using assessment not just to measure and calculate adequate yearly progress, but also to build learner confidence and motivation to learn; to actually be the catalyst for higher student achievement and not merely the dipstick that gauges it.

No parent or educator wants any child to be left behind, and most educators accept the need to improve the quality of the school experience so *all* students are well served. As we noted in Part 1, NCLB counts on accountability-oriented uses of large-scale assessments to improve schools and raise standards. But we can reframe the opportunity it presents, and truly enlist assessment in the service of not leaving children behind by first asking this question: What will it *really* take to realize the goal of NCLB? Can another layer of standardized testing, even one with nationwide high stakes, by itself create schools where all students achieve at high levels? Are there other ways assessment could be used to serve student success?

For the values behind the President's mandate to become reality, it will take much more than another test at grades 3 through 8 in every school in every state, every year. This isn't an argument against accountability or the use of standardized tests. It is rather an argument for a more comprehensive, balanced, and thoughtful approach to the use of assessment in improving schools, one that doesn't allow the score of a single test to determine what we think is good or bad about students and schools. Standardized tests, constructed far from the classroom, cannot provide the level of specificity about individual student achievement that assessment-literate classroom teachers can produce. But, when used appropriately, the standardized assessments *of* learning that are part of NCLB can generate valuable data that can be used to guide programmatic decisions and direct local school improvement. Only when balanced with classroom assessment *for* learning, the daily assessments used by teachers that mirror good instruction and allow students to risk learning without being constantly evaluated, will schools do their job in meeting the information needs of all assessment users, including students.

So, as NCLB plays out in state capitals and school district boardrooms, what can building principals and other administrators do to foster assessment quality and balance? Just as state and district assessment systems need to attend to balancing assessments *of* and *for* learning, leaders can and should attend to issues of quality and balance at the school level. They can begin to create sound assessment practices where they don't exist, and nurture and extend appropriate assessment where it is already in place.

The leadership responsibilities in assessment can be met through the application of a set of 10 competencies. When school leaders put into practice the skills underlying the competencies, they promote the intentional use of accurate, student-involved classroom assessment on a daily basis to improve student learning, and in doing so, they also address the need to raise test scores as measured on standardized tests.

The 10 competencies shown in Table 4 have been revised from a framework designed for educational leaders (Arter, Stiggins, Duke, and Sagor, 1993). Research on assessment to support learning (Black and Wiliam, 1998), and the need to achieve balance between standardized and classroom assessment (Stiggins, 2002) have both influenced the revisions.

**Table 4**

1. The leader understands the standards of quality for student assessments and how to ensure that these standards are met in all assessments.

2. The leader understands the principles of assessment *for* learning and works with staff to integrate them into classroom instruction.

3. The leader understands the necessity of clear academic achievement standards, aligned classroom-level achievement targets, and their relationship to the development of accurate assessments.

4. The leader knows and can evaluate teachers' classroom assessment competencies and helps teachers learn to assess accurately and use the results productively.

5. The leader can plan, present, or secure professional development activities that contribute to the use of sound assessment practices.

6. The leader analyzes student assessment information accurately, uses the information to improve curriculum and instruction, and assists teachers in doing the same.

7. The leader develops and implements sound assessment and assessment-related policies.

8. The leader creates the conditions necessary for the appropriate use and reporting of student achievement information, and can communicate effectively with all members of the school community about student assessment results and their relationship to improving curriculum and instruction.

9. The leader understands the attributes of a sound and balanced assessment system.

10. The leader understands the issues related to the unethical and inappropriate use of student assessment and protects students and staff from such misuse.

What does it look like when school leaders demonstrate competence in each of the 10 areas? There are more ways to work toward the 10 competencies than the activities and resources we suggest to help leaders master and apply these competencies that follow. Our intent is not to offer an exhaustive list, but rather to provide a catalyst for leaders to think about how you fulfill your leadership role in assessment. From there, you can reflect upon what you already know and can do, and upon what needs to be done or learned next in order to implement a quality, balanced student assessment system at the local level.

**Please note:** In the activities and resources that follow, there are several checklists, rubrics, and rating forms included to judge or evaluate educators' understanding of high-quality, student-involved classroom assessment *for* learning. These are all variations on the theme of evaluating teacher confidence and competence in classroom assessment *for* learning, but they each take a slightly different look. You can choose the one(s) most suited to your context and purpose. Here is how they relate to each other:

| Title/Location | What makes it different from the others |
|---|---|
| Auditing Classroom Assessments for Quality—Activity 7 in Competency 1 | This provides a direct analysis of teachers' **application** of the principles of applying high-quality, student-involved classroom assessment *for* learning by examining the assessments actually produced and used by teachers. This is different from asking teachers to self-assess and different from classroom observation. |
| Developmental Continuum—Activity 8 in Competency 1 | This is a teacher or leader assessment tool that emphasizes and details **competence** on assessment quality, with a little bit on assessment *for* learning. It can be used for classroom observation and interviews with teachers. |
| Confidence Questionnaire—Resource 1 in Competency 1 | This is a teacher self-rating form that emphasizes **confidence** in developing and using various assessment methods for various purposes. |
| Nine Principles—Activity 10 in Competency 2 | This is a teacher self-rating tool that emphasizes and details **competence** on assessment *for* learning, with a little bit on assessment quality. |

# Competency 1

## The leader understands the standards of quality for student assessments and how to ensure that these standards are met in all assessments.

It is part of the teacher's professional responsibility to know how to apply standards of quality to classroom assessment development or selection, and it is part of the school leader's assessment responsibility to be able to judge whether an assessment adheres to these standards. Even though teachers lack training in classroom assessment, they are still responsible for developing a majority of their own assessments. Further, selecting ready-made assessments these days is easier than picking questions from the back of the textbook or from other supplementary material. Websites on the Internet offer test items and tasks to teachers in many subjects in many grade levels, and test item banks remain popular software purchases for teacher test construction.

Principals and other school leaders can evaluate any assessment developed or selected by teachers according to the following quality standards:

1. *Clear purpose*: Sound assessments arise from specific information needs
2. *Clear targets*: They arise from explicit standards
3. *Proper methods*: Sound assessments match method to context
4. *Appropriate sample*: Sound assessments are sufficient in scope and coverage
5. *Control for bias*: Bias damages the accuracy of results; sound assessments minimize it

These standards of quality, when applied routinely by assessment-literate teachers ensure the accuracy of classroom assessments. The Black and Wiliam (1998) research described in Part 1 points to the positive effects on learning when assessment quality improves.

It is part of the leader's job to help teachers meet these standards. They can do this only by becoming assessment literate themselves and by ensuring that all assessments provide accurate information. However, too often the assessment job of classroom teachers has been removed from their hands. In place of helping teachers become assessment literate, schools and districts may substitute ready-made assessments that are narrowly designed to prepare for state tests or to generate additional assessment *of* learning data.

Classroom assessment is not about teachers creating or using mini-versions of the state test. Classroom assessment is about giving students information about their own learning on their way to state standards. It enables students to reach the standard on a state test because the scaffolding of learning has been in place in classroom instruction and assessment, allowing them to gain the knowledge and skills necessary to demonstrate mastery of the state standards on the state test. And all assessments along this path, formative and summative, need to reflect standards of quality.

Large-scale assessments also must adhere to standards of quality if they are to be accurate and reliable. Items of poor quality and errors in scoring procedures on state tests are common reports in the media and raise public concern about test quality and the credibility of scores. In 2001, the Commission on Instructionally Supportive Assessment (CISA) released a set of nine requirements that large-scale assessments must adhere to if they are to maximize their usefulness in supporting instruction. Although these guidelines are aimed at state-level accountability tests and therefore are not relevant to classroom assessment, some of the guidelines may have some usefulness for districts constructing assessments to complement the state testing system (pp. iv–v):

1. A state's content standards must be prioritized to support effective instruction and assessment.
2. A state's high-priority content standards must be clearly and thoroughly described so that the knowledge and skills students need to demonstrate competence are evident.
3. The results of a state's assessment of high-priority content standards should be reported standard-by-standard for each student, school, and district.
4. A state must provide educators with optional classroom assessment procedures that can measure students' progress in attaining content standards not assessed by state tests.
5. A state must monitor the breadth of the curriculum to ensure that instructional attention is given to all content standards and subject areas, including those that are not assessed by state tests.

6. A state must ensure that all students have the opportunity to demonstrate their achievement of state standards; consequently, it must provide well-designed assessments appropriate for a broad range of students, with accommodations and alternate methods of assessment available for students who need them.

7. A state must generally allow test developers a minimum of three years to produce statewide tests that satisfy Standards for Educational and Psychological Testing and similar test-quality guidelines.

8. A state must ensure that educators receive professional development focused on how to optimize children's learning based on results of instructionally supportive assessments.

9. States should continually track progress to ensure that tests are a) appropriate for the accountability purposes for which they are used, b) appropriate for determining whether students have attained state standards, c) appropriate for enhancing teaching, and d) not the cause of negative consequence.

## Thinking About Assessment

### Activity 5: Understanding Standards of Classroom Assessment Quality

**Purpose:**    This represents a first step toward helping your leadership team understand the standards of good practice that must guide your work and that of your colleagues.

**Timing:**    30 minutes

**Directions:**    Each member of your leadership team is to return to Door 3 of the self-analysis guide in Part 3 and find the written description of the five standards of assessment quality.  Create your own graphic organizer depicting those standards in a manner that helps you solidify them in your own mind.

Share and compare organizers among team members to further solidify your learning.

## Thinking About Assessment

### Activity 6: ATI Interactive Video, *Creating Sound Classroom Assessments*

**Purpose:** The Assessment Training Institute's interactive training video series for use with school faculties includes one presentation that provides an overview of a practical set of classroom assessment quality standards. These are the same five standards addressed behind Door 3 in Part 3 of this guide:

- Clarify achievement targets.
- Identify assessment users and uses.
- Select a proper assessment method.
- Sample student achievement with high-quality exercises.
- Control for relevant sources of bias.

In this video and its associated trainer's guide, we provide the basis for a workshop experience for a faculty interested in an overview of how these standards lead to gathering accurate information about student achievement day to day in the classroom.

*Important Note:* While this program provides an easy to understand overview of sound classroom assessment practices, it cannot teach teachers how to make those practices operational by itself. That requires further study of the principles of high-quality assessment.

**Timing:** About 2 hours

**Directions:** Obtain a copy of the video and trainer's guide and follow directions provided in the guide.

**Closure:** For those interested in learning more about these ideas and their application in their own classrooms, invite them to form learning teams to study and discuss the practices of assessment-literate teachers.

## Thinking About Assessment

### Activity 7: Auditing Classroom Assessments for Quality

**Purpose:**   Part of being an instructional leader means being able to gauge the quality of classroom assessments to ensure that they are likely to yield accurate results and to be sure that teachers are applying assessment *for* learning techniques. This activity provides leaders with practice in knowing what to look for as they watch assessment in action in the classroom or in other contexts.

Ability to distinguish sound from unsound classroom assessment practices is the heart of competencies being developed throughout all ATI's assessment literacy training materials, including *Student-Involved Classroom Assessment*, *Practice with Student-Involved Classroom Assessment*, and this leadership guide. Completing the activity will not be enough by itself to develop the knowledge and skills needed to be assessment literate, but it will give you a sense of what educators are able to do as a matter of routine after studying the text.

**Time:**   Option A: 30 minutes.  Option B: 60–90 minutes.

**Directions:**   Less experienced leaders and learning teams should complete Option A. More experienced leaders and teams should complete Option B. Enthusiasts may wish to complete both options, using different sample assessments.

*Option A:* Complete the worksheet, "Characteristics of High-Quality Classroom Assessments," page 134. Use the accompanying documents, "Standards of Assessment Quality Summary," page 135, and "Sample Assessment: Reading Rate," pages 136–138, as directed.

*Option B:* Use the information contained in the document, "Classroom Assessment Quality Rubrics," pages 139–146, to analyze a selected sample assessment. You may choose your own sample, or you may use the provided "Sample Assessment: Reading Rate," pages 136–138. If you use your own sample, be sure you understand the following aspects of the assessment context:

- What student learning goals is this assessment intended to cover? Why were these chosen?
- How were the learning goals on which this assessment is based made clear to students?

- For what purpose(s) was this assessment conducted? Who was intended to use the results? Was this an assessment *of* or *for* learning?
- How were students involved in the assessment, if at all?
- How was student learning diversity accommodated, if at all?
- How, if at all, were students and/or others communicated with about the results of this assessment?

1. Individually rate the sample classroom assessment on each of the quality assessment standards using the rubrics. Be specific on the reasons for your ratings—use wording from the rubrics. Use the form "Evaluating Classroom Assessments for Quality," page 147, to record your scores and reasons.

2. When everyone has had a chance to evaluate the assessment individually for each standard, discuss your ratings one standard at a time, and attempt to come to consensus for each. Write the group score in the appropriate space on the form "Evaluating Classroom Assessments for Quality."

3. As a team, write a brief analysis, using the worksheet, "Analysis of a Classroom Assessment," page 148. What are the strengths of the assessment? What things might you improve? Is it appropriate for all students? Use wording from the rubrics and include points made in your discussion.

4. The document, "Sample Assessment: Reading Rate" has been analyzed for quality (pp. 149–152). If you used this sample, you can compare your responses to those we have provided.

**Closure:** Conduct a large-group debriefing by asking the following questions: What did you notice about the assessment you reviewed? What percentage of the classroom assessments with which you are familiar meet these standards of quality? What are the implications for students?

## Option A

---

# Characteristics of High-Quality Classroom Assessments

---

**Step 1 (5 minutes):** Brainstorm a list of qualities of high-quality classroom assessments using the following procedure: Choose a recorder for your group. Give everyone a few moments individually to list characteristics of high-quality classroom assessments. Then, go clockwise with each member of the group supplying one characteristic. Keep going for the remaining time.

> *Brainstormed list of characteristics of a good classroom assessment:*

**Step 2 (about 10 minutes):** Look at document, "Sample Assessment: Reading Rate," pages 136–138. Add to the list of what makes a good classroom assessment.

> *Additional characteristics of a good classroom assessment:*

**Step 3 (about 10 minutes):** Read the "Standards of Assessment Quality Summary" on page 135. Match the characteristics on your lists to the standards on the next page. Where are the matches? Any surprises?

# Standards of Assessment Quality Summary
# Questions to Ask of Classroom Assessments

## Standard 1: Clear and Appropriate Learning Targets
- Does the assessment author have a clear picture of what she or he is trying to measure?
- Are the student learning targets stated and easy to find?
- Are the student learning targets focused—there aren't too many?
- Are they clear? Would teachers agree on what they mean?
- Are they good? Do they represent the heart of the discipline and are they worth the instructional and assessment time devoted to them? Is there a clear connection to standards?
- Do the stated learning targets reflect a bigger plan to cover all important learning targets over time? Do they reflect a bigger plan across grade levels—previous and next learning—in a continuous progress curriculum?

## Standard 2: Clear and Appropriate Users and Uses
- Does the assessment author have a clear picture of how the assessment results will be used and by whom?
- How do the purposes in this assessment fit into a bigger plan that addresses both assessment *of* and *for* learning?
- *Communication:* Will the users of the results understand and find them useful?
- *Student Involvement:* Would student-involvement components be useful in this case? If so, are they present? If not present, could they be easily added? How does the student involvement in this assessment reflect a bigger plan for involving students in their own assessment?

## Standard 3: Choosing the Best Assessment Method
- Has the assessment method been consciously chosen to fit the learning targets to be assessed?
- What types of learning targets are being assessed?
- What are the assessment methods used?
- Are the assessment methods best for the learning targets being assessed? Best = ideal balanced with practical.

## Standard 4: Sampling
- Does the assessment gather enough information to be able to make a generalization about level of student learning on the target? If not, is this assessment part of a bigger plan to gather sufficient information across time/assessments?

## Standard 5: Avoiding Potential Sources of Bias and Distortion
- Do you notice anything in the assessment or way the assessment is carried out that might not allow a student to be able to adequately demonstrate what he or she knows and can do?
- Are the assessment questions or exercises written well—not confusing, the answer to one question doesn't give away the answer to another, etc.?
- If a performance assessment, is the scoring guide (rubric) clear and does it cover the most important aspects of what makes a quality performance? Is the performance task clear? Will it elicit the desired performance on the part of the student so that student performance quality can be assessed using the scoring guide?

# Sample Assessment: Reading Rate

**Intended Grade Level:** Grade 2–3

## Description

The teacher assesses the reading rate of students once each quarter. The teacher chooses a book that she judges is at an appropriate reading level each quarter. All students read the same book each quarter. The students read for one minute while the teacher marks miscues. Reading rate is defined as the total number of words read in one minute minus the number of words that were skipped or misread.

The results for two students follow. Teacher handwritten notes are in italics next to where they occurred in the text; they show miscues and provide other information. An upward arrow (^) denotes how far each student read in one minute.

The teacher uses the information to report progress to parents. Copies of the letter she sends in October and April are attached.

## Student Reading Protocols

| **Watch Out, Ronald Morgan!** (*2.2 level*)* |
| --- |
| It all started when the bell rang. I raced *(rushed)* across the schoolyard and slid *(slide—self corrected OK)* over a patch of ice.<br>"Watch out, Ronald!" Rosemary yelled, but it was too late. I ^ slid into her and she landed in a snow pile.<br><br>*John 10/97     30 – 1 = 29 wpm* |
| It all started when the bell rang. I raced across the schoolyard and slid over a patch *(path)* of ice.<br>"Watch out, Ronald!" Rosemary yelled, but it was too late. I slid into her and she landed in a *(the)* snow pile.<br>When I got to my class I fed the goldfish. I fed Frank, the gerbil, too.<br>"Oh, no," Rosemary said. "You fed the gerbil food to Goldie."<br>"Oh," I said. "The boxes look the same. Billy shook his head. "Can't you read the letters? F is for fish. G is for gerbil."<br>At recess Miss Tyler wouldn't let us go outside. "You'll get snow in ^ your sneakers." She said. We played kickball in the gym. The ball bounced off my head.<br><br>*Lucy 10/97      105 – 2 = 103 wpm* |

*\*Source: From *Watch Out, Ronald Morgan!* by Patricia Reilly Giif and Susanna Natti, 1986, New York: Viking. Reprinted by permission.*

**Letters to Parents**

Date

Dear Parent,

As part of the first quarter assessment of your child, I checked your child to see how many words per minute he/she could read using a story at the **second grade level**. The story was *Watch Out, Ronald Morgan.*

Research shows that when an individual can read at a rate of 150–200 wpm, they are reading proficiently and will comprehend at a high rate. Students should be able to reach that goal by the end of 5th grade. The goal for 2nd graders is 80 wpm, and **the goal for 3rd grade students will be to read 110 wpm at the 3rd grade level**. It only makes sense that the more at ease we are in reading, the more we will understand what we have read.

Next quarter your child will again be tested, but at the 3rd grade level instead of the 2nd grade.

Please read your child's results and see where they are and how they compare with his/her peers. Oral reading at home will greatly improve your child's reading rate.

_____ is currently reading 2nd grade material at a rate of _____ wpm.

**1st Quarter Reading Rates**

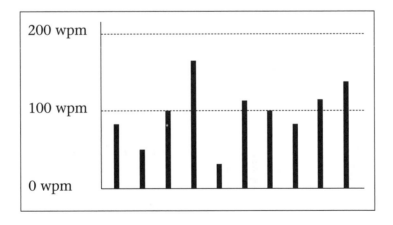

Date

Dear Parent,

Your child was tested last week on the story "The Recital," a story that every child has read twice. It is a story that comes from our third-grade reading book.

As you will recall, our goal is to read 110 wpm by the end of the year. As you can see we have quite a range, from 37 wpm all the way to 208.

Remember that those students who can read at a good rate have a much easier time succeeding in school. Those of you who faithfully listen to your child or read with your child, pat yourself on the back. I applaud you.

Keep reading with your child this quarter. Let's see what percentage of our class can make that 110-wpm goal.

_____ is currently reading 3rd grade material at a rate of _____ words per minute.

**3rd Quarter Reading Rates**

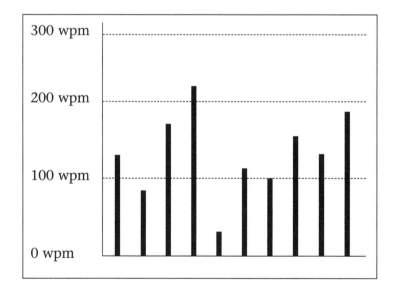

## Option B

| Classroom Assessment Quality Rubrics |
| --- |

### Standards for Quality Assessments

Before using any assessment, the user must ensure its quality. Any standardized test, state or district developed assessment, or classroom assessment must be evaluated through the careful application of specific quality control standards. Good consumers ask tough questions about quality. On the following pages are the questions that an assessment user or author should ask in conducting such an analysis of quality. These questions are framed as a rubric that cover each of the Standards of Assessment Quality expanded on here.

1. **Standard 1**—*What*: A sound assessment arises from clear and appropriate student learning target(s)—achievement expectations are clearly and completely defined and are couched in the best current understanding of the field.

2. **Standard 2**—*Why*: A sound assessment serves clearly articulated and appropriate purposes—why are these targets being assessed, who will use the information, and what will the information be used for? This includes uses that connect directly to opportunities for student learning and motivation (2b), and communication that is appropriate for the audience and use (2c).

3. **Standard 3**—*How*: A sound assessment uses a method appropriate for the targets being assessed and the assessment's audience and purposes.

4. **Standard 4**—*How Much*: A sound assessment samples student achievement appropriately—it provides for gathering just the right amount of information, not too much and not too little.

5. **Standard 5**—*How Accurate*: A sound assessment is developed to avoid potential sources of bias and distortion—there is confidence that the results really reflect what a student knows and is able to do.

### Rationale for the Scale

We have three-point rubrics—an assessment can be "fast-tracked," "on track, but needs work," or "side-tracked" for each of the Standards of Assessment Quality. We decided that three levels of quality are probably enough to help educators understand the nature of quality assessment. The rubrics can, however, easily be converted into a five-point scale. Think of a "4" as having some qualities of a "fast-tracked" and some of an "on track." Likewise, a "2" can be thought of as having some qualities of an "on track" and some of a "side-tracked."

### A Note of Caution

Do not think of these rubrics as checklists—it is not true that everything under a "fast-tracked" has to be present to get a high score. Rather, the statements in each level of the rubrics represent the types of things characteristic of an assessment at each level of quality. Use the rubrics by finding the descriptors that most match the assessment you are reviewing.

## Standard 1—*What:* Clear and Appropriate Student Learning Targets

**Fast Tracked**
- Targets are stated, selective, and easy to find.
- Targets are important—worth the assessment time devoted to them.
- Targets are related clearly to district/state standards/outcomes.
- There is an effort to define targets: examples of student work, definitions, references to performance criteria, and/or a table of specifications.
- The target(s) is clear enough that other educators would more or less interpret the target(s) the same.
- Target descriptions and definitions reflect best thinking in the field.
- There is an appropriate mix of targets and/or there is evidence of long-term thinking—how targets in the current assessment fit with plans for the year.

**On Track, But Needs Work**
- Targets are listed, but they might be stated differently in different places or require some work to find.
- Some of the targets are essential, but there also seems to be some dead wood that might profitably be cut.
- Targets seem to be retrofitted to an already existing test; as a result, one might feel somewhat dissatisfied that the assessment is well thought out.
- Although targets are stated, there is some question as to their meaning—different educators might define the targets differently.
- At first glance there seems to be a connection between stated targets and local content standards, but on closer examination the connection is not clear.
- Some of the targets represent best thinking in the field; others do not.
- Long-term planning—how targets in the current assessment fit with plans for assessing all important targets over time—are implied but must be inferred.

**Side-Tracked**
- Stated targets are broad and/or vague; there is little attempt at clarification.
- No targets are stated.
- There is little focus; everything is listed.
- Statements of targets ramble; the author lists one and later seems to list others. Targets might have to be inferred from the assessment itself.
- Targets are stated, but seem trivial; why spend time assessing this?
- The description of targets doesn't reflect best thinking in the field.
- There is a poor mix of targets: the author might have chosen only the easiest targets to assess; or, there is little evidence of how the targets in the current assessment fit into the overall plan for the year.
- There is no connection to district or state standards and outcomes.

## Standard 2a—*Why:* Clear and Appropriate Users and Uses

**Fast-Tracked**
- It is clear who the intended users and uses are; they are appropriate.
- Users and uses are focused—there aren't too many.
- There are statements relating assessment design to users and uses; these adaptations are appropriate—for example, if an assessment is designed to report student progress to parents, parents actually do understand the report.
- Over several assessments the mix of users and uses is good, including tracking student progress toward important learning outcomes, planning instruction, student involvement, and evaluation of the success of instruction.

**On Track, But Needs Work**
- Users and uses are implied, but not stated; the reviewer has to infer them.
- The author is aware that users and uses are important considerations, but seems to be unsure what to do about it.
- Users and uses are stated, but there is a question about appropriateness.
- Users and uses are stated, but the author doesn't seem to understand the importance of stating them.

**Side-Tracked**
- There are too many users and uses; it would be impossible to satisfy all the stated purposes in a single assessment.
- No purposes are stated; it is not clear why the assessment is being given.
- The stated purpose doesn't seem to match the assessment.
- The only purpose, ever, is grading.
- The author doesn't appear to be aware that an assessment should be designed with users and uses in mind.
- The purposes are inappropriate; you find yourself asking, "Why are they generating information for *this* purpose?"

## Standard 2b—*Why:* Student Involvement

**Fast-Tracked**
- The author has considered how the assessment results, procedures, and/or materials can be used to promote instructional uses; if such student uses are not included, it is reasonable that they should not be—or, it is clear how this assessment is part of a student-involved plan that unfolds over time.
- The assessment results, procedures, or materials help students understand the nature of the learning targets they are to hit through such things as practice with criteria and rubrics, student-friendly versions of rubrics, student development of assessment, or student cross-referencing of assessment questions to targets.
- The assessment results, procedures, or materials assist students with self-assessment, tracking achievement, and communication in a meaningful way—not as something that appears to have been tacked on to look good, but with no real substance.
- There are likely to be other positive side effects for students; e.g., increased student interest in the topic being assessed, increased student motivation to learn, or increased student ability to take control of his or her own learning.

**On Track, But Needs Work**
- Some student-involved procedures are meaningful, some are not.
- It is unclear if the assessment will have positive or negative learning effects for students.
- Student uses are scattered throughout, but have to be searched for or inferred; such use is not consciously stated or related to a larger plan over time.

**Side-Tracked**
- There is no student involvement even though it would be reasonable to include, or, it is not clear how this assessment is part of a student-involved plan that unfolds over time.
- Student-involved uses appear to have been tacked on as an afterthought; suggestions don't promote meaningful student involvement; there is no stated connection to promote learning.
- The assessment might have negative side effects for students; e.g., embarrassment, a feeling of being a failure, or turning students off to learning.
- The author does not seem to believe that students have the ability to assess themselves, nor sees the profit in their trying.

## Standard 2c—*Why:* Communicates Effectively to Users

**Fast-Tracked**
- The author has anticipated the needs of the users—type of information, timing, understandability of symbols and reports, connection to further student learning.
- A description of these considerations is easy to find.
- Possible unintended negative side effects have been anticipated and avoided.

**On Track, But Needs Work**
- The author has considered the communication needs of users, but it still needs work on understandability, timing, descriptiveness, potential for further learning, or possible negative side effects.
- Information about communication is there, but it has to be inferred or searched for.

**Side-Tracked**
- Reporting mechanisms don't seem to fit the needs of the users—the stated users might not understand the information, it is not presented clearly, it is not timely, the only information is judgmental when descriptive feedback would serve the purpose better, connection to further student learning is missing, or presentation might have negative side effects on the recipient.
- The author has not considered communication at all.

## Standard 3—*How:* Target–Method Match

**Fast-Tracked**
- The assessment method matches purpose and target (see table).
- There's a reasonable rationale for the method(s) used and where/why compromises had to be made.
- There's a table of specifications showing how each target is to be measured and its relative importance; this table makes sense.
- There is an appropriate mix of assessment methods; there is balance.
- The author has chosen carefully when and how to use performance assessments; there is clever use of simpler methods.
- There is a good match between the targets the author says are emphasized, instructional emphases, and what is actually on the assessment.

**On Track, But Needs Work**
- The author has used a variety of assessment methods, but it is somewhat unclear why; or, some of the methods might be improved.
- The author seems to have overused performance assessment when a simpler method might be cleverly applied.
- Matching seems to be all right, but this information has to be inferred or searched for.
- There are some matches and some mismatches among targets, instruction, and methods.

**Side-Tracked**
- The method doesn't seem capable of doing the job—one finds oneself asking, "Why did they assess the target *that* way?"
- One type of assessment is used for everything, when various formats would be more appropriate.
- There is no rationale for the methods used.
- The method seems to be "overkill" for the target; for example, performance assessment is used for everything.
- There is over-reliance on assessing only the higher-level skills, without consideration of assessing prerequisite skills, which might require a simpler method.
- There is a mismatch among what the author lists as the targets being assessed, the targets emphasized in instruction, and the targets assessed; or targets don't match criteria.

### Aligning Achievement Targets and Assessment Methods

| | Selected Response | Essay | Performance Assessment | Personal/Communication |
|---|---|---|---|---|
| **Knowledge Mastery** | X | X | | X |
| **Reasoning Proficiency** | X | X | X | X |
| **Performance Skills** | | | X | X |
| **Creating a Product** | | X | X | |
| **Dispositions** | X | X | X | X |

## Standard 4—*How Much:* Sampling

### Fast-Tracked
- The author has defined the domain from which the specific tasks on the assessment have been sampled; this is an appropriate definition (Note: This is where sampling overlaps with clear targets).
- The sample of student performance will accomplish its purpose.
- There are not too many nor too few tasks or exercises, but just enough to get a stable estimate of learning.
- The tasks cover the learning targets (domain) well.
- If this assessment consists of a single task, it is clear how it is part of a bigger plan to gather sufficient information across time/assessments.

### On Track, But Needs Work
- The author seems to have covered the learning targets (domain) well, but has not made a clear enough description of the domain to know for sure.
- In some cases there are too many or too few tasks to get a good estimate of student achievement.
- There is fairly good coverage of the domain of skills needed to make a stable estimate of learning, but the assessment would benefit from a few additions; for example, a writing assessment plan might ask students to write stories and informational text, but no persuasive pieces.
- Although the sampling might be acceptable for some uses, the stakes are such that additional samples would be beneficial.
- Sampling seems OK, but it has to be inferred or searched for.
- Some outcomes are sampled well, some are not.
- The assessment reflects some, but not all of the stated learning targets, or reflects learning of some targets not stated.

### Side-Tracked
- There are not enough tasks to cover the ground and to draw the desired conclusion; e.g., the author draws a conclusion about student ability to read critically on the basis of a single passage.
- The sample doesn't match the breadth of the target or the importance of results.
- The assessment reflects only a few of the stated learning goals.

## Standard 5—*How Accurate:* Avoiding Sources of Bias and Distortion

**Fast-Tracked**
- It is clear what students and assessors are to do during the assessment—instructions are clear.
- Tasks seem to match the targets and criteria—complex target, complex task; simple target, simple task.
- Possible sources of bias and distortion are described or acknowledged; caveats on use are given.
- Performance criteria, when present, are clear, well defined, and cover the most salient features of a performance.
- Paper-and-pencil methods adhere to standards of quality.
- Cultural or gender differences will not interfere with students' ability to accurately demonstrate their learning.
- Tasks and exercises are feasible—it is possible for students to complete tasks successfully.
- There are hardly any obvious sources of bias and distortion; none are too severe.

**On Track, But Needs Work**
- The author is aware that bias and distortion can be a problem, but doesn't completely address potential problems in the assessment.
- Although tasks might have a few features that are vague or confusing, they are generally sound and just require some adjustments or rewording.
- Although criteria may be a little vague or confusing, they are generally sound and just require some adjustments or rewording.
- The assessment might work well for one group of students, but might need to be reworked for use with other groups.
- Information about bias and distortion has to be inferred or searched for.
- Some tasks and exercises are feasible, some are not.
- Some selected response questions adhere to standards of quality, some do not.

**Side-Tracked**
- Tasks are vague or confusing, and it is difficult to see how they might be fixed.
- Tasks (multiple-choice to performance based) don't adhere to standards of quality.
- It would be hard to do the task successfully; e.g., a task requires specialized equipment that might not be equally available to all students.
- The author seems to be unaware of possible sources of bias and distortion.
- The reader can readily identify several possible sources of bias and distortion.
- Criteria for performance assessments don't cover important elements of performance, are vague or confusing, miss the point, or are missing entirely.
- Tasks and procedures might unfairly cause different groups of students to do poorly even when their skills and knowledge are the same.

# Evaluating Classroom Assessments for Quality

Name of Assessment: _____

| Standard | My Score | Group Score | Reasons |
|---|---|---|---|
| 1. Clear and Appropriate Targets | | | |
| 2a. Clear Users | | | |
| 2b. Users—students | | | |
| 2c. Users—communication | | | |
| 3. Target–Method Match | | | |
| 4. Sampling | | | |
| 5. Avoid Bias and Distortion | | | |

# Analysis of a Classroom Assessment

**What are its strengths?**

**What things would you improve?**

**Is it appropriate for all students?**

# Analysis of Sample Assessment: Reading Rate

**Intended Grade Level:** Grade 3

> **Standard 1: Sound assessment arises from clear and appropriate achievement targets.** Has the developer clearly specified the achievement targets to be reflected in the exercises? Do these represent important learning outcomes?

The target *is* clearly stated as being reading rate. The developer even gives a specific target reading rate and the formula for determining rate—number of words read in a minute minus any words read incorrectly. It is stated, selective, and everyone would interpret the target the same.

However, we have some questions. Is reading rate the most important thing to assess in reading? Is it the only thing this teacher assesses in reading? Is it worth the time devoted to it? What about comprehension? The developer's assertion about the relationship between reading rate and comprehension is probably true, but one might read pretty fast in Spanish and not understand much. So, the developer *may* need to review her mix and relative emphasis of targets— there is no evidence of an overall plan to cover all important goals.

There is no link to content standards, but there is a reference to best thinking in the field. For an overall evaluation of how this teacher assesses reading, we would want to explore these followup questions.

**Rating:** We would give this assessment a "2–3" on the trait of clear and appropriate targets, on a scale of 1–5, where 1 is low and 5 is high. Although this target is very clear, we have some questions about its importance (appropriateness).

> **Standard 2a: A sound assessment serves a clear and appropriate purpose.** Did the author specify users and uses, and are these appropriate?

Although the assessment developer didn't specifically list users and uses, it is easy to figure it out. The intended purposes appear to be to (1) help the teacher continuously track student progress toward a well-defined target—110 words a minute; and (2) keep parents informed of the progress of their children about their ability to read grade-appropriate material. In this case, ability to read is measured by reading rate. The users and uses are focused, clear, and appropriate.

**Rating:** We would give this assessment a "4" on the trait of clear and appropriate users and uses, on a scale of 1–5, where 1 is low and 5 is high. Purposes are not specifically stated, but are easy to infer.

> **Standard 2b: Student involvement.** Is it clear how students might be involved in the assessment as a way to help them see and understand intended achievement targets, practice hitting those targets, see themselves growing in their achievement, and communicate with others about their success as learners?

The developer does not mention using the assessment materials or results in this way, but we can certainly see how student involvement could be added: Students could monitor their own rates, track their own progress over time, and describe that progress to their parents. We would like to ask the author if the assessment is used in this manner. If not, why not? Is it because there are other, more important skills that students are monitoring, or the teacher hasn't thought of it, or the teacher doesn't think students are capable of self-monitoring?

An additional question for the author—Do students know the importance of rate? Do they know the target rate? The answers to these questions might imply "next steps" for this assessment.

**Rating:** We would give this assessment a "1" on the trait of student involvement—the potential is there, but the potential is not realized. This rating could be higher depending on the author's answers to the questions posed.

> **Standard 2c: A sound assessment communicates effectively for the intended users and uses.** Is it clear how this assessment helps communication with others about student achievement? Will others understand the message?

The developer appears to have thought this out. The developer has made it very clear what the target is and has set up procedures for continuous reporting to parents. The overall idea is sound.

However, is the graph, as given, the best way to communicate with parents? Will they understand it? Is it useful to have every single student listed separately so that parents can compare their child to all others? Might the average for the class be more useful? Or, maybe the teacher could graph the percentage of students meeting the standard and the percentage not meeting it. Would the tone of the letter put parents off? We would like to ask the author whether she has made sure parents understand and find useful the way reading rate is reported.

**Rating:** We would give this assessment a "2–3" on the trait of communication. Communication has been planned, but we have questions about the format in which the information is presented to parents. If the author demonstrates that parents understand and appreciate this reporting format, then we would raise our rating.

> **Standard 3: A sound assessment relies on an appropriate assessment method.** Is it clear why the developer of the assessment chose the method(s) used? Does the selection of that method make sense given the targets and purposes?

It is clear that the developer picked the best procedure for assessing reading rate—performance assessment. If one wants to see how fast students can read, the best way to tell is to have them read something and time it. The developer has also provided a reasonable rationale for the method chosen.

**Rating:** We would give this assessment a "5" on the trait of target–method match.

> **Standard 4: A sound assessment provides an appropriate sample of achievement.** Is it clear to you how the exercises (tasks, questions) included in the assessment cover the domain of achievement that falls within the target? Are all the important aspects of the target covered?

The reading rate activity described does not cover the domain of achievement implied by the target. It appears that the developer relies on a single, one-minute sample of a single reading selection. Might the average rate over several minutes result in a more stable measure of rate? Might reading rate averaged across several different selections of various types result in a more valid measure of rate? This assessment, as stated, might be one good measure of rate, which, when combined with others, might provide a stable estimate of overall reading rate.

Additionally, there is the lingering question about the role of reading rate in reading comprehension. If the real goal of the assessment is to provide an estimate of reading comprehension using reading rate as a surrogate measure, then the method and sample described are probably not enough to draw a conclusion about comprehension.

Remember, we're not saying that this *is* an issue with this assessment, only that it *might* be, so further scrutiny of the author's reading assessment methods is in order.

**Rating:** We would give this assessment a "1" on the trait of sampling.

> **Standard 5: A sound assessment avoids distortion of scores due to bias.** Are the exercises (tasks, questions) of high quality, given the assessment method used? Would all students have an equal opportunity to shine? When the assessment is constructed response (essay, performance assessment, or personal communication) are the performance criteria of high quality?

The task is certainly clear, aligns with the target, and is feasible. There are, however, several questions with respect to the task. First, how did the developer determine that the selection to be read was at the second- (or third-) grade level? If the determination of level of reading passage is off, then reading rate will be affected. If the selection is too easy, then reading rate might be too high; if the selection is too hard, then reading rate might be too low. We would like to ask the author how the books are selected.

Second, are the books selected appropriate for *all* students? Is knowledge of snow, for example required for understanding the *Ronald Morgan* selection? If so, might students from the South Pacific be at a disadvantage even if their reading rates were the same as students who *do* know about snow? We're not saying that this *is* a problem, it is just that there is no evidence that the assessment developer has asked this question. A solution might be to have several books, equivalent in difficulty, that are matched to students.

Now, on to the performance criteria (since this is a performance assessment). This assessment attempts to measure a fairly straightforward target, so long, extensive rubrics are not needed—simple target, simple rubric. So, the procedure for determining rate is certainly reasonable. However, we'd still like to do a little more research on the formula used to determine rate. Is total number of words read in one minute minus number of words read incorrectly the commonly accepted way to determine reading rate?

Finally, general thoughts about bias and distortion. The developer has not addressed possible sources of bias and distortion. Again, we're not saying that bias and distortion *is* a problem, just that we don't know because the assessment developer doesn't discuss it. For example, does she pick times of day that will let students do their best? Are students at ease when they do their assessment? If the developer were to tackle such issues directly, then we'd be much more assured that she has thought through some of these issues and taken them into account. We'd like to ask the author these questions.

**Rating:** We would give this assessment a "3" on the trait of bias and distortion. If we were to use this assessment, we would want to corroborate the developer's conclusion on the formula and level of books, and supplement the list of selections students can read.

### Overall Judgment

There is enough here to possibly warrant additions and use. The overall idea is good, the communication aspects are considered, the procedures are clear, and the potential for student involvement is great. We'd like to see more justification for the procedures used, more attention given to sampling, revision of the communication with parents, and more of an idea how this fits into a whole program for assessing reading. We'd give it a "2–3" on a scale of 1–5, where 1 is weak and 5 is strong.

## Thinking About Assessment

### Activity 8: Developmental Continua for Teachers

**Purpose:** The attached four developmental continua describe stages of teacher learning about quality assessment. They parallel the five standards for high-quality classroom assessments: "clear targets," "clear users and uses" (including good communication and student-involvement), "appropriate match to targets to methods," and "sampling/bias and distortion," and they can be used in at least two ways.

1. As an activity during professional development for leaders to help you know questions to ask teachers (and the answers to listen for) to explore their knowledge about classroom assessment.

2. As a resource for teachers to self-assess their own learning development in the area of high-quality, student-involved classroom assessment *for* learning. In this latter use are additional purposes:

   ■ To model self-assessment by students through the use of teacher self-assessment on developmental continua

   ■ To help develop teacher understanding of the Standards of Assessment Quality

   ■ To practice what we preach. If we want students to self-assess, it helps if we also self-assess. If we want students to apply criteria to their own performance, then we might do so as well. Likewise, as leaders we shouldn't ask teachers to do anything we haven't done. If we want teachers to define criteria for quality and use them with students, we need to provide teachers with criteria for the quality of their work. These developmental continua are designed to do just that.

**Directions and Closure:** To help you develop your classroom assessment leadership capabilities, brainstorm strong and weak answers that a teacher might supply to each of the questions listed. The questions are divided into the following categories: "clear targets," "clear users and uses," "matching methods to targets," and "sampling and bias/distortion," so that they match the developmental continua.

First, take a few minutes to read through the attached developmental continua. Then divide into pairs or small groups and assign each group one set of questions (clear targets, clear users and uses, etc.). Next, each group brainstorm strong and weak teacher responses to their questions and write them on chart paper. Then groups do a gallery tour—post the charts around the room and have everyone walk around, reading each group's responses.

Finally, have the whole group compare their brainstormed list of teacher responses to the developmental continua. Find matches and ask questions.

Here are the questions in each category:

**Clear targets:**

1. What are your outcomes (targets) for students in general—overall, what do you hope to accomplish with students this year?
2. Why are these the important outcomes you want to emphasize? *and/or* How do your outcomes for students relate to local content standards?

**Clear users and uses:**

1. How do you use the results of your classroom assessments?
2. How do you involve students in their own assessment?
3. How do you communicate assessment results to parents?

**Matching methods to targets:**

1. What is the range of assessment methods to choose from?
2. How do you decide when to use each assessment method?

**Sampling and bias/distortion:**

1. What might go wrong during an assessment that might get in the way of students actually showing what they know and can do? Describe potential sources of bias and distortion (pitfalls), including sampling issues, and how these could affect the accuracy of assessment results.

*To Use the Developmental Continua as a Resource with Teachers*

Teachers who are engaged in studying assessment can use the developmental continua with teachers at any time during learning to self-assess status and growth. This information becomes part of their professional growth portfolio.

## Developmental Continuum Standard 1— Clear and Appropriate Learning Targets

### Skilled

**I know and can articulate the enduring skills and knowledge important for students to master.** I am, myself, a master of the learning targets I teach. The following statements describe me:

- **I know local definitions** of such terms as **content standards, performance standards,** and **benchmarks** and I can provide examples. I can analyze content standards for their implied learning targets; I can relate content standards to classroom instruction and assessment.
- **I can,** without hesitating, **answer the question, "What are your learning goals for students?"**
- **I can describe the five kinds of learning targets** defined in the textbook *Student-Involved Classroom Assessment,* and regularly use this (or a similar scheme) to organize my instruction and assessments. I can list specific examples of each kind of outcome.
- **I consider the targets of instruction before I develop a unit of instruction or assessments.**
- **My learning outcomes for students represent the best thinking in the field** with regard to what students need to know and be able to do.
- **I can provide thorough descriptive details** about the student knowledge, skill, or ability associated with each of my learning targets. For example, if the learning target is becoming a fluent reader, I can define what a fluent reader knows and is able to do.
- **I understand how the achievement targets in my own setting lay the foundation** for students' success in later grades.
- **I can explain to students, parents, and others,** in terms they can understand, which learning targets I plan to achieve during instruction. I can spell it out so that students, parents, and others can accurately explain it back in their own words.
- **I can describe the various levels** of student development toward the learning target—for example, the stages of development in becoming a fluent reader or a strong math problem solver. I can describe the appropriate level(s) for the grade I teach.
- **I model the skills that students are to master.** I am, myself, a confident master of the targets of the achievement targets students are to master.
- **I can show specifically where during instruction** each learning target is addressed and how a sequence of instructional activities develops the required knowledge and skills over time.
- **I have students who can** use precise and common terminology to describe the quality of their work, articulate the criteria for success, explain what I expect them to learn, and describe how the work they're doing is applicable to their lives.
- **I have posted performance criteria** for complex learning targets.

### Practiced

**I know what it takes** to be a master of the targets of instruction, but I need help with the details. The following statements describe me:

- **I cannot readily define** words such as **content standard, performance standard,** and **benchmark,** but I can identify examples when the terms are defined for me.
- **I have tried to explain** to students, parents, and others which learning targets they are to achieve in their instruction, but I am sometimes not entirely successful at the explanation.

- **I link specific learning targets to instructional activities** in general terms, but need to stop and think about specifically where, in an instructional sequence, I am emphasizing different learning targets.
- **I plan instruction by identifying activities that would be engaging for students** and then I go back to identify which learning targets I am emphasizing.
- **I can see glaring barriers (linguistic, cultural, physical, etc.) to some students' success** in some learning target statements but am not always sure how to keep the target that I started with while making it clearer to all of my students.
- **I can list features of a quality performance**, but I need some assistance to distinguish levels of performance. For example, I can state that a piece of writing needs to have voice, but I need assistance to articulate what *strong* or *weak* voice looks like.

## Aware

**I know that it is important** to be clear on student learning targets, and that it is important to have a good "mix" of learning targets, **but I am not sure where to begin or what needs to be done.** The following statements describe me:

- **I need help to clearly state learning targets for students.** I need to develop a better sense of when a learning target is "clear."
- **I need help to relate goals for students to instructional activities.**
- **I need help to differentiate between goals for students and the instructional activities designed to achieve them.**
- **I need help to describe characteristics of strong performance** on a learning target.
- **I'm not always sure if the target statements can be easily understood by all of my students.** Sometimes I can't see potential barriers to their understanding.
- **I need help to distinguish between levels of quality** (or levels of development), and identify those student words or actions that indicate level.
- **I know I need clear criteria**, but I'm not sure that I have them.
- **I know a good mix of learning targets is important**, but I'm not sure I have one.

## Beginner

**I am not sure what learning targets are.** The following statements tend to describe me:

- **I'm not sure I could define what a** learning target for students is. I don't know various types of targets.
- **I count on the textbook**, or a series of prepackaged instructional materials, to define and address the important learning targets for students.
- **I design instruction mostly on what** I like to teach. I'm not sure how it relates to local content standards.
- **I am not convinced** that it is necessary to have clear learning targets.
- **My students have difficulty** explaining why they get the grades they do, self-assessing, and describing what quality work looks like.
- **I feel uncomfortable teaching certain subjects** because I don't understand them myself.
- **I'm not sure I know enough about my students' experiences and linguistic and cultural patterns** to consider how the description of a target might mask the learning required.

# Developmental Continuum Standard 2— Users and Uses of Assessment

## Skilled

**I understand the various purposes (users and uses) of classroom assessment and successfully balance them.** Several of the following describe me:

- **I can describe other uses of classroom assessment information than grading** and believe that these purposes are not only useful, but essential.
- **I monitor student performance and adjust instruction accordingly.**
- **I sometimes gather assessment information just to help refine instruction.**
- **I can explain the important aspects of standards-based education/instruction and the role of day-to-day classroom assessment in this process.**
- **I plan assessments with the end user in mind.** For example, if feedback to parents on student status and progress is important, assessments and reporting are designed to communicate clearly to parents. If assessment materials are used with students as instructional tools, they are "student friendly."
- **I consider the cultural differences of parents and students when planning communication about achievement.**
- I can describe the impact assessment has on students and **I know how to design assessments to involve students** to improve motivation and maximize achievement. For example, I teach students to use rubrics, and/or involve students in student-led conferences.
- **I recognize that instructional support staff and policy makers have legitimate needs for information** and that the type of information they need might be different from the type I need in the classroom. I advocate balance between large-scale and classroom assessment.

## Practiced

**I know about the various users and uses of classroom assessment, and am experimenting.** More than one of the following describes me:

- **I know about many uses for assessment information** other than grading and I'm attempting to implement some, but I'm not sure I completely understand these uses yet.
- **I try to involve students in their own assessment,** but I'm not totally successful yet.
- **I generate assessment information to fine tune instruction,** but I need to do more.
- **I generally know the important aspects of standards-based education,** but I need to fill in some of the details.
- **I try to plan assessments with the end user in mind,** but I'm only partially successful.
- **I try to take cultural background of parents and students into consideration when planning communication about achievement,** but I have only been partly successful.

## Aware

**I am aware of the need to have clear and appropriate users and uses** for assessment, and I know that assessment is more than grading, **but I need assistance in articulating my thoughts.** The following actions and behaviors describe me:

- **I want to use assessment information for more than grading,** but I'm not sure how or what questions to ask of whom.
- **I know that student involvement in their own assessment is important,** but I don't know how to begin.

157

- I would like to make reporting about achievement more powerful, but I'm not sure how to go about it.
- I know that different users need different information, but it is unclear to me how needs differ.
- I know that cultural differences affect the ability to communicate effectively about achievement, but I'm not sure what to do about it.

## Beginner

**I have not yet considered various users and uses for assessment.** The following statements describe me:

- I use assessment mostly for grading.
- I have not thought much about or analyzed my own **information needs**, nor those of students, parents, or others.
- I'm unsure that it makes sense to consider home language, culture, and so forth in planning communication about assessment. Why would their information needs be different?
- I don't see why rethinking assessment procedures is necessary.
- I'm not sure students have the ability to assess themselves, and I'm not convinced that self-assessment is useful. I have not considered involving students in developing assessments.

# Developmental Continuum Standard 3— Matching Methods to Targets

## Skilled

I understand the range of assessment options and when to use each. I use all types of assessment on a regular basis. The following statements describe me:

- I can describe various assessment methods (multiple choice, matching, short answer, essay, performance assessment, personal communication) and show examples. For example, I can give a good definition for "performance assessment" and show some examples.
- I can articulate when to use each assessment method—how to match methods to targets and purposes. The verbs in my student learning targets match the verbs in my assessment approach; e.g., active verbs in an outcome imply performance assessment. I know how to balance an ideal choice of method against a practical choice of method. I know which methods students can use to successfully self-assess.
- I use all types of assessment methods.
- I develop assessments with diverse students in mind so I can identify the kind of assessments that can best portray their learning—without changing the target being assessed.
- I use test blueprints that indicate how each learning target will be assessed and its relative importance.
- I experiment with new methods to find better ways to assess.
- I use "prepackaged" assessments only when I'm sure they'll do the job for me.

## Practiced

I am trying many different types of assessments, but I need to fine tune what I am doing. The following statements describe me:

- I can list various assessment methods, but sometimes I have trouble defining them or identifying examples.
- I use various assessment methods but I sometimes have difficulty explaining why.
- I know that it's important to use a variety of assessments to get honest and accurate information about student learning, but I'm not always certain when a particular type of assessment may mask certain students' achievement.
- I sometimes feel afraid of using "traditional" assessment methods because of the recent hype about performance assessment.

## Aware

I am aware of the need to match assessment methods to learning targets and purposes, and I have the desire to be more intentional about selecting assessment methods, but I'm not entirely sure what needs to be done or where to start. The following statements describe me:

- I have the nagging feeling that I should be using a variety of assessment methods, but I'm not sure what they are.
- I've noticed that students from some cultural and linguistic backgrounds do much better on one type of assessment than another. I'm not sure if this means that I should let them use that form all the time, or if they need to become more able to show their learning in other ways.
- I want to try more performance assessments, but I'm not sure how.

- I think I might already be using performance assessments, but I'm not sure.
- I think I might overuse one form of assessment, but I'm not sure.

## Beginner

**I'm not sure what is meant by matching targets to methods.** The following statements describe me:

- I use mostly prepackaged assessments that come with instructional materials. I'm not sure what to look for to make sure these assessments match my learning targets for students.
- I tend to use the same assessment method all the time.
- My major consideration when selecting an assessment method is that tests are easy to correct.
- I concentrate on using assessment methods that match our standardized test.
- I mostly use the methods used by other teachers; I'm not sure why.
- I haven't thought about how student language, culture, and other experiences fit with various forms of assessment.

# Developmental Continuum Standards 4 & 5—
# Sampling & Eliminating Potential Sources of Bias and Distortion

## Skilled

**I understand the importance of sampling student performance well and of eliminating potential sources of bias and distortion in my assessments. I have some skill in both these areas.** The following statements describe me:

- I can **define sampling and bias and distortion** and describe why they are important to consider when designing classroom assessments.
- I can **readily list and describe potential sources of bias and distortion** in assessment.
- I can **show examples of assessments with various problems** and can describe which problems can be fixed and which have to be lived with.
- I **know how many samples of performance are needed** in order to draw reliable conclusions about student achievement.
- I **seek out assessments that have certain features** and avoid assessments with certain other features. For example, I seek portfolio systems that have clear and appropriate performance criteria and avoid portfolio systems with skimpy or no performance criteria; or, I look for assessment tasks that relate to the real word and can be approached in different ways by different kinds of learners.
- I can **analyze existing assessments to identify linguistic and cultural barriers** and can adjust and adapt these assessments to remove the barriers to accuracy.
- I **modify my assessments** if I don't get what I wanted from students.
- I **plan for multiple assessments of complex targets** and use a variety of assessments so that all of my students have opportunities to demonstrate their learning fully.
- I **have modified assessments developed by others** because of observed problems such as unclear instructions, obvious answers, wording that is too difficult, or features that might not allow each student to do their best.
- I have **pilot tested assessment questions to make sure they work.** I discard questions that don't.
- I **have asked others to critique my assessments.**

## Practiced

**I can do many of the above things, but I need to fine tune.** The following statements tend to describe me:

- I can **describe at least some of most common potential sources of bias and distortion**, but I don't always understand how to address these issues.
- I can **identify potential problems in real assessments and I have tried to fix them**, but I may not always know the best way to fix the problem.
- I'm **experimenting with alternative ways to assess the learning of students** whose language, culture, or other characteristics differ from my own without losing vital information about the target, but I'm not sure if I'm doing it right.
- I **don't use the assessment results I know are biased**, but I'm not sure what to do about it.
- I **have tried to sample student performance**, but I'm not sure I do it well.

## Aware

**I understand that sampling and bias and distortion can be a problem,** and I want to improve my classroom assessments, **but I'm not quite sure how to proceed.** The following statements tend to describe me:

- **I'm not sure I can define "sampling" and "bias and distortion."**
- **I have noticed possible problems** in some of the assessments I use, but I don't quite know what to do about it, or even if it is a *real* problem. ("The assessment developers must know what they are doing; I'm probably wrong.")
- **I am uncertain about how to prevent problems.**
- **I don't know what to look for to determine if sampling or bias and distortion are problems.**
- **I think there are some problems** in prepackaged assessments, but I'm not real sure what to do about it.
- **I know that assessments can contain barriers that mask some students' learning,** but I'm uncertain what to do about it.

## Beginner

**I know that such things as sampling and bias and distortion exist, but I don't quite see how it applies to me.** The following statements tend to describe me:

- **I thought that sampling and bias and distortion are mainly problems with large-scale assessments.**
- **I use prepackaged assessments uncritically.**
- **What's "sampling"? What's "bias and distortion"?**
- **Why should assessing students from different cultural or linguistic backgrounds be any different than assessing any other student?**

## Applying the Skills

### **Resource 1:** Confidence Questionnaire

**What this resource is:**

This resource is a self-rating form for teachers on the degree to which they feel confident with respect to standards of assessment quality:

- Being clear on the achievement targets students are to hit.
- Being able to translate these achievement targets into high-quality assessments that yield accurate and dependable results.
- Involving students in assessment to improve their motivation and learning.
- Communicating effectively with others about student learning.

**Ideas for making it useful:**

Teachers who are engaged in the study of assessment can use this resource at the outset to determine where learning emphasis should be placed. They can also use it to track their learning progress about high-quality, student-involved classroom assessment. When summarized across teachers, results can help to gauge the impact of professional development in assessment.

## CLASSROOM ASSESSMENT CONFIDENCE QUESTIONNAIRE

**INSTRUCTIONS:** We designed this questionnaire for use by those involved in professional development or coursework using *Student-Involved Classroom Assessment,* 3d ed., by Richard Stiggins. It's designed to assist learners to track changing self-perceptions over time, as assessment learning proceeds. It's also designed to practice what we preach—that dispositions (such as confidence and attitudes) are worthy and useful learning targets. Confidence and attitudes, whether toward reading, writing, science, or classroom assessment, can make or break learning. Therefore, it is in your best interests to be as honest as possible in your responses.

Complete the questionnaire by circling the number that corresponds to your answer. Many of us are reluctant to give ourselves a top score. Remember that when you choose "2" it does not imply that everything is perfect; it just means that you are well on your way or that you are feeling confident. No one but you will see your responses unless you want them to.

**A. Clear Achievement Targets for Students. I can describe what it means to succeed academically in my classroom.** I have...

|  | I'm uncertain if I've done this yet | I haven't done this yet | I've started | I'm well on the way |
|---|:---:|:---:|:---:|:---:|
| 1. Outlined in writing the *subject matter content knowledge* my students are to master. | ? | 0 | 1 | 2 |
| 2. Differentiated content students are to *learn outright* from content they are to *learn to retrieve* later through the use of references. | ? | 0 | 1 | 2 |
| 3. Defined in writing the specific *patterns of reasoning* students are to master. | ? | 0 | 1 | 2 |
| 4. Articulated in writing the *performance skills* I expect students to learn to demonstrate (where it is the actual doing that counts). | ? | 0 | 1 | 2 |
| 5. Defined the key attributes of *products* I expect students to learn to create. | ? | 0 | 1 | 2 |
| 6. Thought through and defined *academic dispositions* (school-related attitudes) I hope my students will develop. | ? | 0 | 1 | 2 |
| 7. Met with other teachers across grade levels to merge my expectations into a *continuous progress curriculum.* | ? | 0 | 1 | 2 |

B.  **Assessing Student Achievement. I can translate my learning targets for students into dependable assessments.** I am confident that...

|  | I'm uncertain about my confidence | I am not very confident | I am somewhat confident | I'm very confident |
|---|---|---|---|---|
| 8. I can define key standards of assessment quality in commonsense, understandable terms. | ? | 0 | 1 | 2 |
| 9. I can develop high-quality *Selected Response/Short Answer Assessments* (multiple choice, true/false, matching, fill-in). | ? | 0 | 1 | 2 |
| 10. I can develop high-quality *Essay Assessments* (traditional essay requiring a written response). | ? | 0 | 1 | 2 |
| 11. I can develop high-quality *Performance Assessments* (observation and judgment). | ? | 0 | 1 | 2 |
| 12. I can develop high-quality *Personal Communication–based Assessments* (interviews, oral exams, etc.). | ? | 0 | 1 | 2 |
| 13. I can understand and use the results of *Standardized Achievement Tests*. | ? | 0 | 1 | 2 |

C.  **Student-Involved Classroom Assessment.** I am confident that I can turn the following assessment methods into instructional interventions by involving students...

|  | I'm uncertain about my confidence | I am not very confident | I am somewhat confident | I'm very confident |
|---|---|---|---|---|
| 14. *Selected Response/Short-Answer Assessments* | ? | 0 | 1 | 2 |
| 15. *Essay Assessment* | ? | 0 | 1 | 2 |
| 16. *Performance Assessment* | ? | 0 | 1 | 2 |
| 17. *Personal Communication Assessment* | ? | 0 | 1 | 2 |

**D. Communicating Effectively and Accurately About Student Achievement.** I am confident that...

| | I'm uncertain about my confidence | I am not very confident | I am somewhat confident | I'm very confident |
|---|---|---|---|---|
| 18. I understand and can apply *principles of effective communication* about student achievement. | ? | 0 | 1 | 2 |
| 19. I can use *report card grades* to communicate accurately and effectively. | ? | 0 | 1 | 2 |
| 20. I can use *other written report cards* to communicate accurately and effectively. | ? | 0 | 1 | 2 |
| 21. I can use *portfolios* to communicate accurately and effectively. | ? | 0 | 1 | 2 |
| 22. I can use *parent–teacher conferences* to communicate accurately and effectively. | ? | 0 | 1 | 2 |
| 23. I can use *student-involved conferences* to communicate accurately and effectively. | ? | 0 | 1 | 2 |

**E. Final Reflections**

24. I have the most skill and confidence in the following assessment areas:

25. I want to work most on the following assessment skills:

26. I have the following burning questions about assessment:

27. These are things I want to be able to do by the time I've finished my learning experience on classroom assessment:

---

**SCORING YOUR SURVEY:** For questions 1–23, add up the numbers you circled to determine your score. Before you begin your professional development or coursework, your score may be very low. However, as you learn about and implement effective assessment and communication procedures over time, your score should go up. Complete the Survey at least twice—once at the beginning and once at the end of study. You can also complete the Survey at the end of study of each major section of the textbook.

# Competency 2

## The leader understands the principles of assessment *for* learning and works with staff to integrate them into classroom instruction.

Over the years educators have been encouraged to think about assessment and instruction as hand-in-glove, to think about teaching as one seamless act melding curriculum, instruction, and assessment. This is easier said than done. Let's begin with a vision of what it means. We've created a list of nine principles that clarify instruction-embedded assessment, or assessment *for* learning. These nine principles are our best answer to teachers' frequently asked question, "Exactly how do I integrate assessment with instruction and truly make one an extension of the other?" The application of these principles achieves just that in the classroom, with assessment becoming another form of good teaching. Following are the nine principles of assessment *for* learning:

1. Teachers understand and can articulate *in advance of teaching* the achievement targets students are to hit.

2. *Students are informed regularly* about those targets in terms they can understand, in part through the study of the criteria by which their work will be evaluated, and samples of high-quality work.

3. *Students can describe what targets they are to hit* and what comes next in their learning.

4. Classroom teachers can transform those targets into *dependable assessments* that yield accurate information.

5. Both the teacher and the student use classroom assessment information to *revise and guide* teaching and learning.

6. Feedback given to students is descriptive, constructive, frequent, and timely; *helping students identify their strengths and know how to plan and improve* their work.

7. *Students are actively,* consistently, and effectively *involved in assessment,* including learning to manage their own learning through the skills of self-assessment.

8. *Students* actively, consistently, and effectively *communicate with others* about their achievement status and improvement.

9. Teachers understand the relationship between assessment and student motivation and u*se assessment to build student success* and confidence rather than failure and defeat.

Of the 10 leader competencies, Competency 2 is most clearly focused on your capacity to guide the development of an assessment-literate faculty. Each of the nine principles of assessment *for* learning in Competency 2 has behind it a set of specific skills and teaching strategies. It is the consistent application of those skills and strategies throughout a school or district that produces significant gains in student achievement. And although all students in the classroom stand to benefit, it is those that typically are the lowest achievers who gain the most (Black and Wiliam, 1998). Instructional leaders create communities of teachers who learn to do these things as a matter of routine.

Here are some examples of what assessment-literate teachers do when applying the nine principles:

■ Translate learning targets into student-friendly terms, to clarify what students are expected to learn.

■ Gather accurate information about student achievement on a regular basis using high-quality formative assessments that adhere to standards of quality. In this process, teachers consider which assessment method will give the most accurate picture of student achievement on the specific learning targets.

■ Provide students descriptive feedback linked directly to the intended learning, giving them insight about current strengths and how to do better next time, rather than giving evaluative feedback consisting only of marks and letter grades. Students have an opportunity to practice, using this feedback, before a summative assessment.

- Keep students connected to a vision of quality as the learning unfolds, continually defining for students what the learning expectations are for the lesson/unit (Chappuis and Stiggins, 2002).

- Involve students in their own assessment in ways that require them to think about their own progress, communicate their own understanding of what they have learned, and set goals to close the gap between where they are now relative to the intended learning and where they need to be to meet standards. Assessment-literate teachers teach students the skills of self-assessment, and involve students in conferences, have students create practice test items, and evaluate anonymous classroom work for quality—all examples of students being involved in assessment.

- Have students communicate the status of their own learning to interested adults through written journals, student-involved parent conferences, and portfolios that focus on growth toward the standards.

## Thinking About Assessment

### **Activity 9:** Classroom Assessment *for* Learning

**Purpose:** Begin to identify examples of what the principles of assessment *for* learning look like when integrated into classroom instruction.

**Time:** 30 minutes

**Directions:** Read the following article, "Classroom Assessment *for* Learning" reprinted from ASCD's *Educational Leadership* and after reading, answer the following questions:

- Of the classroom practices listed in the article, which do you most commonly see in classrooms in your school/district?
- Which practices are least evident?
- What other teaching strategies do you see in your school/district that might support assessment *for* learning? Relate them to the nine principles of assessment *for* learning.
- How might you help teachers begin to incorporate some of these strategies into their classroom routine?

**Closure:** Many of the teaching strategies described in the article (and other strategies not included that also reflect assessment *for* learning practices) are present in many classrooms already. We can help teachers expand their repertoire of strategies and ensure they use them intentionally by beginning to see how their current practices relate to the nine principles and by providing the professional development opportunities needed to make the nine principles part of everyday teaching practice.

# Classroom Assessment *for* Learning

*Classroom assessment that involves students in the process and focuses on increasing learning can motivate rather than merely measure students.*

STEPHEN CHAPPUIS AND RICHARD J. STIGGINS

IMAGINE a classroom assessment as a healthy part of effective teaching and successful learning. At a time when large-scale, external assessments of learning gain political favor and attention, many teachers are discovering how to engage and motivate students using day-to-day classroom assessment for purposes beyond measurement. By applying the principles of what is called *assessment for learning,* teachers have followed clear research findings of the effects that high-quality, formative assessment can have on student achievement.

We typically think of assessment as an index of school success rather than as the cause of that success. Unfortunately, largely absent from the traditional classroom assessment environment is the use of assessment as a tool to promote greater student achievement (Shepard, 2000). In general, the teacher teaches and then tests. The teacher and class move on, leaving unsuccessful students, those who might not learn at the established pace and within a fixed time frame, to finish low in the rank order. This assessment model is founded on two outdated beliefs: that to increase learning we should increase student anxiety and that comparison with more successful peers will motivate low performers to do better.

STEPHEN CHAPPUIS is Director of Professional Development and RICHARD STIGGINS is President and Founder of the Assessment Training Institute, Portland, OR.

By contrast, assessment for learning occurs during the teaching and learning process rather than after it and has as its primary focus the ongoing improvement of learning for all students (Assessment Reform Group, 1999; Crooks, 2001; Shepard, 2000). Teachers who assess for learning use day-to-day classroom assessment activities to involve students directly and deeply in their own learning, increasing their confidence and motivation to learn by emphasizing progress and achievement rather than failure and defeat (Stiggins, 1999; 2001). In the assessment for learning model, assessment is an instructional tool that promotes learning rather than an event designed solely for the purpose of evaluation and assigning grades. And when students become involved in the assessment process, assessment for learning begins to look more like teaching and less like testing (Davies, 2000).

## STUDENT-INVOLVED ASSESSMENT

Research shows that classroom assessments that provide accurate, descriptive feedback to students and involve them in the assessment process can improve learning (Black and Wiliam, 1998). As a result, assessment for learning means more than just assessing students often, more than providing the teacher with assessment results to revise instruction. In assessment for learning, both teacher and student use classroom assessment information to modify teaching and learning activities. Teachers use assessment information formatively when they

- Pretest before a unit of study and adjust

*Source:* From "Classroom Assessment for Learning," by S. Chappuis and R. J. Stiggins, 2002, *Educational Leadership, 60*(1), pp. 40–44. Copyright 2002 by ASCD. Reprinted by permission of ASCD.

instruction for individuals or the entire group.

- Analyze which students need more practice.
- Continually revise instruction on the basis of results.
- Reflect on the effectiveness of their own teaching practices.
- Confer with students regarding their strengths and the areas that need improvement.
- Facilitate peer tutoring, matching students who demonstrate understanding with those who do not.

We tend to think of students as passive participants in assessment rather than engaged users of the information that assessment can produce. What we should be asking is, How can students use assessment to take responsibility for and improve their own learning?

Student involvement in assessment doesn't mean that students control decisions regarding what will or won't be learned or tested. It doesn't mean that they assign their own grades. Instead, student involvement means that students learn to use assessment information to manage their own learning so that they understand how they learn best, know exactly where they are in relation to the defined learning targets, and plan and take the next steps in their learning.

---

*Student-involved assessment means that students learn to use assessment information to manage their own learning.*

---

Students engage in the assessment for learning process when they use assessment information to set goals, make learning decisions related to their own improvement, develop an understanding of what quality work looks like, self-assess, and communicate their status and progress toward established learning goals. Students involved in their own assessment might

- Determine the attributes of good performance. Students look at teacher-supplied anonymous samples of strong student performances and list the qualities that make them strong, learning the language of quality and the concepts behind strong performance.

- Use scoring guides to evaluate real work samples. Students can start with just one criterion in the guide and expand to others as they become more proficient in scoring. As students engage in determining the characteristics of quality work and scoring actual work samples, they become better able to evaluate their own work. Using the language of the scoring guide, they can identify their areas of strength and set goals for improvement—in essence, planning the next steps in their learning.

- Revise anonymous work samples. Students go beyond evaluating work to using criteria to improve the quality of a work sample. They can develop a revision plan that outlines improvements, or write a letter to the creator of the original work offering advice on how to improve the sample. This activity also helps students know what to do before they revise their own work.

- Create practice tests or test items based on their understanding of the learning targets and the essential concepts in the class material. Students can work in pairs to identify what they think should be on the test and to generate sample test items and responses.

- Communicate with others about their growth and determine when they are nearing success. Students achieve a deeper understanding of themselves and the material that they are attempting to learn when they describe the quality of their own work. Letters to parents, written self-reflections, and conferences with teachers and parents in which students outline the process they used to create a product allow students to share what they know and describe their progress toward the learning target. By accumulating evidence of their own improvement in growth portfolios, students can refer to specific stages in their growth and celebrate their achievement with others.

## EFFECTIVE TEACHER FEEDBACK

"You need to study harder." "Your handwriting is

very nice." "Good job." Traditionally, teachers use such statements to register their approval or disapproval of student performance. But such evaluative feedback, long a classroom staple, is of limited value for improving student learning and can actually have negative effects on students' desire to learn. And grades, those traditional coded symbols and markings—B-, 71 percent, 4/10, Satisfactory, F—actually communicate even less about what students have done well or need to do to improve. By contrast, teacher comments that focus on student work and not on individual student characteristics can increase student's motivation and desire to learn.

Black and Wiliam (1998) point to the benefits of replacing judgmental feedback with specific, descriptive, and immediate feedback. When the goal is to increase student motivation and learning, productive feedback tells students what they are doing right, pinpointing strengths and helping learners develop those strengths even further. For some students, receiving this feedback in writing and having time to reflect on it is sufficient. Other students need face-to-face teacher feedback to reinforce what they have done well.

Effective teacher feedback describes why an answer is right or wrong in specific terms that students understand. Students can also generate their own descriptive feedback by comparing their work with teacher-provided examplars or posted examples. They can then compare their own feedback with that of their teacher.

Descriptive feedback should provide ways for students to improve in clear, constructive language. Instead of simply labeling student errors or omissions, effective feedback guides students to better performance throughout the learning process. Useful comments focus specifically on improving only one area at a time.

Finally, teacher feedback for learning draws an even bigger picture by telling students where they are now relative to the defined learning targets— and where teachers ultimately want them to be. By modeling for students a variety of suggestions designed to narrow the gap between where they are and where they should be headed, teachers can help students learn to generate their own strategies for improvement.

## THE SKILLS OF SELF-ASSESSMENT

Eventually, we want students to be able to direct their own learning. Yet it often seems unclear just how students will achieve this goal. Assessment for learning helps students become self-directed learners by developing their self-assessment skills. The principles of assessment for learning are interrelated: Just as involving students in the assessment process helps make assessment more like instruction, students need to learn to self-assess so that they can use the descriptive feedback from the teacher to its best advantage. Sadler (1989) and Atkin, Black and Coffey (2001) describe a model of formative assessment in which learners continually ask themselves three questions as they self-assess.

### Where Am I Trying To Go?

Students need clearly articulated, concise learning targets to be able to answer this first question. Learning is easier when learners understand what goal they are trying to achieve, the purpose of achieving the goal, and the specific attributes of success. Teachers should continually help students clarify the intended learning as the lessons unfold—not just at the beginning of a unit of study. Teachers share learning intentions with students when they

• Phase objectives in terms that begin with "We are learning to…" or "I can…"

• Ask students to read the objectives aloud and ask clarifying questions.

• Separate what they want students to do—the instructions for completing the task—from what they want students to learn. Otherwise, the directions might overshadow the intended learning.

• Inform students why they need to learn what comes next and how it connects to previous and future learning.

• Display the learning objectives in the classroom.

• Provide students with examples of outstanding work as well as samples of lesser quality so that they can see the differences.

● Ask students to rephrase the learning targets or describe what attainment of a target looks like (Arter & Busick, 2001; Clarke, 2001).

### Where Am I Now?

Students can practice comparing their work to models of high-quality work and trying to identify the differences. They can use teacher feedback from formative assessments to gather evidence of what they know and can do relative to the defined learning target. They can use questions designed to prompt students to reflect on what they have learned individually relative to the intended learning. All of these strategies help students ascertain—and, even more important, learn *how* to ascertain—where they are and where they need to be, an awareness that is central to their ultimate success.

*Teachers share learning intentions with students when they separate what they want students to do—the instructions for completing a task—from what they want students to learn.*

### How Do I Close The Gap?

Assessment for learning helps students know what to do to move from their current position to the final learning goal. To meet learning goals, students must participate fully in creating the goals, analyzing assessment data, and developing a plan of action to achieve the next goal (Clarke, 2001).

Students should learn question-and-answer strategies that they can use to close the gap: What do I need to change in my work to improve its quality? What specific help do I need to make these changes? From whom can I get help? What resources do I need?

Sadler (1989) notes that a steady flow of descriptive feedback to students encourages continual self-assessment around what constitutes quality. Keeping students connected to a vision of quality as the unit of study progresses helps them close the gap by formulating their next steps in learning.

## ALL STUDENTS LEARNING WELL

The habits and skills of self-assessment are within the grasp and capabilities of almost every student. Students take greater responsibility for their own learning when they regularly assess themselves (Shepard, 2001). In the hands of trained teachers, assessment for learning breeds confidence in learning. It provides students with opportunities for monitoring and communicating to others their own progress.

Educators open the door to using assessment in more productive ways when they acknowledge that students respond differently to the use of test scores as threats of punishment or promises of reward. Those who succeed keep striving; those who fail may give up. By contrast, most students respond positively to classroom assessment environments that promote success rather than simply measure it.

Students demonstrate unprecedented score gains on standardized assessments when their teachers apply the principles of assessment for learning in the classroom (Black and Wiliam, 1998). With appropriate training, teachers can improve the accuracy of their day-to-day assessments, make their feedback to students descriptive and informative, and increase the involvement of students in the entire assessment process. In this way, classroom assessment for learning becomes a school improvement tool that helps create responsible, engaged, and self-directed learners.

### References

Arter, J. A., & Busick, K. U. (2001). *Practice with student-involved classroom assessment.* Portland, OR: Assessment Training Institute.

Assessment Reform Group. (1999). *Assessment for learning. Beyond the black box.* Cambridge, England: University of Cambridge.

Atkin, J. M., Black, P., & Coffey, J. (2001). *Classroom assessment and the National Science Education Standards.* Washington, DC: National Academy Press.

Black, P., & Wiliam, D. (1998). Inside the black box: Raising standards through classroom assessment. *Phi Delta Kappan, 80*(2), 139–148.

Clarke, S. (2001). *Unlocking formative assessment*. London: Hodder and Stoughton.

Crooks, T. (2001). *The validity of formative assessments*. Leeds, England: British Educational Research Association.

Davies, A. (2000). *Making classroom assessment work*. Merville, British Columbia, Canada: Connections Publishing.

Sadler, R. (1989). Formative assessment and the design of instructional systems. *Instructional Science, 18,* 119–144.

Shepard, L. A. (2000). The role of assessment in a learning culture. *Educational Researcher, 29*(7), 4–14.

Shepard, L. A. (2001, July). *Using assessment to help students think about learning*. Keynote address at the Assessment Training Institute Summer Conference, Portland, OR.

Stiggins, R. J. (1999). Assessment, student confidence, and school success. *Phi Delta Kappan, 81*(3), 191–198.

Stiggins, R. J. (2001). *Student-involved classroom assessment* (3d ed.). Upper Saddle River, NJ: Merrill-Prentice Hall.

## Thinking About Assessment

### Activity 10: Principles of Assessment *for* Learning: A Self-Analysis

**Purpose:**     This activity is helpful in charting next steps for learning and professional development by identifying which principles of assessment *for* learning are already in place and which principles need additional attention in order to be applied consistently in the school/classroom. This activity can be done individually by leadership team members and then summarized, or an entire faculty can get together and rate their school or district as a group. The point is to identify strengths and potential areas for growth among the nine principles.

**Time:**     30 minutes

**Directions:**     Using the checklist provided in this activity, select the level of your educational organization (district, building, classroom) with which you are most familiar and analyze it. Each participant rates each principle on a scale of 1–5 using the following descriptors:

$$1 \quad = \quad \text{doesn't happen}$$
$$2 \quad = \quad \text{infrequently happens}$$
$$3 \quad = \quad \text{sometimes}$$
$$4 \quad = \quad \text{frequently happens}$$
$$5 \quad = \quad \text{routinely done}$$

Then tally the results.
- Which principles came out strongest? How do you account for that?
- Which principles appear like they need the most improvement or work?
- How could you go about organizing improvement in those areas?

**Closure:**     When using this as a group activity, especially with teachers, participants need to have more than a passing familiarity with the nine principles before doing a self- or school analysis. Having discussions about each principle, reading about assessment *for* learning, and sharing ideas with each other help clarify each of the principles, making it easier to judge the current state of affairs regarding the level of school or district implementation. Further, allow people to rate anonymously to create a safe environment for those who may need a level of personal privacy. This will also help maximize the accuracy of the responses, and therefore, the profile of the group.

One engaging way to use this activity and to maintain anonymity is to have participants rate themselves low to high using a scale of 1–5 on a separate blank sheet of paper. No names are written on the paper. When participants are all finished, ask them to crumple up the paper into a snowball, give it a toss, and then pick one up, making sure it isn't their own.

At this point, have participants create a "human histogram." Tape big numbers 1 to 5 on the wall. Then ask participants to line up by the number that is shown on their sheet, starting with the first principle. When everyone is lined up, a bar graph emerges that represents the group's rating on that particular principle. Do this for each of the nine principles. This can lead to discussions about strengths and weaknesses, patterns, and professional development priorities.

# Assessment Training Institute
# Principles of Assessment *for* Learning

1. I understand and can articulate in advance of teaching the achievement targets students are to hit.
   Low 1_____ 2_____ 3_____ 4_____ 5_____ High

2. My students are informed regularly about those targets in terms they can understand, in part through the study of the criteria by which their work will be evaluated and samples of high-quality work.
   Low 1_____ 2_____ 3_____ 4_____ 5_____ High

3. My students can describe what targets they are to hit and what comes next in their learning.
   Low 1_____ 2_____ 3_____ 4_____ 5_____ High

4. I can transform those targets into dependable assessments that yield accurate information.
   Low 1_____ 2_____ 3_____ 4_____ 5_____ High

5. I use classroom assessment information to revise and guide teaching and student learning, and share this information with students.
   Low 1_____ 2_____ 3_____ 4_____ 5_____ High

6. The feedback I give to students is descriptive, constructive, frequent, and immediate, helping students know how to plan and improve.
   Low 1_____ 2_____ 3_____ 4_____ 5_____ High

7. My students are actively, consistently, and effectively involved in assessment, including learning to manage their own learning through the skills of self-assessment.
   Low 1_____ 2_____ 3_____ 4_____ 5_____ High

8. My students actively, consistently, and effectively communicate with others about their achievement status and improvement.
   Low 1_____ 2_____ 3_____ 4_____ 5_____ High

9. I understand the relationship between assessment and student motivation and use assessment to build student success and confidence rather than failure and defeat.
   Low 1_____ 2_____ 3_____ 4_____ 5_____ High

## Thinking About Assessment

## Activity 11: Converting Learning Targets to Student-Friendly Language

**Purpose:**  One key principle of assessment *for* learning requires the development of student-friendly versions of achievement targets. This activity shows teachers how to think about that translation.

**Time:**  30–45 minutes

**Directions, Part A:**  Gather a sample of two or three grade-level learning targets from your district or state and turn them into student-friendly "I can" statements like those in the Ohio example here. (You might want to use your reading curriculum and find *predict, summarize,* and *infer* learning targets so you can use the wording here.) Share the examples with participants, showing how we first identify the terms to be defined, then define them, and then turn the learning target into one or more "I can" statements, using language our students will understand.

### Ohio Sixth-Grade Reading Grade-Level Indicators

- Predict from information in the text, substantiating with specific references to textual examples that may be in widely separated sections of text.
- Summarize the information in texts, recognizing important ideas and supporting details, and noting gaps or contradictions.
- Answer inferential questions to demonstrate comprehension.

### Turning Grade Level Indicators into Student-Friendly Language
*Predict from information in the text.*
1. Word to be defined: *Predict*
   *Predict:* to make a statement saying that something will happen in the future.
2. Student-friendly language: I can predict from information in the text. This means I can use information from what I read to guess at what will happen next. (Or, to guess what the author will tell me next.)

*Summarize the information in texts.*
1. Word to be defined: *Summarize*
   *Summarize:* To give a brief statement of the main points, main events, or important ideas.

2. Student-friendly language: I can summarize the information in texts. This means I can make a short statement of the main points or the big ideas of what I read.

### *Answer inferential questions.*

1. Word to be defined: *inferential*

   *Inferential*: Requiring a conclusion drawn using the information available and reasoning.

2. Student-friendly language: I can answer inferential questions. This means I can use information from what I read together with my own reasoning to draw a conclusion.

**Directions, Part B:**

Using the local curriculum, ask participants to identify a learning target that would be unclear to most of their students. Then have them identify and define key elements. Last, have them turn the learning target into one or more "I can" statements. An example using Ohio's Grade-Level Indicators follows.

**Clarifying Grade-Level Indicators for Yourself:**
**Identifying and Defining Key Elements**

Select one of the Grade-Level Indicators on the next page to work with—one with wording you think would be UNCLEAR to many students at that grade level. Write it in the box below, identify and define the key elements, then turn it into one or more "I can" statements.

| GL INDICATOR | Key Elements IDENTIFIED AND DEFINED |
|---|---|
|  |  |

Clarifying Grade-Level Indicators for Students:

Turn the Key Elements into one or more "I can" statements:

| "I Can" Statements |
| --- |
|  |

## A Sample of Ohio's Grade-Level Indicators

### 5th Grade:

■ Identify the connotation and denotation of new words. (Reading)

■ Make predictions based on experimental and theoretical probabilities. (Mathematics)

### 6th Grade

■ Analyze information from primary and secondary sources in order to summarize, make generalizations, and draw conclusions. (Social Studies)

■ Evaluate simple expressions by replacing variables with given values, and use formulas in problem-solving situations. (Mathematics)

### 7th Grade

■ Analyze examples of cause and effect and fact and opinion. (Reading)

■ Formulate and identify questions to guide scientific investigations that connect to science concepts and can be answered through scientific investigations. (Science)

### 8th Grade:

■ Extend the use of variables to include covariants where $y$ depends on $x$. (Mathematics)

■ Establish a thesis statement for informational writing or a plan for narrative writing. (Writing)

### The Process

1. Find important learning target.
2. Identify word(s) needing definition.
3. Define word(s).
4. Rewrite the learning target in student-friendly language.
5. Try it out on a partner or students; get feedback.
6. Refine as needed.

**Closure:** Participants may wonder about the amount of time it takes to clarify learning targets. Ask them to discuss how they might economize in this process, set priorities, or manage it effectively. If they do not come up with ideas, you might prime the pump by suggesting that (1) a good place to start is with a learning target that students generally do not do well on, and (2) you can have students share in this work on some learning targets as an introduction to the learning.

Close with a discussion of the benefits to students. Bring the discussion back to the necessity of students' knowing where they are going.

## Thinking About Assessment

### Activity 12: Ways That Teachers and Students Use Formative Assessment

**Purpose:** To introduce participants to the range of formative uses of assessment—ways to operationalize the use of assessment *for* learning.

**Time:** 20–30 minutes

**Directions:** After providing a brief summary of the Black and Wiliam (1998) research on the effects of formative assessment on student learning, ask participants to think of the formative assessment strategies they are familiar with—methods they use in the classroom, or have seen, or have heard of.

| Formative assessment strategies I'm familiar with: |
|---|
| |

Then ask participants to read through the accompanying three lists of assessment practices, marking those practices with which they are familiar.

**Closure:** Ask participants to reflect on and share any surprises or new ideas.

## Formative Assessment Practices

### *Teacher*

Just as we want a balance of assessment methods used in classrooms to reflect the different kinds of learning targets we hold for students, we also want a balance of summative (assessment *of* learning) and formative (assessment *for* learning) practices in the classroom. Many teachers are delighted to agree with this statement, but may not know just how to go about putting **formative** assessment—assessment *for* learning—into action. Or, they may be engaging in formative assessment without knowing it's what they're already doing. Here is a list of ways the **teacher** can function as a formative assessor:

- Use diagnostic assessments, designed to reflect the intended learning targets, to make preinstruction decisions.

- Share learning targets/objectives/goals in advance of teaching lessons, giving assignments, or doing activities. (Okay, if it's a pure discovery learning activity, you can hold off. But you need to know what you're aiming for, unless you regularly run out of things to teach before you run out of year. And eventually, they'll need to know too.) Use language students understand, and check to make sure they understand; e.g., ask "Why is it we are doing this activity? What is it we are learning?"

- Let students know the purpose of each assignment or activity. Is it for practice? What kind of feedback will they get on it? Informal? Formal? Where does it fit in the grading scheme?

- Provide descriptive feedback (oral or written) in place of summative grades during learning, including on homework, *especially if the homework is intended to reinforce concepts taught that day*. Everything that moves does not have to be graded.

- Focus feedback on learning targets/objectives/goals. Let students know what they *have* learned well before launching into what they need to work on. Consider how much corrective feedback the learner—especially the struggling learner—can reasonably be expected to act on at one time.

## *Student*

Teacher feedback functions as a model for students—to teach them how to begin thinking about their own work. We provide descriptive feedback and encourage students to join us in that endeavor, gradually reducing our role as their own capabilities grow. Here is a list of ways **students** can learn to become formative assessors:

- Respond to the questions, "What did you do in Music today? What did you learn?" (oral or written response).

- Determine, with the teacher, attributes of a good performance or product.

- Use criteria to evaluate the quality of anonymous work and then to identify strengths and weaknesses in their own work.

- Before a discussion or conference with the teacher, identify their own perception of strengths and weaknesses on a specific piece of their work.

- Write letters home to parents explaining what they've learned that day/week/month.

- Write letters home to parents explaining how they can help them with a piece of work.

- Offer feedback to peers.

- Engage in self-assessment, self-reflection, and goal-setting

- Accumulate evidence of their improvement in growth portfolios. (This means **students** are able to identify samples that constitute evidence of improvement.)

- Participate in conferences with parents.

- Talk about their growth: identify their progress and explain what they need to do to improve.

## Summative Assessment Practices

Preparing and administering **summative** assessments comes with the job. That does not doom them to necessary-evil status; summative assessments can be used formatively in service of increased student learning. For example, have **students** do the following:

- Develop practice test blueprints based on their understanding of the learning targets they are to hit and the essential concepts in material to be learned.

- Self-assess on learning targets or test blueprint a few days prior to the test, then create a study plan and/or study group based on what each student needs to learn. (See Stiggins, 2001, p. 150.) Remember, it is the student creating the plan. You can help with the grouping.

- Generate and answer questions they think might be on the test, based on their understanding of the content/processes/skills they were responsible for learning.

- Create practice tests, based on understanding of what was taught. This is a good small group activity—different groups can answer each others' test questions as a way to review.

- Use item formulas and a test blueprint or list of learning targets to construct 3–4 test items for a particular topic that will be on the test.

- Assign each cell of the test blueprint to a small group of students and have them write propositions for that cell. Then have another group write test questions for the cell. Have each group take another's "test."

- Before a test ( a few days in advance is a good idea), practice "positive talk" by answering the following questions:
  - Why am I taking this test? Who will use the results? How?
  - What is it testing?
  - How do I think I will do?
  - What do I need to study?
  - With whom might I work?

To think about why using the summative assessment formatively might be a good idea, *just remember what happens to your own clarity about the intended learning* when **you** engage in activities such as the following:

- Creating a test plan
- Preparing a quiz to help students know what to study
- Writing propositions from which to develop test items
- Generating test questions
- Explaining to students what's going to be tested without giving away the exact contents of the test

Also, think about where the balance of work is in your classroom when it comes time to review for a summative assessment. Who does the majority of the reviewing work? Who needs to do it?

## Applying the Skills

**Resource 2:** Student Survey to Study Assessment *for* Learning Practices in the Classroom

**What this resource is:**

This resource is a survey that can be given to students in grades 4–12 as one measure of the extent to which assessment *for* learning practices have been implemented in the classroom. The survey is recommended to be used for teacher action research and self-reflection, for professional growth—rather than as a supervisory tool the principal might use for teacher evaluation.

The questions on the survey correspond to entries 3, 5, 7, and 8 of the nine principles of assessment *for* learning. Teachers can use the student survey to examine the impact of their efforts to implement principles 3, 5, 7, and 8, such as through pre/post-assessment administration of the survey.

■ Survey items 1, 2, and 6 relate to Principle 3—"My students can describe what targets they are to hit and what comes next in their learning."

■ Survey items 4 and 5 relate to Principle 5—"I use classroom assessment information to revise and guide teaching and student learning, and share this information with students."

■ Survey items 3–5 and 7–11 relate to Principle 7—"My students are actively, consistently, and effectively involved in assessment, including learning to manage their own learning through the skills of self-assessment."

■ Survey item 12 relates to Principle 8—"My students actively, consistently, and effectively communicate with others about their achievement status and improvement."

■ Survey items 13 and 14 relate to student attitude toward assessment as an indicator of how teachers use assessment to motivate students to want to learn.

**Time:**

It will take students no longer than 10 minutes to complete this survey.

**Ideas for making it useful:**

The survey was pilot tested with students in grades 5–8 as part of a study ATI conducted for the National Board on Professional Standards. Here are instructions that teachers can use when they administer the survey to their students.

1. Introduce the survey in whatever way that you are used to doing when you ask students to give you feedback about their learning.

2. Students should not put their names on their papers. This is anonymous.

3. Read the instructions with students.

4. Point out that each statement begins with the words "In this class..." Therefore, students will only be answering the questions in relationship to this single classroom, not others in which they are involved.

5. Tell students there are no right or wrong answers. Assure students that you just want to know their opinion. So, please be honest.

6. Remind students to fill in the bubble that represents their answer.

7. It's OK to answer student clarifying questions and help students read the questions. (Note: On item 10 of the survey there is a reference to rubrics and scoring guides. If these are not the terms used in your classroom, tell students what term to substitute.)

**Closure:**

Tally results by item. Then pool results across items within a principle. Then draw conclusions about how students regard each of the four principles, 3, 5, 7, and 8. Make adjustments in classroom practice as needed.

Dear Student:

We are interested in how YOU see your learning and assessment in this class. Your opinions will help improve classroom assessment. There are no right or wrong answers. Read each statement and rate how you feel using the following rating scale. "1" means that you disagree with the statement, and "5" means that you agree. If you feel somewhere in between, select the number that best represents how you feel. Fill in the circle that best describes how you feel. Thank you for answering these questions honestly.

**Disagree  1 / 2 / 3 / 4 / 5  Agree**

**In this class . . .**

1. . . . I understand what I am supposed to learn.  ① ② ③ ④ ⑤
2. . . . I know whenever a test is coming up, and I know for sure what will be covered.  ① ② ③ ④ ⑤
3. . . . I learn to judge how good my work is.  ① ② ③ ④ ⑤
4. . . . I know what subjects and skills I'm good at.  ① ② ③ ④ ⑤
5. . . . I know what I need to get better at.  ① ② ③ ④ ⑤
6. . . . I know what I will learn next.  ① ② ③ ④ ⑤
7. . . . I work with my teacher to set goals for my learning.  ① ② ③ ④ ⑤
8. . . . I learn how to look back on my work to see how I have improved.  ① ② ③ ④ ⑤
9. . . . I know how to assemble a portfolio of my work.  ① ② ③ ④ ⑤
10. . . . I can write or use scoring guides or rubrics to judge how good work is.  ① ② ③ ④ ⑤
11. . . . I learn how to write practice test questions that cover what I am learning.  ① ② ③ ④ ⑤
12. . . . I have learned how to lead a conference with my parents or other adults on what I have learned.  ① ② ③ ④ ⑤
13. . . . I enjoy the experience of taking tests and assessments.  ① ② ③ ④ ⑤
14. . . . I enjoy learning how I did on my tests and assessments.  ① ② ③ ④ ⑤

## Thinking About Assessment

### Activity 13: Using Feedback to Set Goals

**Purpose:**   To help teachers learn more about providing descriptive feedback. For students to set meaningful goals for their work, they need to understand what they have accomplished as well as what, specifically, they need to work on. To prepare them to do this thinking, it is helpful if the teacher models it for them first by offering descriptive feedback on a sample of their work. In the activity, students think about their work sample's strengths and needed improvements. Then the teacher offers either written or verbal feedback on strengths and improvements. Last, the student makes a plan for what to work on and where to get feedback from next.

**Time:**   20–30 minutes

**Directions:**   Start with a sample of typical student work that requires a performance rating, for example, a piece of writing. Have teachers score it using your building, district, or state scoring guide. Then have teachers pair up. One becomes "Partner A," the other is "Partner B." Activity directions for teachers:

1.  Do this first item independently (about 5 minutes):
    **Partner A:**  You are a student. You have just produced this sample of work. Take a few moments to prepare to confer with your teacher about your sample. Use the language of the scoring guide to identify your sample's strengths and problems, if any. Write the strengths and problem(s) on the form, "Using Feedback to Set Goals," page 193, under "My Opinion."

    **Partner B:**  You are Partner A's teacher.  She or he has just produced this sample of work. Take a few moments to prepare to confer with Partner A about her or his sample. Use the language of the scoring guide to identify the sample's strengths and problems, if any. Write the strengths and problems on the form "Using Feedback to Set Goals," page 193, under "My Teacher's Opinion."

2. Read the description of a three-minute conference on page 194.

3. Conduct a three-minute conference with your partner. Let the student be the writer on the form.

**Closure:** Ask teachers to discuss how this form could be used in their classrooms, and what problems it might solve.

# Using Feedback to Set Goals

TRAIT(S): _____     NAME: _____

NAME OF PAPER: _____     DATE: _____

**MY OPINION**

My strengths:

_____

_____

What I think I need to work on:

_____

_____

**MY TEACHER'S OPINION**

Strengths:

_____

_____

Work on:

_____

_____

**MY PLAN**

What I will do now:

_____

_____

Next time I'll ask for feedback from:

_____

_____

## Using Feedback to Set Goals

### The Three-Minute Conference

If you confer with students as a way to offer feedback on their work, consider asking them to do some thinking prior to meeting with you. This causes the conference to take less time and your feedback to be more meaningful.

1. Identify a focus for the feedback—narrow it, if needed. Have them focus only on a few aspects of quality—either you choose the aspects of quality based on what you have been teaching them to do or let them choose, depending on their level of sophistication. (For example, in writing, a teacher may be focusing minilessons on how to include details that are interesting, important, and informative, which is part of the trait of "Ideas and Content" in her scoring guide. So she may ask students to think about the quality of their details.)

2. Before meeting with you (or submitting their work for your feedback) have students use the scoring guide (or whatever description of quality you have taught) to identify what aspects of quality are present in a particular piece of their work. Encourage them to use the language of the scoring guide.

3. Have them follow the same procedure to identify one or two aspects of quality they think need work.

4. Offer your feedback. If you agree, it's simple. If you can, point out a strength the student overlooked. Add to or modify what the student needs to work on, if needed.

5. Ask students to take their own and your opinions into account and decide what to do next. At first, students may set large, unmanageable, or nonspecific goals. Help them, if needed, focus their plan on what is doable in the short term.

6. If your students have practiced giving formative feedback, encourage them to use each other as feedback providers.

*Offering Written Feedback*

You can also use the form, "Using Feedback to Set Goals," as a vehicle for offering written feedback. The student completes the top information and "My Opinion" before turning in the work. You fill out the teacher portion as you are reviewing the work, hand it back, and the student fills in the plan.

*How does this activity benefit you and your students?* Engaging in self-assessment prior to receiving feedback and in action planning afterwards shifts the primary responsibility for improving the work to the student, where it belongs. If you use this as part of your conferences, you will notice that gradually you will have fewer students to confer with and more students thinking about how the elements of quality you are teaching relate to their own work. In either written or verbal feedback situations, if you are spending time providing feedback, you want it to be used. Students are more likely to understand and act on your suggestions because you have asked them to think about quality in advance, which provides a mental "hook" for your feedback.

## Applying the Skills

**Resource 3:** Using Test Results to Self-Assess and Set Goals

**What this resource is:**

A chart that students complete to analyze the results of a test they have already taken and determine areas for further study, along with a simulation to introduce it to staff. Students often take tests without knowing what the test measures beyond the most general level: "reading," "social studies," or "science." If called on to use test results to set goals, without more specific understanding of what learning the test represents, students write the most general of goals: "study more," "take my book home," or "try harder." Although noble, these goals do not focus on what students actually need to learn, and therefore are of limited use.

This activity requires that a teacher administering a test first make a numbered list of the learning targets to be assessed. Then the teacher transfers that information to the chart, "Identifying Your Strengths and Focusing Further Study," page 198, by filling out the "Learning Target #" column, which identifies the learning target addressed by each item. Last, the teacher copies the chart for each student and hands it out with the test.

As students take the test, they note on the chart whether they feel confident or unsure of the correct response to each item. The teacher corrects the tests as usual and hands them back to students, along with the numbered list of learning targets. The students are now ready to identify their own specific strengths and areas for further study by following the steps explained on the form, "Analyzing Your Results," page 199.

This activity addresses principles of assessment *for* learning 1, 3, 5, 7, and 9, with a primary emphasis on principles 3, 5 and 7.

**Ideas for making it useful:**

*Preparation:*

To introduce this resource to staff, plan an activity where they use it just as students would. First, obtain a corrected test. Next, identify which learning target each item addresses and create a numbered list of all of the targets tested. Then,

196

fill out the two lefthand columns of the chart. In the first column, write the test item number (done for you in the example). In the second column, write the number corresponding to the learning target that item tests. Last, make copies of the corrected test, this chart, and the numbered list of learning targets to pass out to each participant.

*The activity:*

1. For purposes of this simulation, have participants pretend they are students, marking "Confident" or "Unsure" for each item on the chart, as though they had done so while taking the test.

2. Then have them complete the section entitled "Analyzing Your Results."

3. Last, ask participants to discuss when this would be useful for students to do and what it would accomplish.

**Student chart, to be handed out as students take a test:**

## IDENTIFYING YOUR STRENGTHS AND FOCUSING FURTHER STUDY

As you answer each question on the test, decide whether you feel confident in your answer or are unsure about it, and mark the corresponding box.

| Problem | Learning Target # | Confident | Unsure | | Right | Wrong | Simple Mistake | Further Study |
|---|---|---|---|---|---|---|---|---|
| 1 | | | | | | | | |
| 2 | | | | | | | | |
| 3 | | | | | | | | |
| 4 | | | | | | | | |
| 5 | | | | | | | | |
| 6 | | | | | | | | |
| 7 | | | | | | | | |
| 8 | | | | | | | | |
| 9 | | | | | | | | |
| 10 | | | | | | | | |
| 11 | | | | | | | | |
| 12 | | | | | | | | |
| 13 | | | | | | | | |
| 14 | | | | | | | | |
| 15 | | | | | | | | |
| | | | | | | | | |
| | | | | | | | | |
| | | | | | | | | |
| | | | | | | | | |
| | | | | | | | | |
| | | | | | | | | |
| | | | | | | | | |

**Student analysis activity, to be completed using the same chart after receiving the correct test:**

## ANALYZING YOUR RESULTS

1. After your test has been corrected, identify which problems you got right and which you got wrong by putting *X*s in the "Right" and "Wrong" columns.

2. Of the problems you got wrong, decide which ones were due to simple mistakes and mark the "Simple Mistake" column.

3. For all of the remaining wrong answers, mark the "Further Study" column.

4. To identify your areas of strength, write down the learning target numbers corresponding to the problems you felt confident about *and* got right. Then write a short description of the target or problem.

**MY STRENGTHS:**

| Learning Target # | Learning Target or Problem Description |
|---|---|
|  |  |
|  |  |
|  |  |
|  |  |

5. To determine what you need to study most, write down the learning target numbers corresponding to the marks in the "Further Study" column (problems you got wrong *not* because of a simple mistake). Then write a short description of the target or problem.

**MY HIGHEST PRIORITY FOR STUDYING:**

| Learning Target # | Learning Target or Problem Description |
|---|---|
|  |  |
|  |  |
|  |  |
|  |  |

6. Do the same thing for the problems you were unsure of and for the problems on which you made simple mistakes.

**WHAT I NEED TO REVIEW:**

| Learning Target # | Learning Target or Problem Description |
|---|---|
|  |  |
|  |  |
|  |  |
|  |  |

## Applying the Skills

### Resource 4: Student Self-Assessment and Goal-Setting Activities

**What this
resource is:**   A collection of ideas for what students can do to self-assess and set goals for
further learning.

**Ideas for
making
it useful:**   Handout of ideas for teachers to use with students (after a discussion about self-
assessment and goal setting).

### TRACKING THEIR OWN LEARNING*

Give students a blank sheet of paper (11" x 17") before you begin a new unit of study. Have
students sketch, write, or diagram anything they think they already know on the topic.
Collect these sheets.  Partway through the unit, return the sheets to students and ask them to
add information they now know on the topic using a different colour of ink.  At the end of
the unit, repeat the process.

| What I know about fractions |
|---|
| April 17 |
| April 26 |
| May 5 |

*Source: From *Self-Assessment and Goal-Setting* (p. 25), by K. Gregory, C. Cameron, and A. Davies, 2000, Merville, BC:
Connections. Reprinted with permission.

**SELF-ASSESSMENT**

**"Traffic-Light Icons"**

Students mark their work with a large dot—either a green, yellow, or red dot—to judge it. The colors, analogous to traffic lights, can represent variations on the basic meanings of "go," "exercise caution," and "stop" (Atkin, Black, and Coffey, 2001).

For example, when a student uses a rubric to evaluate her solution to a complex mathematics problem, she might use a key such as this:

Green dot = High-quality solution, "ready to go"

Yellow dot = Some difficulties present, "rework"

Red dot = Solution stopped dead in its tracks, "need help"

Or, students might use the colors to assess their understanding of a concept, in which case the key could look like this:

Green dot = My work shows strong understanding of _____ (concept).

Yellow dot = My work shows partial understanding of _____ (concept).

Red dot = I am struggling mightily with _____ (concept).

The teacher can then group students by colors. The "greens" and "yellows" pair up to sort through their problems together, while the teacher meets with the "reds" to reteach whatever is needed (Black, Harrison, Lee, Marshall, and Wiliam, 2002).

**GOAL SETTING\*\***

We model how to fill out planning frames so students can see how using a frame can help them set long-term goals. Then we help students complete their own individual frames.

| |
|---|
| To get better at _____, I could… |
| ■ |
| ■ |
| ■ |
| One thing I am going to start doing is… |
| ■ |
| I'll start doing this on _____ and work on it until _____ |
|                   date                 date |
| One way I'll know I'm getting better is … |

\*\**Source:* From *Self-Assessment and Goal-Setting* (p. 45), by K. Gregory, C. Cameron, and A. Davies, 2000, Merville, BC: Connections. Reprinted with permission.

| Goal | Steps | Evidence |
|---|---|---|
| What do I need to get better at? I've | How do I plan to do this? | What evidence will show achieved my goal? |

**Time Frame:** Begin _____ End _____

Date _____ Signed _____

# Competency 3

## The leader understands the necessity of clear academic achievement standards, aligned classroom-level achievement targets, and their relationship to the development of accurate assessments.

The third competency asks leaders to ensure that classroom instruction aims directly at learning targets that are crystal clear to all stakeholders: teachers, students, and parents. It's fair to assume that if the curriculum floor of the house is in disarray then the assessment floor of the house is going to be equally messy. The fact that we might already have a written curriculum may not be good enough.

- To what extent is it implemented in each classroom?
- Is it intentionally aligned with state standards?
- Is there a match between what is taught and what is tested, between what is written and what is learned?
- Is it high-quality curriculum, written with clarity and at a level of specificity to support instruction?
- Is the curriculum balanced among the four different types of learning targets (knowledge, reasoning, skill, product), resulting in the use of a variety of assessment methods?

Students learn more when they know what they are expected to achieve. Many students come to school every day prepared to learn yet are not given a clear sense of what is expected of them. Those who cannot clearly see the target will have difficulty hitting it. Even with state standards, supporting curriculum frameworks, grade-level and subject-area documents, and guides aligning standards to textbook material, many teachers are adrift in a sea of standards because they are not given the training, support, and time needed to transfer it all into everyday teaching (Schmoker, 2002). Strong leaders demonstrate Competency 3 when they support teachers in curriculum mapping (see Jacobs, 1997) or grade-level/subject-area articulation activities to further clarify what is taught and assessed, and when they provide structured time for teachers to work together to develop lessons geared toward the standards and aligned assessments.

It is also important to ensure the curriculum is available to parents and students in versions written specifically for them. Curriculum documents translated to everyday language and in a user-friendly format can be posted on the refrigerator at home, and help parents not only know what their children are learning but support them in that effort. In addition, as discussed in Part 3 of this guide behind Door 1, it is essential for leaders to ensure that all teachers are masters of the content knowledge they are assigned to teach. Effective leaders arrange for subject-area professional development where needed and institute hiring practices that place a high priority on selecting candidates with strong backgrounds in curricular content.

Beyond verifying that content standards drive classroom instruction and that daily lessons deliver the scaffolding students need to attain mastery of those standards as reflected on assessments *of* learning, strong leaders can also break down group achievement data into standard-by-standard information, so they can report individual student progress based on those same content standards. And to the greatest extent possible, leaders can also ensure instruction is aimed at all targets in the written curriculum, not just those assessed by the state for accountability purposes.

## Applying the Skills

### Resource 5: Implementing the Written Curriculum

**What this resource is:** By making sure the written curriculum of the state/district/school is used to plan and deliver instruction, school leaders help ensure that students receive instruction that matches the written curriculum. To increase the probability that the learning expectations for students are consistent across schools and classrooms, the written curriculum must be uniformly implemented. This resource provides ideas on how different roles/positions in the organization can help achieve that goal.

**Ideas for making it useful:** Before this tool can be of any value, you will need to gather some information on the level of curriculum implementation in your school or district. There may be uniformity in certain schools and not others, in certain grade levels and departments and not others, or implementation issues may exist systemwide. It mat be that teachers already use the written curriculum for its intended purpose. But in schools and/or districts where that is not the case, the plan that follows can be used to solidify curriculum implementation. We suggest that you use these lists of responsibilities as the basis for self-study—to see if all roles are being fulfilled.

# Teaching the Written Curriculum

Ensuring implementation and continued use of district-adopted curricula in every classroom of the school district is a responsibility best shared. The roles-based plan below defines responsibilities for each member of your district's education team.

| Curriculum Office: | Building Principal: |
|---|---|
| ■ Make the written curriculum readily available in multiple ways and easily read for all subjects, all grade levels, K–12.<br><br>■ Provide ongoing inservice training for teachers in understanding and teaching all learning targets.<br><br>■ Provide targeted ongoing training for teachers new to the district.<br><br>■ Provide "at a glance" sheets to teachers and other public documents like parent handbooks to use with parents during back-to-school nights, conferences, etc.<br><br>■ Provide skill continuum documents when appropriate.<br><br>■ Over time, provide evidence that the new curriculum improves student learning.<br><br>■ Provide sample classroom assessments linked to the written curriculum.<br><br>■ Carefully review all instructional materials for clear alignment and support of the written curriculum.<br><br>■ Ensure alignment of local curriculum with state standards. | ■ Focus supervision and evaluation of classroom teaching on use of the curriculum in planning and delivering instruction and in assessing student progress.<br><br>■ Frequently observe the curriculum in action in the classroom.<br><br>■ Provide teachers common planning time to work together to plan lessons leading to the accomplishment of the standards.<br><br>■ Act as conduit between Curriculum Office and school staff.<br><br>■ Promote use of the written curriculum through personal knowledge of the specific objectives.<br><br>■ Help connect and align adopted curriculum with classroom practice through staff development, faculty meetings, vertical teaming groups, etc.<br><br>■ Help secure resources for teachers to help understand/teach the curriculum, as needed.<br><br>■ Call on curriculum specialists or master teachers to assist as necessary.<br><br>■ Encourage teachers to follow a process to "audit" classroom curriculum against the adopted curriculum, if necessary.<br><br>■ Help ensure instructional materials support the written curriculum. |

| **Classroom Teacher:** | **School Board Policies:** |
|---|---|
| ■ Teach and assess the written curriculum.<br>■ Use district documents as the basis for daily planning and formative and summative assessment.<br>■ Communicate the learning expectations to students and parents, regularly and in understandable terms.<br>■ Possess detailed knowledge of subject-area objectives and be able to classify the type of learning target.<br>■ Monitor each student's progress toward the content standards.<br>■ In summary: know it, teach it, and assess it. | ■ Develop curriculum implementation policy.<br>■ Align district policies/curriculum to state goals.<br>■ Ensure professional development policies support subject-specific training. |
| | **Others:** (department heads, learning specialists, management team, etc.)<br>■ Site-based teams support and problem-solve implementation issues. |

In addition, the following functions have roles to play in implementing the written curriculum:

| **Staff Development:** | **Teacher Evaluation:** |
|---|---|
| ■ Clearly focus on curriculum implementation through a common training model for schools to follow.<br>■ In instrumental strategies training, use essential learning as context/examples.<br>■ Offer professional development in content areas, linked to identified standards/curriculum.<br>■ Continue teacher involvement in curriculum revision/improvement.<br>■ Provide school-based training on units of study based on the new curriculum.<br>■ Develop enrichment units/lessons and distribute them.<br>■ Continue training related to specific curricula.<br>■ Offer teachers an audit of building/classroom materials to ensure curriculum alignment. | ■ Continue to encourage staff to write professional growth goals related to curriculum implementation for formative evaluation.<br>■ Summative evaluation criteria/indicators relate to planning lessons, teaching, and assessing the written curriculum.<br>■ Pre/post conferences always focus in part on the intended learning. |

| **Curriculum Documents:** | **Texts/Supplemental Materials:** |
|---|---|
| ■ Readily available, user friendly, similar formats for all subjects.<br>■ Curriculum at-a-glance documents provided.<br>■ Aligned to state standards.<br>■ Available electronically through district website as well as hard copy. | ■ Must reflect and support standards and curriculum.<br>■ Selection requires support and alignment.<br>■ Requires appropriate level of introduction/training for teachers |
| **Special Education, LAP, Title 1:**<br>■ IEP's (academic portion) and LAP instructional plans need to be tied to district curriculum. | **Principal Evaluation:**<br>■ Accountability for curriculum implementation through the School Learning Plan. |
| **Reporting Student Progress and Student Work:**<br>■ Link report card phrases to the written curriculum. | |

## Thinking About Assessment

### Activity 14: Deconstructing Standards into Classroom-Level Achievement Targets: Practice for School Leaders

**Purpose:** To prepare students to demonstrate mastery of state standards, teachers need to help them progress over time through the ascending levels of achievement that lead up to those standards. The purpose of this activity is to show school leaders how to map those ascending levels of achievement with real classroom-level achievement targets.

*Important Note:* We refer to the process of identifying the enabling classroom targets as "deconstructing" standards. It is our contention, however, that the work of transforming standards into classroom-level targets that ascend within and across grade levels should be done by school districts as part of the curriculum function and not by each individual teacher working alone. This activity is designed to show you what is involved.

**Time:** 1 hour

**Background Information:** The goal of state standards is to set priorities on what students need to know and be able to do. Sometimes standards are broken down into *benchmarks* to further define what is meant. But, have you ever looked at content standards or benchmarks and asked yourself any of these questions?

■ What am I going to teach here?

■ How do I explain the target to students?

■ Will my colleagues interpret this the same as I do?

■ What do I *do* to enable students to do well on *this*?

No matter how careful we are in listing, describing, and breaking down content standards, they still need to be translated into daily classroom teaching. We've found that it's helpful to "unpack," or break down, unclear standards to see what knowledge, reasoning proficiencies, skills, and/or products underpin student success.

**The Process:** 1. Choose a standard or benchmark that is unclear—it isn't immediately clear what you might teach or teachers might have different interpretations of what the indicator might mean. For example, "Knows the binomial theorem" might mean

    a. Knowledge interpretations: (1) Knows it by sight—can pick it out of a list. (2) Can reproduce it when asked.

    b. Reasoning interpretations: (1) Can use it to solve a problem when instructed to do so. (2) Can choose the problems which would best be solved by using the binomial theorem. (3) Can write a problem that would require the binomial theorem to solve.

Each of these interpretations would have different implications for instruction. Which interpretation is correct?

2. The ultimate intent of a benchmark might be any of the four types of achievement targets. Determine the "ultimate" type of learning target embodied in the benchmark. Each of the types of learning targets—knowledge, reasoning, skills, and products—is defined in the accompanying list, "Types of Achievement Targets."

To help determine the "ultimate" target type of a particular benchmark, look for key words. Key words are included in the chart, "Types of Achievement Targets—Key Words." However, key words won't always identify the "ultimate" target type of a benchmark. For example, what is the ultimate goal of "Knows the binomial theorem"? The word *knows* indicates that it's a knowledge target, but is it ultimately a reasoning target?

3. For a benchmark that you judge to be reasoning, skills, or products, consider the knowledge, reasoning, and/or skills prerequisite to and underpinning competence on that benchmark. What are these? Ask yourself the following four questions. Don't list every little piece of knowledge or itty-bitty skill, just the major ones.

    1. What does a student need to *know and understand* to attain mastery on this benchmark?

    2. What *patterns of reasoning*, if any, are required to attain mastery on this benchmark?

3. On what specific *performance skills*, if any, must students attain proficiency to attain mastery on this benchmark?

4. What *products*, if any, would students be proficient in creating if they were masters of this benchmark?

For example, "Knows the binomial theorem" has knowledge underpinnings—knows what the binomial theorem is and when to use it. It also has reasoning underpinnings that need to be practiced—use the binomial theorem to solve problems, identify problems best solved using it, etc. All of these things would be incorporated into instruction.

**Key Points to Remember:**

1. **Not all benchmarks embody all types of learning targets.** Knowledge targets embody no reasoning, skill, or product underpinnings. Reasoning targets require knowledge but no skills or products. Skills targets require underlying knowledge and reasoning, but not products. Product targets might be underpinned by all four types of learning targets.

2. You are looking at what the benchmark requires students to know and be able to do, **not** how you will assess it. Because the import of this statement might not be immediately obvious, consider "Compare and contrast democracies with other forms of government." This is a reasoning target. It requires knowledge of what a democracy is and knowledge of other types of government—purposes and how power is acquired, used, and justified; and how government can affect people. It also requires practice in comparing and contrasting—a reasoning target—using the knowledge of different forms of government. You might assess these knowledge and reasoning underpinnings through an oral presentation (a skill) or a report or a poster (a product). These oral presentations or reports require a lot of other skills—writing, art work, delivery, etc. So, you might be tempted to list all these. **But don't.** All of this extra information is not required for the benchmark, just for the assessment. The benchmark requires only knowledge and reasoning.

## Types of Achievement Targets

Use this list to help you understand and identify the different kinds of classroom learning to be developed and assessed as students work toward achieving state standards:

**Master Factual and Procedural *Knowledge***
   Some to be learned outright
   Some to be retrieved using reference materials

**Use Knowledge to *Reason* and Solve Problems**
   Analytical or comparative reasoning
   Synthesizing
   Classifying
   Induction and deduction
   Critical/evaluative thinking

**Demonstrate Mastery of Specific *Skills***
   Speaking a second language
   Giving an oral presentation
   Working effectively on a team
   Science process skills

**Create Quality *Products***
   Writing samples
   Term projects
   Artistic products
   Research reports
   Shop projects
   Science exhibits

**Acquire Positive *Affect/Dispositions***
   Positive self-concept
   Desire to learn/read/think critically
   Positive attitude toward school
   Good citizenship
   Respect toward self and others
   Flexibility
   Perseverance

## Types of Achievement Targets—Key Words

| Target Type | Explanation | Content Standards/Benchmark Key Words | Examples |
|---|---|---|---|
| **Knowledge/ Understanding** | Some knowledge/facts/ concepts to be learned outright; some to be retrieved using reference materials | Explain, understand, describe, identify, recognize | Vocabulary<br>Measurement concepts<br>U.S. government structure<br>Patterns of growth and development |
| **Reasoning** | Thinking profieciences; using one's knowledge to solve a problem, makea decision, plan, etc. | *Analyze:* components, parts, ingredients, logical sequence<br>*Compare/contrast:* discriminate between/ among; alike and different, relate<br>*Synthesize:* combine into<br>*Classify:* categorize<br>*Infer/deduce:* interpret, implications, predict<br>*Evaluate:* justify, support opinion, think critically, debate | Think critically<br>Analyze authors' use of language<br>Solve problems<br>Compare forms of government<br>Self-evaluation<br>Analyze health information |
| **Skills** | Behavioral demonstrations; where the doing is what is important; using one's knowledge and reasoning to perform skillfully | Observe, focus attention, listen, perform, do, question, conduct, work | Read fluently<br>Oral presentations<br>Play an instrument<br>Use laboratory equipment<br>Conduct investigations |
| **Products** | Where the characteristics of the final product are important; using one's knowledge, reasoning, and skills to produce a final product | Design, produce, create, develop | Writing<br>Artistic products<br>Research reports<br>Make a map<br>Personal fitness plan<br>Make a model that represents a scientific principle |

213

## Examples

### Learning to Drive a Car

| | |
|---|---|
| **Knowledge/ Understanding** | Know the law<br>Understand informal rules of the road, e.g., courtesy<br>Understand what different parts of the car do<br>Read signs and understand what they mean<br>Understand what "creating a danger" means<br>Understand what "creating a hazard" means |
| **Reasoning** | Analyze road conditions, vehicle performance, and other driver's actions, compare/contrast this information with knowledge and past experience, synthesize information, and evaluate options to make decisions on what to do next.<br>Evaluate "am I safe" and synthesize information to take action if needed. |
| **Skills** | Steering, shifting, parallel parking, looking, signaling, backing up, etc.<br>Fluidity/automaticity in performing driving actions |
| **Products** | None (undamaged car...?) |

### History Example

Distinguish fact from judgment and opinion; recognize stereotypes; compare and contrast historical information

| | |
|---|---|
| **Knowledge/ Understanding** | What facts are and how to identify them<br>What opinions are and how to identify them<br>What stereotypes are and how to identify them<br>What it means to compare and contrast things<br>The basis (bases) or criteria on which to compare and contrast (events, people, conditions, events, consequences?) |
| **Reasoning** | Distinguish facts from opinions in the context of news reporting.<br>Recognize novel stereotypes.<br>Find the correct information on which to compare and contrast.<br>Compare and contrast the historical information specified on the bases specified. |
| **Skills** | None required |
| **Products** | None required |

## Examples from State Standards

**Sample State Standard 1—History: Students will evaluate different interpretations of historical events.**

*Knowledge and Understanding:* Students must know and understand key features of each historical event, and must understand each of the alternative interpretations to be evaluated. The teacher must determine if students are to know those things outright or if they can use reference materials to retrieve the required knowledge.

*Reasoning:* Evaluative reasoning requires judgment about the quality of each interpretation. Thus students must demonstrate both an understanding of the criteria by which one judges the quality of an interpretation and the ability to apply these criteria.

*Performance Skills:* None required

*Products:* None required

**Sample State Standard 2—Writing: Students will use styles appropriate for their audience and purpose, including proper use of voice, word choice, and sentence fluency.**

*Knowledge and Understanding:* Writers must possess appropriate understanding of the concept of style as evidenced in voice, word choice, and sentence fluency. They need to know what voice, word choice, and sentence fluency are, why they are important, and the ways they can vary. They need to understand various audiences and purposes for text and how these might influence style. In addition, students must possess knowledge of the topic they are to write about.

*Reasoning:* Writers must be able to reason through voice, word choice, and sentence fluency choices for novel audiences and purposes. They also must figure out how to make appropriate voice, word choice, and sentence construction decisions while composing original text for various audiences and purposes.

*Performance Skills:* Students will either write longhand or will compose text on a keyboard. Each requires its own kind of skill competence.

*Products:* The final evidence of competence will be written products that present evidence of the ability to write effectively for different audiences and purposes.

*Directions:*

Listed here are several more state benchmarks. Pick one where it is not immediately clear what you would teach, or for which teachers might disagree. Analyze it for the Knowledge/ Understanding, Reasoning, Skill, and Product prerequisites needed to perform well on the benchmark. Ask yourself, "What would students need to know and understand to perform well? What reasoning, if any, does this standard require? What skills, if any, would the students need to practice? What products, if any, would students need practice producing?" Practice deconstructing as many as you need to understand the curriculum development task at hand.

1. **Reading, Comprehension Processes, Grades 2–3**—Relate critical facts and details in narrative or information text to comprehend text.

2. **Reading, Comprehension Processes, Grades 6–8**—Interpret text(s) from multiple perspectives (e.g., historical, cultural, gender, political).

3. **Writing, Rhetoric, Grades 4–5**—Convey meaning, provide important information, make a point, fulfill a purpose.

4. **Writing, Rhetoric, Grades 9–12**—Have an organizing structure that gives the writing coherence (e.g., weaves the threads of meaning into a whole).

5. **Social Studies, Political Science/Civics, Grades K–3**—Create and use surveys, interviews, polls, and/or tallies to find information to solve a real problem or make a decision, e.g., create tally sheets to monitor frequency and amount of littering.

6. **Social Studies, Political Science/Civics, Grades 6–8**—Explain and apply tools and methods drawn from political science to examine political issues and/or problems.

7. **Science, Domain I, Inquiry, Grades 4–5**—Design and conduct simple investigations to answer questions or to test ideas about the environment.

8. **Science, Domain I, Inquiry, Grades 9–12**—Communicate and defend scientific explanations and conclusions.

9. **Science, Domain II, Grades K–3**—Explain how sanitary practices, vaccinations, medicines, and other scientific treatments keep people healthy.

10. **Science, Domain II, Grades 6–8**—Describe and exemplify how information and communication technologies affect research and work done in the field of science.

11. **World Languages, Cultures, Grades 4–5**—Identify and use appropriate gestures and other forms of nonverbal communication.

12. **World Languages, Comparisons, Grades 9–12**—Use knowledge of contrasting structural patterns between the target language and the student's own language to communicate effectively.

13. **Music, Singing, Grades K–3**—Sing expressively with appropriate dynamics and phrasing.

14. **Music, Singing, Grades 6–8**—Sing expressively with appropriate dynamics, breath control, phrasing, and nuance, demonstrating understanding of text and style.

## Thinking About Assessment

### Activity 15: Using Interviews to Hire Teachers with Content Knowledge and Assessment Competence

**Purpose:** Interviews of prospective teachers often leave out questions that check for competence in classroom assessment. Questions related to classroom management, instructional skill, and issues of student discipline are common; less common are questions about the teacher's assessment beliefs, grading practices, and knowledge of standards of assessment quality. Also sometimes overlooked is the candidate's mastery of the content knowledge necessary for the specific teaching assignment. Frequently, evidence of content mastery is gathered from college transcripts, previous teaching assignments, or candidate portfolios to help inform the hiring decision. This activity asks participants to think about what questions could be included in the interview that would help school leaders evaluate the assessment literacy of teacher applicants, as well as their academic preparation to teach the assigned subject(s).

**Time:** 1 hour

**Directions:** Think about and discuss the following questions:

- What should we reasonably expect the interview component of the overall hiring process to produce in terms of useful information about the candidate's subject matter knowledge and assessment competence?

- Given that, what questions could we design that would help inform us about the applicant's subject matter knowledge? What is the range of acceptable answers to those questions?

- What questions could we design that would inform us about the applicant's assessment competence? What answers would we consider acceptable for that set of questions?

**Closure:** Look at the questions on some of the interview forms currently in use in your school/district and see if they include questions related to assessment. If they do, are the questions related to assessment *of* learning, assessment *for* learning, or both? If your district has a comprehensive assessment plan, check it to see if it spells out classroom assessment competencies. Also, consider asking teachers whom you believe already understand the principles of quality assessment to tell you what questions they think should be included in the interview.

*Important note:* The stronger your foundation of understanding of the principles of sound assessment (Competency 1), the easier it will be to formulate your answer.

Finally, whatever questions you might ask about subject matter knowledge, and especially about assessment competence, consider the following points:

- Is there a link between what questions are asked in the interview and subsequent teacher evaluation? If not, should there be? Why or why not?
- Is there a link between those same questions, which in part act as our expectations of teacher skills and knowledge, and the staff development program of the school or district? If not, should there be? Why or why not?

## Thinking About Assessment

### Activity 16: Auditing Your Classroom Curriculum

**Purpose:** When introduced to a new standards-aligned curriculum, teachers swiftly and accurately identify the primary roadblock to implementation: "When am I going to find time to teach *all this*?" The following activity provides a process by which teachers can compare what they currently teach and assess to the content of a new curriculum, in order to determine the following:

- Where their instruction and assessment already align
- What parts of the new curriculum they need to insert
- Which instructional activities and assessments they can eliminate

**Preparation:** To complete the activity, teachers need to have created a personal curriculum map for the year or course, including the content and skills they will teach and assessments they will use for each. In addition, you will need to provide them with a numbered list of the new curriculum standards/grade-level learning targets for each subject to be addressed.

**Directions:** *Data Gathering*

1. *New and current curriculum—Where's the match?* Compare your curriculum map's list of content and skills to the numbered list of the new curriculum standards/grade-level learning targets. On your curriculum map, highlight those content and skill entries that show up on the list. Next, go back through the highlighted content and skill entries and write the number of the new curriculum standard(s)/grade-level learning target(s) next to each highlighted content and skill on your curriculum map to show the match.

2. *Instruction—How's the balance?* Working with the content and skill entries you highlighted on your curriculum map in Step 1, determine the amount of emphasis each new standard or grade-level learning target receives in your current teaching. Is it about right, given its relative importance to everything else students must learn, and its emphasis in state and district assessments? Is it over-represented? Under-represented? Not present at all? Mark the cor responding column on the chart, "Comparing the Classroom Curriculum to District/State Standards."

219

3. *Assessment—How's the balance?* Again working with the content and skill entries you highlighted in Step 1, refer to the assessments students take over the course of the year. Is each new standard or grade-level learning target sufficiently sampled, given its relative importance to everything else students must learn, and its emphasis in state and district assessments? Is it over-sampled? Under-sampled? Or, not assessed at all? Mark the corresponding column on the chart, "Comparing the Classroom Curriculum to District/State Standards."

*Decision Making*

4. *What to leave out?* Examine the content and skills you **didn't** highlight in Step 1 to determine which can and should be eliminated from your curriculum map. If you can address the new curriculum in less than the full year, consider which of these content and skills can and should remain in your teaching plan.

5. *What to adjust?* Use the information on the chart, "Comparing the Classroom Curriculum to District/State Standards" gathered in Steps 2 and 3, to rework your curriculum map.

## Comparing the Classroom Curriculum to District/State Standards

| Standard/Grade-Level Learning Target | Instruction and Activities | | | | Assessment | | | |
|---|---|---|---|---|---|---|---|---|
| | Right amount of emphasis | Too much emphasis | Not enough emphasis | Not present | Sufficient sample | Over-sampled | Under-sampled | Not assessed |
| 1. | | | | | | | | |
| 2. | | | | | | | | |
| 3. | | | | | | | | |
| 4. | | | | | | | | |
| 5. | | | | | | | | |
| 6. | | | | | | | | |
| 7. | | | | | | | | |

## Competency 4

## The leader knows and can evaluate teachers' classroom assessment competencies, and helps teachers learn to assess accurately and use the results productively.

Evaluating teachers' classroom assessment competencies presents a problem. Whether teacher evaluation is summative in nature, using the traditional observational checklists of criteria and indicators, or whether it is a formative model that relies on personal/professional growth goals as the structure for the evaluation, accountability for assessment competence is often absent. Whatever supervision and evaluation model is in place, if something is worth knowing and doing properly in the classroom, especially something that can either harm or help students, solid guidance is essential. Specifically, principals need to know how well teachers do the following:

1. Attend to the purpose of each assessment given, who will use the results, and in what way.
2. Address the learning targets being assessed and explain why they are important to assess.
3. Select proper assessment methods for the content.
4. Assure accuracy of the results.
5. Involve students in assessment.
6. Communicate assessment results to meet the needs of a variety of audiences.

Further, do students receive the evaluation criteria in advance, and are the criteria written in terms they understand? Do students receive descriptive feedback?

When evidence suggests that teachers do these things well a principal knows that high-quality assessment is a priority in the classroom, and that the teacher understands the use of assessment *for* learning to improve student learning. When the principal holds regular discussions with teachers about these practices and is capable of providing supportive, meaningful feedback to staff, regardless of the teacher evaluation model in place, conversations in the school begin to center on the importance of using assessment in ways that contribute to learning, beyond final report card grades.

## Thinking About Assessment

**Activity 17:** Should Teachers Be Held Accountable for Assessment Competence Through Evaluation?

**Purpose:**     Teacher evaluation criteria and instruments vary greatly and may or may not contain indicators of classroom assessment competence. This leadership team activity asks you as school leaders to think about whether teachers should be evaluated for assessment competence and if so, what the criteria for that evaluation should include.

**Time:**     45–60 minutes

**Directions:**     Collect copies of the forms used for teacher evaluation in your school/district. Using the forms, make a separate list of the criteria that relate to assessment competence that are currently included.

In your group, discuss the following question:

■  Should teachers be held accountable for assessment competence through evaluation?

1. If your answer is "Yes," begin to list criteria, in addition to what may already be included, that you believe should be part of the evaluation document. The criteria would describe the specific knowledge and/or skills that you would want teachers to be able to demonstrate routinely in assessment. Several resources and activities in this guide can be used as references.

2. If your answer is "No," explain why you do not believe assessment competence should be part of teacher evaluation.

**Closure:**     This issue, and therefore the activity itself, may be complicated by the fact that many schools and districts no longer use a summative form or process for teacher evaluation. The traditional classroom observation by the principal and checklist with criteria/indicators used for pre-/post-evaluation conferences about individual strengths and areas for improvement has been replaced in some schools. In many cases, new evaluation systems rely more on formative processes, where the teacher selects a few, focused professional-growth goals or instructional goals, sometimes in partnership with the supervisor. Indicators of assessment competence would not necessarily be part of that model or others similar to it. If that is the case in your system, what other ways can schools and districts ensure each teacher is a competent assessor of student learning?

To assist those who wish to add assessment competence to their summative evaluation, the main question to be addressed is, "What are the indicators of competence we want to see demonstrated?" You can compare answers generated in this activity to indicators in several of the other activities in this guide, as well as to the list of principles of assessment *for* learning.

Activities/resources in this guide that may be relevant or helpful include
- Activity 7: Auditing Classroom Assessments for Quality
- Activity 8: Developmental Continua for Teachers
- Resource 1: Confidence Questionnaire
- Activity 10: Principles of Assessment for Learning: A Self-Analysis

However, we encourage school systems that either have indicators of assessment competence in their evaluation procedures already, or that plan to add them to the list of proficiencies teachers must demonstrate, to provide teachers the support and professional development needed before holding them accountable for the knowledge and skills. Likewise, if administrators are to be asked to observe these proficiencies in teachers, they too, should have the requisite training in sound classroom assessment practices.

# Competency 5

## The leader can plan, present, or secure professional development activities that contribute to the use of sound assessment practices.

This competency links the school or district's staff development program with the leader's goal of every instructional staff member becoming assessment literate. If, for example, a principal wants to establish common quality standards for all end-of-course tests in every subject area, then he or she must secure the professional development necessary to ensure teachers have the ability to create tests that meet those standards.

To be effective, leaders should attend to both the content and form of professional development. Professional development needs to offer teachers opportunities for continuous learning focused on school/district goals, about what we want students to know and do and how to assess it. Teachers need to learn about and practice developing and using formative classroom assessments, individually and with peers. The learning team model combines research-based assessment content with an adult learning process that honors teacher professionalism, fosters collaboration, and takes place over time, allowing for focus and concentrated effort. The nine principles of assessment *for* learning in Competency 2 all lend themselves to learning-by-doing in a learning team model of staff development.

Professional development in classroom assessment often connects to professional development in other school/district initiatives and priorities. Finding and establishing those connections and helping teachers see the relationships among them brings coherence to a professional development program that often can be seen as isolated events entirely disconnected from each other. (See Activity 30.) For example, when teachers become assessment literate they learn to begin assessment planning with the established learning targets. As a result, training in classroom assessment can also be a strategy to assist in implementing the written curriculum. And as we help teachers understand and teach the content standards of a given discipline, helping them understand the principles of assessment *for* learning at the same time introduces assessment not just as a vehicle to collect reliable evidence of student learning but also as a form of good instruction.

225

We all want our professional development programs to, in the end, demonstrably raise student achievement. Evaluating our programs for their effectiveness becomes a leader's responsibility, and we'll address that in more detail in Part 5.

## Thinking About Assessment

### Activity 18: Analyzing Your Professional Development Program

**Purpose:** This activity helps you profile your school's or district's professional development program by using a set of guidelines for sound, effective programs. Having conducted the analysis, leaders can take whatever next steps they deem necessary to improve the quality of the program and its impact on student learning.

**Time:** 1 hour

**Directions:** Using the "Guidelines for Effective Professional Development," page 229, profile your own staff development program. There are several ways you can do this:

1. For each of the eight guidelines, rate the overall professional development program in your school/district using a scale of 1–5 for each guideline, with 1 being low and 5 being high.

   1 = We have not considered this or it is never present
   2 = We rarely see this characteristic
   3 = We see or apply this guideline some of the time
   4 = We see this frequently but not always
   5 = This is built into our professional development program

2. Make a list of those staff development models used most in your school or district. A sample has been started for you in Table 5, which includes such models as early release/late arrival days, summer institutes, local workshops/conferences, etc. You will need to add other models used in your school/district. Rank each of those models against the eight guidelines. When using the guidelines as evaluative criteria, which of your local models appear to be effective? Which forms of professional development in use appear to be less effective?

3. Discuss with teachers the eight guidelines. Ask them to identify which ones they value most and which ones have contributed most to their learning.

227

**Closure:**   Certainly there are other considerations that go into thinking about and improving professional development. As financial resources become increasingly stretched, what are the most cost effective models? What does current research tell us about model effectiveness?

# Guidelines For Effective Professional Development

Productive programs of teacher and administrator professional development do the following:

1. Focus on improving student learning by enabling teachers to reflect on and improve their classroom practice in specific ways that lead to higher student achievement.

    1_____    2_____    3_____    4_____    5_____

2. Arise from an analysis of discrepancies between current student achievement and desired achievement as reflected in standards.

    1_____    2_____    3_____    4_____    5_____

3. Are ongoing, promoting continuous increments of improvement over time.

    1_____    2_____    3_____    4_____    5_____

4. Rely on the investigation of sound new perspectives and strategies, collaborative inter-action, study of the research, and hands-on practice as adult learning tactics.

    1_____    2_____    3_____    4_____    5_____

5. Merge comfortably into what all consider to be the normal work of teachers.

    1_____    2_____    3_____    4_____    5_____

6. Are flexible, accommodating differences in teachers' knowledge bases as well as rate of learning.

    1_____    2_____    3_____    4_____    5_____

7. Are supported with sufficient resources and are economical in that they provide maximum impact for resources invested.

    1_____    2_____    3_____    4_____    5_____

8. Are evaluated for effectiveness.

    1_____    2_____    3_____    4_____    5_____

## Table 5

| | Professional Development Days | Early Release Days for Common Planning | Summer Institute | Local Workshop | Conference | Learning Teams | Other |
|---|---|---|---|---|---|---|---|
| Focus on improving student learning by enabling teachers to reflect on and improve their classroom practice in specific ways that lead to higher student achievement. | | | | | | | |
| Arise from an analysis of discrepancies between current student achievement and desired achievement as reflected in standards. | | | | | | | |
| Are ongoing, promoting continuous increments of improvement over time. | | | | | | | |
| Rely on the investigation of sound new perspectives and strategies, collaborative interaction, study of the research, and hands-on practice as adult learning tactics. | | | | | | | |
| Merge comfortably into what all consider to be the normal work of teachers. | | | | | | | |
| Are flexible, accommodating differences in teachers' knowledge bases as well as rate of learning. | | | | | | | |
| Are supported with sufficient resources and are economical in that they provide maximum impact for resources invested. | | | | | | | |
| Are evaluated for effectiveness. | | | | | | | |

## Thinking About Assessment

### Activity 19: Learning Teams for Assessment Literacy

**Purpose:**    Leadership teams or school faculties may use the accompanying article reprint as a foundation for staff development programs relating to assessment literacy.

**Time:**    45 minutes

**Directions:**    The accompanying article, reprinted from the *Journal of Staff Development,* explains the need for staff development in the area of classroom assessment, defines assessment literacy and the skill set it requires, explains the range of staff development options available, and makes the case for learning teams as the most effective and efficient vehicle for developing an assessment-literate faculty.

Take 20 minutes to read the article. Then work together as a team to address the following questions:

1. Does the idea of learning team–based professional development make sense in our context?
2. Has anyone had experience with this process? What was the result?
3. What resources would we need to allocate to implement learning teams for assessment literacy?

# Learning Teams For Assessment Literacy

BY RICK STIGGINS

Teachers will be expected to be far more assessment literate in the future than they are today or have been in the past. Virtually every set of standards of teacher competence developed recently, including those developed separately by the NEA, AFT, NCATE, CCSSO and NBPTS (Wise, 1996), holds the expectation that teachers will be competent in assessment.

This trend is corroborated by our recently completed survey of state teacher licensing standards. As Table 1 reveals, twenty-five of the fifty states have now instituted certification requirements holding that teachers either (a) attain specific competence standards in assessment or (b) complete assessment course work during their preparation. This is up sharply from previous surveys in 1983, 1988, and 1991 (Wolmut, 1988 and O'Sullivan & Chalnick, 1991).

But even more importantly, this trend aligns licensing requirements with what we have long known to be the reality of assessment life in classrooms. Teachers can spend a third of their professional time or more involved in assessment related activities (Herman & Dorr-Bremme, 1982; Crooks, 1988; and, Stiggins & Conklin, 1992). An appropriate level of assessment competence is required to do this job well.

These new standards of professional excellence place significant new pressure on colleges of education to prepare their graduates to be assessment literate—a challenge they have long failed to meet (Noll, 1955; Roeder, 1972; Gullickson, 1984; Shafer & Lissitz, 1987; and Stiggins & Conklin, 1992).

Until higher education responds to this demand, local school district staff development professionals will continue to face the challenge of filling this long-standing gap in assessment literacy.

---

**Table 1**
**State Licensing and Certification Requirements**
**(As of January 1998)**

States with teacher certification standards requiring competence in assessment:
Colorado, Connecticut, Delaware, Florida, Hawaii, Indiana, New York, Ohio, Oklahoma, Oregon, Texas, Utah, Vermont, Virginia, Washington (15 states)

States explicitly requiring assessment course work during training:
Alabama, Alaska, Arizona, California, Iowa, Montana, North Dakota, Texas, Wisconsin, Wyoming (10 states)

States holding no expectation of competence in assessment:
Arkansas, Georgia, Idaho, Illinois, Kansas, Kentucky, Louisiana, Maine, Maryland, Massachusetts, Michigan, Minnesota, Mississippi, Missouri, Nebraska, Nevada, New Hampshire, New Jersey, New Mexico, North Carolina, Pennsylvania, Rhode Island, South Carolina, South Dakota, West Virginia (25 states)

---

*Source:* Adapted from the *Journal of Staff Development*, Volume 20, Number 3, 1999, pp. 17–21. Adapted by permission from the National Staff Development Council. All rights reserved.

And, lest we think that teachers can turn to their building principals to lead this effort, we need only turn to Trevisan's (1998) analysis of their licensing requirements. In this case, we find that only three of the fifty states require assessment competence as a condition for principal certification.

The purpose of this paper is to provide local staff development specialists, many of whom may lack assessment literacy themselves, with an efficient, flexible, and very effective means of facilitating this key dimension of professional growth. The strategy suggested is the use of learning teams, in which teachers and administrators team up to take joint responsibility for their collective professional development.

## ASSESSMENT LITERACY DEFINED

Teachers and administrators who are assessment literate understand the difference between sound and unsound assessment, evaluation and communication practices. Those who are assessment literate:

- Understand what assessment methods to use in order to gather dependable information about student achievement;
- Communicate assessment results effectively, whether using report card grades, test scores, portfolios or conferences; and
- Understand how to use assessment to maximize student motivation and learning by involving students as full partners in assessment, record keeping and communication.

## WHAT TEACHERS NEED TO KNOW

Professional development in classroom assessment must build a deep understanding of the difference between sound and unsound assessment and a complete understanding of how to use assessment as a teaching tool. This translates into the following six classroom assessment competencies for educators (Stiggins, 1997).

First, they must understand the full range of users and uses of assessment. Users are found in the classroom, in instructional support roles and in the ranks of policy makers. Different users in different contexts need different information about student achievement in different forms and at different times to do their jobs. No single assessment can meet everyone' needs. Assessment literate educators understand and appreciate those differences.

Second, educators must be crystal clear about the achievement targets that they want their students to hit. Different forms of achievement (i.e., mastery of content knowledge, reasoning proficiency, performance skills and product creation proficiencies) require the application of different modes of assessment. Assessment literates know that the first question they must answer is, "What do I want to assess?" Only with that answer in mind can they determine how best to assess it.

---

*"Professional development in classroom assessment must build a deep understanding of the difference between sound and unsound assessment . . ."*

---

Third, they must be prepared to use the full range of assessments to track student achievement, including selected response, essay, performance, and personal communication-based assessment formats. Teachers must know how to select an appropriate assessment method for their particular context and understand when to use it and why it fits best.

Fourth, they must understand how to assemble the exercises of whatever method they choose in order to sample student performance effectively and efficiently. Assessment literates can gather just enough evidence of student achievement to lead them to a confident conclusion without wasting time gathering too much.

Fifth, they understand the sources of bias that can creep into each assessment and they know what specific actions to take to prevent those potential problems from distorting their assessment results.

And finally, assessment literate teachers understand the relationship between assessment and student motivation. They know how to bring students into the processes of assessment and communicating results, thus turning these into confidence-building instructional interventions. They understand that this kind of deep student involvement greatly boosts the chances of student success.

## PROFESSIONAL DEVELOPMENT OPTIONS

What kinds of adult learning environments and experiences are most likely to help teachers and administrators learn to design, develop, and implement quality classroom assessments in these terms? Whatever approach(es) we use must meet certain standards of excellence in professional development practice. To be specific, they must provide:

- An *infusion of new ideas* regarding effective assessment practices—specific things competent assessors need to know and do to maximize the quality and impact of their classroom assessment;

- Opportunities to *practice applying* the principles of sound assessment, providing teachers with the chance to make newly-acquired assessment ideas and strategies come alive in their own classrooms;

- Assessment tactics that *deliver concrete benefits almost immediately* to teachers and their students so as to provide positive motivation to continue learning;

- Ways for educators to *take responsibility for their own training*—honoring their professionalism in the pursuit of excellence in assessment;

- *Flexibility to adjust* to various learning styles, training schedules, and paces of professional development;

- Opportunities for *collaborative learning* and collegial support groups, because adults learn most effectively when individuals share the lessons they have learned (support groups that include both teachers and administrators can be important here); and

- *Efficiency of training*, minimizing the amount of time and energy practitioners must invest to derive maximum benefit, because resources for professional development will always be thin.

We must select from three choices in planning professional development to meet these standards:

*workshops, learning teams, and individual study.* Given the above standards, a development strategy for assessment literacy should combine these elements in the following proportions:

- 10 percent in workshops that generate excitement about the potential of assessment literacy;

- 25 percent in learning team meetings sharing lessons learned in the classroom; and

- 65 percent in individual study, classroom experimentation and reflection on "what works in my classroom."

*Workshops:* Workshops serve to introduce educators to the importance of being assessment literate. They also can reveal the potential benefits of adopting new classroom assessment strategies. Further, we can use workshops to encourage the formation of learning teams. But taken alone, workshops fall far short of meeting the professional development standards listed above. Suffice it to say that we cannot rely on workshops to help teachers attain the depth of understanding they need to meet emerging assessment responsibilities.

Similarly, we must remain circumspect about the benefits derived from hiring external consultants to be our "assessment trainers." Expert consultants can help in planning instructionally relevant assessment systems. They can offer motivational workshops to energize a faculty into wanting to become assessment literate. They can even provide guidance in mapping the route. But they cannot take the journey to assessment literacy for us. Each individual educator must take responsibility for getting there themselves. It takes that kind of personal investment of cognitive energy.

*Learning Teams:* This is why, after two decades of experimentation with all options, I strongly recommend an assessment literacy development plan that relies heavily on teacher (and administrator) learning teams as the basis of interaction and growth. A small group of three to seven teachers and administrators agrees to meet regularly to manage and promote their own professional development. They study together to fill the gaps in assessment literacy with the team's goal to help all members become as assessment literate as possible.

> *" . . . Three quarters of the time needed to become assessment literate must, of necessity, be contributed by the adult learner."*

***Individual Study:*** However, my recommended strategy relies even more heavily on *individual study.* Here's why, and the reason is critical: In between team meetings, each team member must agree to complete agreed upon assignments designed to advance the team's collective knowledge and skills in classroom assessment. These assignments might be the same for all team members. For example, they might read and reflect on the same pieces of professional literature or try the same assessment strategy, bringing the lessons they have learned from that experience to share in the group meeting. Or team members might complete different assignments, learning different lessons, so meeting time can be used to "jigsaw"or share a variety of insights for the benefit of all.

- This is where most of the personal professional growth takes place. Think about the work that is to be done. We must:
- Take time to read about and reflect upon new assessment ideas;
- Shape them into applications that make sense in our personal classrooms;
- Experiment with those applications, trying strategies, observing effects, interacting with students and drawing inferences about what works and what doesn't; and
- Finally, collect our thoughts, reactions and conclusions into some summary form to share with the learning team at the next meeting.

Incidentally, here is a brief but very important message to district administrators charged with allocating resources for professional development: Regard the percentages listed above once more. Note that three quarters of the time needed to become assessment literate must, of necessity, be contributed by the adult learner. If staff is willing to make this major personal investment in the collective assessment literacy of the organization, wouldn't it be appropriate for that organization to ante up a little something too? How about paying for time for team meetings by providing substitutes, early release time or extended contract time? It seems only fair!

## ASSESSMENT LITERACY TRAINING

To begin with, the value of being assessment literate must be fixed in the minds of all educators. Then, interested teachers and administrators must be given the resources and opportunity for teachers and administrators to independently, and as a group, become assessment literate.

To stimulate interest within faculty and staff, a leadership group might offer an introductory workshop on the importance of high-quality classroom assessment. Any experienced staff development specialist can lead this workshop with little advanced preparation. This kind of introductory session might culminate with the announcement that classroom assessment learning teams or study groups will be formed for all interested teachers and administrators.

## ORGANIZING LEARNING TEAMS

Within any district, learning teams can be configured in any of a variety of ways. Groups might be formed from among faculty members and administrators within one building, formed on the basis of grade level (within or across levels) or discipline (math, science, arts, etc.). Principals and vice-principals from various buildings might assemble to create a team for preparing to provide building-level leadership in this arena. Learning teams might come into existence as opportunities arise—for example, when an ad hoc committee is assembled to evaluate and consider revising a report card or when a curriculum-development team decides to deal with some underlying assessment issues. Participants might work together only for the period of time needed to complete their study. But all such instances represent opportunities for learning.

Some school districts have found it prudent to also set up a "leadership study team" comprised of a few key teachers and administrators from across the organization. This team's mission might include four parts:

1. Experiencing the learning team process so as to be able to share it with others;
2. Developing high levels of assessment literacy in order to lead others in their learning;
3. Devising a plan for forming and supporting multiple learning teams within the district; and
4. Conducting an ongoing evaluation of the professional development effort to discern its impact.

Other districts have issued the invitation to team up and ask those who are interested to form teams as they wish. They encourage teams to form and start at their convenience, pacing their work in a manner consistent with the schedules of team members. The flexibility of this professional development process is clear.

In any case, as members complete an initial learning team experience, they can then fan out and lead a team effort involving others. Then, those participants might do the same, and so on, building a professional development pyramid. As time passes, those not involved at the outset will begin to see others around them managing assessment with renewed confidence. This will motivate them to learn valuable assessment lessons.

## SPECIFICS ABOUT TEAM WORK

To advance their assessment literacy, team members could complete group study of assessment materials designed for this purpose by ATI. To do this they would schedule a series of meetings, agree on topics to cover, and plan a series of assignments to complete in between team meetings to increase their understanding of sound assessment practices.

But whatever the topic or reference the team decides to center on, team members must understand from the start that these are not merely books to be read and discussed. *A learning team is not a book club.* Rather, these are books to be read, reflected upon, worked through, experimented with,

discussed, and culled for ideas that work in each teacher's individual classroom learning environment. They contain no prescriptions, only possibilities from which teachers choose—pieces of clay to be molded to fit each individual teacher's needs.

This is why we recommend such a heavy allocation of time to individual study, classroom experimentation, and reflection between learning team meetings. Team meetings are times for sharing lessons learned in the classroom assessment process; not merely lessons learned from reading the book. It is a time to share successes, to discuss those strategies that worked and why. It also is a time to share difficulties team members may have experienced, to figure out why problems came up, and to find solutions.

## MOTIVATING PARTICIPATION IN LEARNING TEAMS

The learning team method of professional development takes advantage of four factors that can encourage participation. It offers:

1. Individual study for participants who have an interest in experimenting on their own (with minimum risk of embarrassment if things go wrong);
2. Collaborative study for those who like to work together to share experiences and lessons learned;
3. Training when members feel it is an appropriate part of their overall professional development plan; and
4. Time to concentrate on one important topic long enough to internalize some new and useful ideas.

For many educators, the promise of these four will be incentive enough to encourage their participation. But for those who need additional incentive, the district might provide release time or extended contract time to permit teachers to participate in these efforts.

Another option includes establishing an ongoing working relationship with a higher education institution to offer graduate credit. It has been our experience at Assessment Training Institute that colleges of education are most willing to enter into productive working relationships with districts to make such an offering possible.

## A FINAL THOUGHT

One need only contemplate the dangers to students of the inaccurate day-to-day classroom assessment of their achievement to understand how critical assessment literacy is to the effective functioning of schools. If we mismeasure achievement, we might fail to identify important learner needs, group students inappropriately, place faith in instructional strategies that really don't work, assign inaccurate grades, leave students with a sense of failure when they really succeeded, or leave students feeling successful when they really failed. In short, we place students directly in harm's way.

Yet, even in the late 1990s, we cannot assure our students and their families that we accurately assess achievement. We have yet to invest the resources needed to build an assessment literate school culture. We know what teachers need to know to function effectively as classroom assessors, and we know how to help them become assessment literate. We have very flexible and efficient professional development options available to us. Teachers just need the opportunity to team up and learn.

Crooks, T. J. (1988). The impact of classroom evaluation on students. *Review of Educational Research*, 58(4), 438-481.

Gullickson, A. (1984). Matching teacher training with teacher needs in testing. A paper presented at the annual meeting of the American Educational Research Association, New Orleans, LA.

Herman, J. & Dorr-Bremme, D. (1982). Assessing students: Teachers' routine practices and reasoning. A paper presented at the annual meeting of the American Educational Research Association, New York, NY.

Noll, V. H. (1955). Requirements in educational measurement for prospective teachers. *School and Society*. 80, 88-91.

O'Sullivan, R. & Chalnick, M. (1991). Measurement-related course work requirements for teacher certification and recertification. *Educational Measurement: Issues and Practice*, 10(2), 17-19, 23.

Roeder, H. H. (1972). Are today's teachers prepared to use tests? *Peabody Journal of Education*, 59, 239-240.

Schafer, W. D. & Lissitz, R. W. (1987). Measurement training for school personnel: Recommendations and reality. *Journal of Teacher Education*, 38(3), 57-63.

Stiggins, R. (1997). *Student-Centered Classroom Assessment*, 2nd Ed., Columbus, OH: Merrill, an imprint of Prentice Hall.

Stiggins, R. & Conklin, N. (1992). *In teachers' hands: Investigating the practice of classroom assessment*. Albany, NY: SUNY Press.

Trevisan, M. (1998). Administrator certification requirements for student assessment competence, *Applied Measurement in Education*. (In press).

Wise, A. E. (Ed.) (1996). Quality teaching for the 21st century. A special issue of *Phi Delta Kappan*, 78, (3), 190-224.

Wolmut, P. (1988). On the matter of testing misinformation. A paper presented at the SRA, Inc., Invitational Conference, Phoenix, AZ.

## Applying the Skills

### Resource 6: How Principals Can Support Learning Teams

**What this
resource is:**

This resource assumes that teachers will join learning teams to study the ATI program built around the text, *Student-Involved Classroom Assessment* (Stiggins, 2001). It offers an explanation of the content that teachers will be studying, along with suggested actions principals can take to support implementation of the content and of the learning team.

**Ideas for
making
it useful:**

Read through the two lists of suggestions, "What Principals Can Do to Support the Content of the Program" and "What Principals Can Do to Help Teams Succeed." Select actions that suit your context.

## WHAT PRINCIPALS CAN DO TO SUPPORT THE CONTENT OF THE PROGRAM

- First, make sure you can articulate the big ideas of what the teams are studying:
  1. *Quality*—How to select and create high-quality (accurate and efficient) assessments for classroom use.
  2. *Balancing Assessments* of *and* for *Learning*—How to meet parents', teachers', and students' information needs.
  3. *Student Involvement*—How to use student-involvement strategies to increase student motivation and achievement.
- Get a schedule of your teams' meeting dates and assigned readings. Ask questions about the specific chapters they are reading. (See "Content Highlights to Discuss/Reinforce.")
- Identify a "concept of the week (or month)." Highlight it at a staff meeting, such as through examples, an activity, testimonials, or student work. Consider co-planning the meetings with the team facilitator or the whole team.
- Be quick to notice success. If someone tells you, "I tried this out, and it really worked!" do something with that information. Email a response. Recognize small successes; make those small but important changes visible in some way. Get them into faculty meetings—plan a short (5 minute), regular "Successful Assessment Ideas Sharing Time" to help people realize that huge successes build on small ones, and that we/they are learning one step at a time. Celebrate the steps!
- Ask members of the team to invite you into the classroom the next time they try a new idea. Get in there to watch student involvement in action. "I'm intrigued by... and wondered if you would let me know the next time you..." Write a short note commenting on one positive aspect of what you saw.
- Release teachers to watch each other. Sub for them if need be. Schedule joint planning time for team members to create and/or critique an assessment together. Apply all the tactics you already have in your bag of tricks for making sure an important initiative gets off the ground (and stays aloft...).

## WHAT PRINCIPALS CAN DO TO HELP TEAMS SUCCEED

- First, make sure you understand the "why" and the "what" of learning teams—the rationale for this model of professional development and what process learning teams will be following. Then follow these suggestions for actions you can take to support the process.
- The most effective step you can take to support learning teams in your school is to *join a learning team yourself.* More than any words you can put together, this act telegraphs that you believe assessment literacy to be a high priority, a skill set worthy of your own time.

- Your team(s) will have regularly scheduled meeting times. Hold that time sacred for them. Avoid asking individuals to do something else during their meeting time.

- Members of the learning teams have committed a great deal of their own time, as well as team time, to become assessment literate. They may also be willing to assist you on other committees/teams, but consider not asking them for additional time commitments this year.

- They are acting on intrinsic motivation. The greatest reward for them will be seeing the changes in their students. Help them track those changes by asking about them. Encourage members to document students' changes for their own personal growth portfolios. If this seems overwhelming, ask them to select three students—one strong learner, a midrange learner, and a struggling learner—and look for changes in them.

- If you are a member of a team, consciously adopt a "learner stance." In team or committee settings, some people watch the principal to see how she or he responds and then pattern their actions after the principal's. You want your team members to feel safe enough to admit that something doesn't work well and to try new ideas. Model this: "I always did _____ when I was teaching, and now I see why it wasn't the best choice. If I had it to do over again, I think I'd try _____." In a learning team setting, it can work to your advantage to be a learner along with your staff, and it can work against you if they see you as the "expert," because you are not there to teach the class, you are there to learn along with them.

## STUDENT-INVOLVED CLASSROOM ASSESSMENT

### Content Highlights to Discuss/Reinforce

### Part I: Overview of Assessment Literacy

#### Purpose – Chapters 1 and 2

- Think about the purpose of assessment differently, not just as a vehicle for getting a grade for the report card.
- Think beyond teachers as the main users of assessment information.
- Consider the student as the most important user of assessment information, whose information needs must be met. What are those information needs?

#### Targets – Chapter 3

- Thinking about assessment begins in the planning stages of a unit, when we identify the targets we'll be teaching to.
- It's important to know what kinds of learning targets we hold for students, and to understand them, in order to teach and assess them well.
- It's important to communicate those targets clearly to students, in advance of teaching.

240

### Methods – Chapter 4

- How we select an assessment method depends on the kind of target we want to assess and the purpose for the assessment.
- When choosing an assessment method, we are going for accuracy and efficiency (keeping our purpose in mind).
- We need to be comfortable with using all four methods.

## Part II: Each Assessment Method

### Selected Response – Chapter 5

- Creating a test plan, in advance of teaching (or along the way), is a good thing.
- We don't need to become full-time item writers, but we do need to know how to audit a test for quality, which includes its match to what was taught (and the learning targets). And we need to know how to revise a selected response test so that it adheres to standards of quality.
- Using student-involvement strategies with selected response testing is not cheating.
- How much summative assessment information about student achievement is enough for grading purposes? How much is too much?

### Essay Assessment – Chapter 6

- We need to pay attention to guidelines for writing essay test questions (extended response items), because a poorly worded, or poorly thought out question can cause students to write a poor-quality answer.
- We need to have in place a scoring mechanism (points or rubrics) for essay questions that we communicate to students prior to giving the test.
- We need to know how to involve students productively in essay assessment.
- How much summative assessment information about student achievement is enough for grading purposes? How much is too much? Too little?

### Performance Assessment – Chapter 7

- Performance assessment cannot do everything, but it does provide us with the opportunity to engage students in "life beyond school" applications of subject-matter knowledge.
- Adhering to guidelines for creating the task is as important as adhering to guidelines when devising or selecting criteria.
- We need to know how to involve students productively in performance assessment.
- How much summative assessment information about student achievement is enough for grading purposes? How much is too much? Too little?

### Personal Communication – Chapter 8

- Assessing with personal communication provides a great opportunity to offer descriptive feedback.
- How much summative assessment information about student achievement is enough for grading purposes? How much is too much? Too little?

## Part III: Assessing Different Kinds of Targets

### Reasoning Learning Targets – Chapter 9

- We need to be able to define clearly for ourselves and for our students the kinds of reasoning targets we hold for them.
- We need to be able to teach students how to work through each pattern of reasoning we intend to assess.
- We need to assess reasoning targets explicitly.

### Skill and Product Learning Targets – Chapter 10

- We need to attend carefully to the quality of both the *task* and the *criteria* we use in a performance assessment. There are rubrics we can use to evaluate the quality of each.

### Dispositions – Chapter 11

- It is equally important to adhere to standards of assessment quality when making decisions about dispositions.

## Part IV: Communication About Learning

### Standardized Testing – Chapter 12

- Some of our problems with standardized testing come from misuse of the information—it's not the test, it's what we try to make the results do that confounds us.
- Classroom teachers and building-level administrators are the first line of defense against misuse of standardized test information.
- Anyone giving *or taking* a standardized test must understand what it measures and how the results are to be used (refer back to "Purpose").

### Report Cards – Chapter 13

- Level of achievement on the subject learning targets is the only factor that belongs in a subject-area report card grade.
- Practice activities should not be figured into the report card grade.
- Factoring in a zero for late or missing work misrepresents achievement.

### Portfolios – Chapter 14

- It needs to be clear at the outset what the purpose for a particular portfolio is.
- The learning targets the portfolio represents need to be stated clearly.

- Having a portfolio without student involvement, such as student self-reflection, is of extremely limited instructional use.

**Conferences – Chapter 15**
- Student involvement in conferences benefits all ages and all levels of students.

# Competency 6

## The leader analyzes student assessment information accurately, uses the information to improve curriculum and instruction, and assists teachers in doing the same.

In this guide we have established the need for balance between large-scale standardized tests and classroom assessments, while emphasizing the power of classroom assessment and the principles of assessment *for* learning. That does not mean that standardized testing doesn't have an important role to play in a balanced assessment system. It absolutely does; decisions about program effectiveness and professional development needs, among others, require this kind of information. Large-scale assessment results also offer evidence of system success, indicators that schools and districts can use to show the fruit of their efforts, solid proof that students are learning.

State and local testing systems together combine to create huge amounts of student test data, and all school leaders must be prepared to interpret, manage, and use that data productively. (We'll examine how to coordinate local and state assessment systems in Activity 27.) Now more than ever, leaders have a responsibility for conducting meaningful data analyses and providing clear, accurate reports of student assessment results. At the school level, principals need to work with the building instructional staff to use test results to identify patterns in group achievement strengths and weaknesses. Principals need to be able to produce annual learning improvement goals and identify the specific instructional strategies and professional development teachers need to reach those goals, based on the analyzed data. The use of data for these purposes supplants the use of hunches and intuition about what to do next to improve student learning, and places the data in the center of decision making. While teachers should receive appropriate training in data analysis and review, more importantly they need structured, collaborative time to review disaggregated test data and consider answers to the questions it raises, under the leadership of the building principal.

The leader's first step in achieving Competency 6 is to conduct an audit of all standardized assessments used in the school/district to ensure the information needs of all users are being met. The audit, also described in Door 2 in Part 3 of this guide, provides information about each test, including the purposes for giving the test, the standards assessed by the test, and how the results will be used. The audit can be used to ensure that standardized assessments will function as a system, rather than as isolated, unconnected measurement events (Office of the Superintendent of Public Instruction [OSPI], 1996).

As a part of the audit, each test must be analyzed to determine the content standards and curriculum objectives assessed. This analysis creates the foundation for accurate data interpretation, reveals information gaps and overlaps (which standards are going unassessed and which standards appear to be over-assessed), and focuses attention on which assessments yield the most useful information. Test specifications, which identify the objectives tested, are frequently available from test publishers. Such information, often underutilized, is crucial to our ability to do anything meaningful with test scores. We protect student well-being when we identify the match between standardized test content and what students are learning through our local curriculum, and ensure that every educator in the school knows what specific standards each score represents, enabling them to use the test information appropriately.

To analyze data and to communicate the information to all who need it, many principals form school data teams. These teams, comprised of representatives of the building's instructional staff (and sometimes parents as well), are given the responsibility for collecting useful data and asking questions about what test results and other data tell the staff about the student' performance. Here is a sample of the questions that a data team might ask about assessment *of* learning data:

- How do the results for our school compare with other groups: schools, district, state?
- Are there some groups in the school that outperformed others? Which subgroups need further data analysis?
- In what areas is student performance improving? Not improving?
- What learning targets do students struggle with most?
- Is there a particular assessment method that appears to cause students difficulty?
- What does the data from our feeder school(s) suggest?
- How do students who have been in our school the longest perform relative to students who have been in the school only a short time?

- Are the test results from one test consistent with other tests given in the school? Are they consistent with report card grades/GPAs?
- What needs for improvement can we infer from the data?
- What is currently in place that addresses those needs?
- What else do we need to know, and what data do we need to get the answers?

Software programs are now readily available to help analyze and present data in multiple ways. Many are user friendly and can help compare test scores by subgroup (gender, ethnicity, etc.), examine data at the individual test-item level, and assist in conducting program evaluations or gauging the effectiveness of one instructional model over another. And when the test results are linked to individual student identification numbers, longitudinal analysis becomes possible. If your state or district doesn't offer training on data analysis, there are multiple print and media resources available to help you through the process, including the following:

- *Getting Excited About Data*, by Edie Holcomb (Thousand Oaks, CA: Corwin, 1999)
- *Data Analysis for Comprehensive Schoolwide Improvement*, by Victoria L. Bernhardt (Larchmont, NY: Eye on Education, 1998)
- *The School Portfolio Toolkit*, by Victoria L. Bernhardt (Larchmont, NY: Eye on Education, 2002)
- *The Handbook for SMART School Teams*, by Anne Conzemius and Jan O'Neill (Bloomington, IN: National Educational Services, 2002)
- *Using Data to Close the Achievement Gap*, by Ruth S. Johnson (Thousand Oaks, CA: Corwin, 2002)
- *Using Data to Improve Student Achievement: A Handbook for Collecting, Organizing, Analyzing and Using Data*, by Deborah Wahlstrom (Suffolk, VA: Successline, 1999)

Standardized testing information is less useful, however, when it comes to informing the continuous instructional decisions that help each student attain state standards. For that we need classroom assessment information, based directly on the content standards and curriculum objectives taught. Common grade-level or department assessments, diagnostic assessments, classroom formative assessments, collaborative examination of student work, and data from teachers' observations can all be used to make decisions about curriculum and instruction and reveal why some students are learning better than others. It is the principal's role here to provide teachers time to meet to interpret the information they have and make instructional decisions on its basis, in both job-alike teams and in articulation teams with groups of teachers from adjoining grade levels.

The following resources also may be of value:

- *Professional Learning Communities at Work: Best Practices for Enhancing Student Achievement,* by Rick DuFour (Bloomington, IN: National Educational Service, 1998)
- *Results: The Key to Continuous School Improvement,* 2d ed., by Mike Schmoker (Alexandria, VA: Association for Supervision and Curriculum Development, 1999)

## Applying the Skills

### Resource 7: Conducting an Assessment Audit

**What this
resource is:**
As described in Part 3, Door 2, schools and districts need to map the "big picture" of the tests administered in local assessment systems to ensure that the information needs of all stakeholders are being met. The audit will capture such information as what learning expectations are being measured in each assessment, when assessments are given, how often, how much time each one takes, and the purpose of each assessment. When completed with the relevant information, the templates provided with this resource act as such an assessment inventory. Administrators can then use it to manage the local assessment system, analyze its contents, and find the testing gaps and the redundancies relative to the academic standards (OSPI, 1996; Stiggins, 2001).

You can create other grids, depending on your local program, to help gather and catalogue the information that will paint a picture of the total testing program in the school/district. We include here three templates that will help you begin to analyze your assessment program.

**Ideas for
making
it useful:**
The results of an assessment audit can also be a valuable tool to use when communicating with parents about standardized test administration and results. Once each test is catalogued, the information about that test (time, purpose, standards assessed, methods used, scoring procedures, etc.) is all in one place and can all be transferred into a letter home to parents to provide the necessary information.(See Resource 9.)

If you're trying to merge a local and state assessment system and ensure they work together and don't overlap (see Activity 27) the information collected through the audit is essential.

## A Model for Identifying Gaps in Your Assessment Plan

| Name/form of each standardized test or other assessment administered (list by content area or test battery separately) | Grade level(s) tested | Time of year given | Total testing time | Specific state standards assessed by this instrument | Assessment method(s) used | Connection to the district curriculum | Intended uses and users of test results | Communication plans |
|---|---|---|---|---|---|---|---|---|
| | | | | | | | | |
| | | | | | | | | |
| | | | | | | | | |
| | | | | | | | | |
| | | | | | | | | |
| | | | | | | | | |

## Record of Required State, District, and School Assessments*

| | Math | Language | Reading | Science | Social Studies | Other | Total State Required | Total District Required | Total School Required | Total |
|---|---|---|---|---|---|---|---|---|---|---|
| Grade 2 | | | | | | | | | | |
| Grade 3 | | | | | | | | | | |
| Grade 4 | | | | | | | | | | |
| Grade 5 | | | | | | | | | | |

* Developed with Dr. Linda Elman, Central Kitsap School District, WA.

## Assessments in <u>Math</u> (or other content area)*

| Test Name | Test Uses: Purpose | Test Users | School Level | District Level | Classroom Level | Methods Used | Time Needed | K | 1 | 2 | 3 | 4 | 5 | 6 | 7 | 8 | 9 | 10 | 11 | 12 |
|---|---|---|---|---|---|---|---|---|---|---|---|---|---|---|---|---|---|---|---|---|
| | | | | | | | | | | | | | | | | | | | | |
| | | | | | | | | | | | | | | | | | | | | |
| | | | | | | | | | | | | | | | | | | | | |
| | | | | | | | | | | | | | | | | | | | | |
| | | | | | | | | | | | | | | | | | | | | |
| | | | | | | | | | | | | | | | | | | | | |
| | | | | | | | | | | | | | | | | | | | | |
| | | | | | | | | | | | | | | | | | | | | |
| | | | | | | | | | | | | | | | | | | | | |
| | | | | | | | | | | | | | | | | | | | | |

* Adapted from OSPI, 1996.

# Competency 7

## The leader develops and implements sound assessment and assessment-related policies.

Many policies at both the school and the district level have the potential to either support or hinder the effective use of high-quality, balanced assessment. Further, policies can either support each other, acting in concert as a system of beliefs and practices, or they can act in opposition to each other, creating inconsistency and even conflict. It is part of the school leader's assessment responsibilities to revise policies so they provide a framework for sound assessment practice and act in unison with each other. In fact, without policy support, assessment reform initiatives may flounder. Leaders are more likely to succeed at this task if they approach it with three perspectives in mind:

1. How we view the role of the policy manual is critical. School and district policy needs to be seen as more than the regulatory compliance arm of the organization. Beyond fulfilling the legal requirements of the state and federal governments, policy can serve as an implementation tool for strategic planning efforts and can be used as one of many strategies to help the vision become reality. It provides an opportunity to set and communicate standards, expectations, and the priorities most relevant to student achievement, and can help educate the local community. The integration of district planning and priorities with policy making is especially necessary in a standards-based assessment system (California School Boards Association, 1999).

2. As mentioned in Part 2, assessment systems need to be planned as just that: *systems* with connected parts all working toward a common goal. District policy manuals and faculty handbooks should be approached from the same perspective. The elements all need to fit together, which requires thinking about policies beyond revising one at a time or revising each only in response to some district crisis or legislative enactment.

3. A written comprehensive assessment plan clarifies the purpose of assessment and how it fits into effective teaching and learning. We will say more about this in Part 5, but a document that states assessment beliefs and provides guiding principles and policies for both large-scale testing and classroom practice based on that set of beliefs is essential for assessment reform.

Policies that have a strong connection with student assessment and that should be reviewed for appropriateness and congruence include the following:

| | |
|---|---|
| Grading | Attendance |
| Homework | Student placement |
| Lesson planning | Graduation requirements |
| Hiring | Promotion and retention |

Following are three global guidelines to follow when formulating assessment policy:

- In a standards-based educational environment, what grades mean should be unambiguous. If the grading policy allows effort, attitude, tardies, absences, or other variables having nothing to do with achievement of content standards to be factored into the grade, many students' achievement will be inaccurately reported.

- If grading policies dictate the practice of averaging the marks in the gradebook to calculate the final grade, if formative homework counts in the grade the same way summative quizzes or tests do, or if marks early in the grading period always carry the same weight as marks in the latter part of the grading period, the same risk of, if not certainty of, inaccurate reporting of student achievement will result (O'Connor, 2002).

- Basing a promotion/retention decision (or any other high-stakes decision, for that matter) on a single test score or other measure of student learning may lead to an ill-informed decision. Any single test is limited in its capability to show what students know and are able to do. The use of multiple measures is always preferred in order to increase the dependability of the evidence.

## Thinking About Assessment

**Activity 20:** Using School/District Policies to Support Quality
Assessment

**Purpose:**     This activity requests that your team review a series of school/district policies, all of which have a connection in some way to assessment. Some are more complete than others; some are more current and better written than others. All are examples of policies at the district level, although school-level administrators can also make use of this activity simply by shifting the emphasis to school-level policies contained in a faculty handbook. By reviewing the policies with an eye toward how they could be rewritten or improved to be more supportive of quality assessment, your team and other school leaders practice building the framework for a productive assessment environment through the use of sound school/district policies.

One of the objectives of this activity and in working with policy in general is to see policies as a systemic whole, where the elements (in this case the policies themselves) hang together, all working toward a common purpose. Without approaching the policy manual in that way we risk having policies in opposition to each other: an attendance policy may contradict a grading policy, or a promotion/retention policy may conflict with a policy on student assessment that is grounded in a specific set of belief statements.

Lastly, the district-level policies in this activity are just that; without the implementation procedures that usually accompany policies and provide the specifics of how the policy is to be applied, we lack some context. However, the underlying concepts and ideas are apparent in each example. The intention of the activity is not to perfect each policy, but rather to get some practice in reviewing policies with quality assessment as the filter.

**Time:**         90 minutes

**Directions:**   Before starting this activity, it will be helpful for your team to list a set of criteria to use when reviewing these policies (and any other policies you may choose to use from your local school/district). What is the group looking to achieve in assessment through school or district policies? What would constitute a strong policy? For example, your team might generate policy review criteria in the form of questions. The list that follows is a start, but other considerations may be important to your team.

Does this policy

- Support the vision of assessment in the school/district?
- Have a direct impact on student learning?
- Have an impact on or connection to other policies that need to be considered?
- Encourage the use of multiple measures of student learning, creating judgments made about students with combinations of data sources?
- Require clear, meaningful, and frequent communication about learning?
- Link standards, instruction, and assessment?
- Require any specialized professional development?

Recognize that each of these criteria or those your team may generate might not be relevant or apply to each policy under review. After finalizing your list of criteria, read the first policy in this activity. Then pause and consider the following three questions with your team. Do this with the remainder of the sample policies in this activity. Use the criteria developed by your team to help answer the questions for each policy review.

1. What are the strong points of the policy the way it is currently written?
2. What are the weak areas of the policy?
3. What language could be omitted, and what language might be added to make it more supportive of sound assessment?

**Closure:** Completing this activity gives team members some experience in reviewing policies with assessment in mind. Your next step can be to undertake a similar activity using current policies from your school/district. Remember, if you find policies in need of reworking, improving them as a set of connected policies is more likely to result in policies that work in concert, whereas dealing with each in isolation can bring about conflicts in language and ideas.

## POLICY 2101 – STUDENT RETENTION/PROMOTION

As the ability to read proficiently is the basic foundation for success in school, as it is indeed throughout life, it is the goal of the primary school, the first three (3) grades, to teach each child to read independently with understanding by the time he/she finishes the third grade. It is within this period when retention of a youngster in a grade can be most valuable. Teachers, taking into account factors such as achievement, mental age, chronological age, emotional stability, social and physical maturity may find it advisable in the case of some students to retain a child once or twice during this period. By following this policy, the District will find some children completing the first three grades in four (4) years and some in five (5) as well as the majority who will finish in the regular three (3) year period.

With the above as a basic policy, retention after the third grade should only be a problem in those cases where a student is not achieving and meeting the grade standards of which he is capable. In cases where it is contemplated holding a student in the same grade for an extra year, the teacher should notify the parents as early in the year as possible, but not later than the end of the third quarter.

No student shall be retained for more than two (2) years in the same grade.

Since it is the responsibility of the school to adjust the work in each grade to the child's individual needs and ability to provide an equal educational opportunity for all children, no arbitrary policy of promotion is suggested. Promotion should be made for grade to grade, based upon a consideration of the best interest of the student concerned.

The following factors shall be taken into consideration: achievement, mental age, chronological age, emotional stability, social and physical maturity. The curriculum should be so broad on each grade level that the needs of bright students are met, as well as the needs of average and slow students. Therefore, when accepting pupils who are new to District schools, the principal should make the best placement possible on the basis of the information he/she can obtain.

## POLICY 2102– LESSON PLANS

To ensure proper planning and continuity of instruction, the Board requires that each teacher prepare lesson plans for daily instruction. To facilitate more effective instruction, lesson plans must be prepared in advance of the actual class presentation. The format for the lesson plan will be specified by the building principal and shall be reviewed on a regular basis. The plan book must be readily available when a substitute teacher is needed.

## POLICY 2103– CLASS RANK

The Board acknowledges the usefulness of a system of computing grade point averages and class ranking for secondary school graduates to inform students, parents, and others of their relative academic placement among their peers.

The Board authorizes a system of class ranking, by grade point average, for student in grades 9–12. Class rank shall be computed by the final grade except that non-numerical marks/grades shall be excluded from the calculation of the grade point average.

A student's grade point average shall be reported on his/her term grade report. Such calculations may also be used for recognizing individual students for their achievement.

## POLICY 2104—HOMEWORK

The Board believes that homework is a constructive tool in the teaching/learning process when geared to the age, health, abilities, and needs of students. Purposeful assignments not only enhance student achievement but also develop self-discipline and associated good working habits. As an extension of the classroom, homework must be planned and organized; must be viewed as purposeful to the students; and must be evaluated and returned to the student in a timely manner.

The purposes of homework assignments, the basis for evaluating the work performed and the guidelines and/or rules should be made clear to the student at the time of the assignment.

The school principal shall establish guidelines that clarify the nature and use of homework assignments to improve school achievement.

Make-up work, due to illness, is not to be considered as homework. Students shall be given the opportunity to make-up assignments missed during excused absences.

## POLICY 2105—COMPREHENSIVE STUDENT ASSESSMENT SYSTEM

The school district's comprehensive student assessment system will focus on measuring student learning, specifically student achievement of the academic and technical skills and knowledge essential to meeting four student learning goals:
- Read with comprehension, write with skill, and communicate effectively and responsibly in a variety of ways and settings;
- Know and apply the core concepts and principles of mathematics; social, physical, and life sciences; civics and history; geography; arts; and health and fitness;

- Think analytically, logically, and creatively, and integrate experience and knowledge to form reasoned judgments and solve problems; and
- Understand the importance of work and how performance, effort, and decisions directly affect future career and educational opportunities.

The district will utilize a variety of assessment strategies to assess student performance including but not limited to norm-referenced tests, criterion-referenced tests, district-level and classroom-based performance assessments. The district believes that a variety of measures will give the most accurate picture of student performance. Staff will be trained in the administration of assessments, including tests required by the state. The district will adopt performance assessments as the state board of education implements these assessments.

## POLICY 2106—GRADING AND PROGRESS REPORTS

The Board believes that the cooperation of school and home is a vital ingredient in the growth and education of the student and recognizes the responsibility to keep parents informed of student personal development/work habits, as well as academic progress in school.

The issuance of grades and progress reports on a regular basis serves as the basis for continuous evaluation of the student's performance and determining changes that should be made to effect improvement. These reports shall be designed to provide information that will be helpful to the student, teacher, counselor, and parent.

For grades 9–12, the district shall comply with the marking/grading system incorporated into the statewide standardized high school transcript. The superintendent may consider alternative grading/progress reports. A student's grade point shall be reported for each term, individually and cumulatively.

The Board directs the superintendent to establish a system of reporting student progress and shall require all staff members to comply with such a system as a part of their teaching responsibility.

If classroom participation is used as the basis of mastery of an objective, a student's grades may be adversely affected by an absence, provided that on the day of the excused absence, there was a graded participation activity. If the teacher does not so advise students in writing, the teacher may not use attendance and participation in the grading process. Teachers shall consider circumstances pertaining to the student's inability to attend school. No student grade shall be reduced or credit denied for disciplinary reasons only, rather than for academic reasons, unless due process of law is provided. Individual students, who feel that an unjust application of attendance or tardiness factors has been made, may follow the appeal process for resolving the differences. Academic appeals have no further step for appeal.

## POLICY 2107—INSTRUCTION

<u>Effective Communication about Student Achievement</u>

_____ School District is a standards driven district with the goal of communicating effectively about student achievement. It is the intent of the District to provide timely, understandable, and meaningful information about student progress towards clearly articulated achievement standards to students, parents, educational professionals and third parties with interest. Grading and reporting practices represent one of a variety of ways to communicate student progress towards standards and may serve the following purpose(s).

■ Communication of the achievement status of students to parents/guardians in ways that describe progress toward district standards and provide an accurate focus on learning.

■ Information students can use for self-evaluation and improvement.

■ Data for the selection, identification, or grouping of students for certain educational paths or programs.

■ Information for evaluation of the effectiveness of instructional programs.

Grading and reporting provide important information about student progress, but there is no single best way of communicating about student achievement. The District will use a variety of ways to deliver information about student achievement to intended users. All information users are important and are entitled to timely and accurate achievement data: some may require greater detail about achievement than can be provided by grades and test scores to make informed decisions. The following illustrate different types of communication about student achievement:

■ Checklists of standards

■ Narrative descriptions

■ Portfolios of various kinds

■ Report card grades

■ Student conferences

All practices related to communication about student achievement should be carried out according to the best current understanding and application of the research. The District will provide staff members on-going professional development needed to gain that understanding.

### Grading and Reporting

The District's policy and procedures on communication about student achievement, specifically grading and reporting practices, are based upon the principles that

■ Individual achievement of clearly stated learning targets should be the only basis for grades, providing an accurate reflection of what each student knows and can do; the effectiveness of the communication is determined by the accuracy of the information about student achievement.

- Other characteristics (effort, behavior, attendance, attitude, etc.) should not be included in grades but should be reported separately.
- Different users and decision makers of achievement data need information in different forms at different times in order to make their decisions.
- Grading and reporting should always be done in reference to specified achievement targets, comparing students' performance against a standard rather than against other students in the class (on a curve).
- Grades should be calculated to ensure that the grade each student receives is a fair reflection of what he/she knows and can do, emphasizing the most recent summative assessment information.
- Consideration shall be given to the use of appropriate grade calculation procedures to ensure that assigned grades reflect the intended importance of each leaning goal.
- Grades have some value as incentives but no value as punishments.

During the first week of classes, teachers shall provide students and parents with a written syllabus of learning expectations and grading criteria in clear, easily understandable language, indicating how summative assessment throughout the grading period will be calculated into course grades. Teachers shall discuss classroom assessment practices with students, in an age appropriate manner, at the beginning of instruction.

The Superintendent shall develop written procedures that support the District policy on Communicating Effectively about Student Achievement.

# Competency 8

## The leader creates the conditions necessary for the appropriate use and reporting of student achievement information, and can communicate effectively with all members of the school community about student assessment results and their relationship to improving curriculum and instruction.

Because test scores and report card grades will not be sufficient communication vehicles about how well students are learning in an era of standards-based instruction, educational leaders need to understand the principles of effective communication as they relate to student achievement. They also need to know when and how to use the variety of communication options available, including using students as communicators of their own progress toward standards (Stiggins, 2001).

Helping parents and community members understand what is underneath the grades and test scores they receive is an important practice in this competency. (See ATI's parent and community guide to assessment, *Understanding School Assessment* [Chappuis and Chappuis, 2002].) Parents learn about the results of their children's assessments *of* learning taken at school in a variety of ways, including through the local media. School leaders need to help parents understand assessment in ways that go beyond the scoreboard presented in the newspapers. Each time a standardized test is administered at school, whether at the department, school, district, or state level, we need to communicate with parents/guardians about the purpose of the assessment. To help parents put assessment in context, we can send a letter home (see Resource 9) explaining what is being assessed and why, how the results will be used and by whom, and the relationship between the assessment and the improvement of the instructional program at the school.

We recommend the following components be included in communication with parents:

- Explanation of what the test items measure
- How long the test takes, if it is timed (and why or why not)
- What assessment methods are used

- How items are scored
- Sample test items showing what the test looks like
- Written tutorials on how to interpret the results
- Sample interpretations of the results
- How the results are intended to be used, and how you will use them (linking the uses you will make of the information to the kinds of uses for which the test is designed)

Schools also can hold parent meetings to review these topics, as well as where each test fits into the total assessment program, and what the results mean for individual students as they progress through the system. This helps create a foundation for common understanding and effective communication between the school and home. We also can help parents use the test information wisely by cautioning them about how too much attention given to any one indicator of student achievement can skew the picture of individual or group progress. When we clearly communicate the results of standardized testing in relation to state standards, and use report cards that communicate progress toward those same standards, parents get a more complete picture from the school about what students know and can do relative to a predetermined standard (Chappuis and Chappuis, 2002).

The report card grading issues raised in the policies reviewed in Activity 20 also extend to the quality of school-to-home communication. If grades are to reflect something meaningful and serve a useful communications function they must be based on accurate assessments. But beyond this, grading practices themselves also present many difficult and potentially contentious issues. Unless resolved, these issues can result in faulty communication about student learning. Some software grading programs, while on the surface appearing fair and precise, can use computerized routines to generate grades that are neither fair nor precise (Guskey, 2002). When the report card grade obscures more than it reveals about achievement, the school leader must take action to create the conditions needed to institute clarity and accuracy in both grading (see Activity 21) and communication about achievement that goes beyond grades (see Activity 25).

Schools and districts that have moved or are moving to new reporting systems based on student attainment of content standards can take steps to ensure both students and parents understand how student progress will now be reported.

That understanding can be built by comparing and contrasting for parents a traditional report card based on A–F letter grades with a new standards-based model, describing the characteristics of and the philosophical foundation for each type of system. Informing students and parents of what is factored into the report card grade and what isn't also is important in building a common understanding. And we can also ensure our systems use as few coded messages as possible (B-, 79%, satisfactory, emerging), and always provide clear definitions of what those coded symbols mean.

## Thinking About Assessment

### Activity 21: Grading Scenarios

**Purpose:**     Communication about student achievement often relies on grades and report cards. The grading scenarios in this activity help leaders understand grading issues to help teachers use grades to accurately reflect student learning. This activity is intended as a tool for you, but if you use it with staff, don't use the results for formal teacher evaluation. Rather, use the results to plan professional development.

**Time:**     Each scenario takes about 15 minutes.

**Directions:**     Users can work through scenarios one by one or they can be divided up among groups in a staff meeting or workshop setting.

     For each scenario choose the course of action one should take when assigning an overall grade for a grading period, and explain why. Use the "Report Card Grading Guidelines," page 268.

**Closure:**     Discuss both the "Grading Guidelines" and your responses to each scenario. Discuss how your local grading policies reflect guidelines for grading in a standards-based system. Are any changes needed?

## Grading Scenarios*

Each of the following scenarios describes a decision a teacher has to make about assigning the report card grade. The teacher is unsure of what to do and has asked you for some advice. What issues does the teacher's situation raise? What questions ought the teacher consider before making a decision? What might be missing in the teacher's grading schemes?

Use the "ATI Report Card Grading Guidelines," page 268, to help make decisions. Our responses are included after each scenario to help facilitate the discussion.

Guideline 8—Relating grading procedures to learning goals (e.g., standards) rather than to sources of information (e.g., quizzes, exams, projects, homework) is a consideration for all scenarios. It is more difficult to decide what to do if one doesn't know what learning targets each source of information is addressing.

### Scenario 1

In her 7th grade social studies class Ms. Nguyen's report card grades are based on quizzes, tests, and an out-of-class project that counted as 25% of the grade. Terry obtained an A average on his quizzes and tests, but has not turned in the project despite frequent reminders. In this situation, should Ms. Nguyen

a. Exclude the missing project and give Terry an A?
b. Assign Terry a 0 for the project and D on his report card because his average would be 68%?
c. Assign Terry a lower grade than A, counting off some for not turning in the project?
d. Something else...

Scenario 1: Not b because of Guideline 6. Zeros distort true level of achievement. Not c because of Guideline 2—Only count achievement. Answer c would count a behavior—not turning in work—as part of the grade. We would choose d—assign an incomplete because there is not enough information to make a true estimate of student learning.

### Scenario 2

Mr. Marlowe's 9th grade English class has students of varying abilities. During this grading period, the students' grades are based on quizzes, tests, and homework assignments that involve practice exercises. Kelly has not turned in any homework assignments despite frequent reminders. His grades on the quizzes

*Scenarios adapted from *Grading* (pp. 188–191), by S. Brookhart, 2004, Upper Saddle River, NJ: Pearson Education. Scenarios based on unpublished survey instruments, B. H. Loyd, 1991. Reprinted with permission.

have ranged from 65% to 75%, and he received a D on each of the tests. In this situation, should Mr. Marlowe

a.  Assign Kelly a 0 for the homework assignments and include this in the grade, thus giving him an average of F for the grading period?
b.  Ignore the missing homework assignments and assign Kelly a D?
c.  Ignore the missing homework assignments and give Kelly a C?
d.  Something else...

Scenario 2:  Not a because of Guideline 6. Zeros distort true level of achievement.  We would choose b or c because of Guideline 3—do not include all scores in grades, especially scores on practice work.  Base grades on summative assessments.  We don't know whether a grade of C or D is more appropriate because we don't know the grading scale.  The only caveat is if the homework would provide additional information about student achievement; then we might assign an incomplete.

## Scenario 3

Mr. Paderewski is the teacher in a 6th grade heterogeneously grouped class. Chris, one of his students, has strong academic abilities as shown by her previous work, tests results, reports of other teachers, and his own observation. As he looks over her work for the grading period he realizes that the quality of her work is above average for the class, but it doesn't represent the best that she can do. The effort shown has been minimal, but, because of her ability, the work is reasonably good. In this situation, should Mr. Paderewski

a.  Grade Chris on the quality of her work in comparison to the class, without being concerned about the quality of work she could have done?
b.  Lower Chris's grade because she did not make a serious effort in this class; she could have done better?
c.  Give Chris a lower grade to encourage her to work harder?
d.  Something else...

Scenario 3:  Not a because of Guideline 1—don't grade on a curve, (norm referenced) use criterion-referenced grades.  Not b or c because of Guideline 3—include only achievement in the grade.  We would choose d—grade on a preset criterion-referenced standard.

## Scenario 4

Ms. Quantum has a heterogeneously grouped 7th grade science class. Barbara is one of her lower performing students, as measured by her previous performance and the observation of her previous teachers. Throughout this grading period Barbara has worked very hard. She has turned in her assignments on time and has often come to Ms. Quantum for extra help before tests. Her average for this grading period is two points below what she would need to get a D on Ms. Quantum's grading scale. In this situation, should Ms. Quantum

a.  Give Barbara a D for the effort she has shown?

b.  Grade Barbara according to the grading scale and give her an F?

c.  Something else...

Scenario 4: Not b because of Guideline 2—only include achievement in grades. We would choose c because we would want to make sure we have the best available evidence of achievement before failing a student. So, we would check for Guideline 4—use quality assessments and properly recorded evidence of achievement. Was there something in the assessment procedure that made test results inaccurate? We might also collect more information, perhaps from an oral exam (Guideline 5—use the most current information).

*Scenario 5*

Ms. Exponent is teaching high school algebra. In her class she gives two tests each grading period. David received an F on the first test and a low B on the second. In this situation, should Ms. Exponent

a.  Assign David an overall grade of D based on the average of his performance on the two exams?

b.  Assign David an overall grade of C because he showed improvement on his performance?

c.  Assign David an overall grade of B because that was his level of performance at the end of the term?

d.  Something else...

Scenario 5: The answer to this one depends on whether the second test covered material also covered on the first test. If the student really did use the F on the first test to learn the material, then Guideline 5 holds—use the most current information; so we'd choose c. If the tests covered different material then we'd choose a or b depending on the relative weight of the two tests.

*Scenario 6*

Ms. Phylum is teaching a heterogeneously grouped introductory biology class. In this class she gives two exams each term. In calculating Bernie's grade for this term, she notices that on the first exam he obtained a score equivalent to an A and on the second exam he received a low C. In this situation, should Ms. Phylum

a.  Assign Bernie an overall grade of B, which is the average of his scores on the two exams?

b.  Assign Bernie an overall grade of C, noting that there was a definite decline in his performance?

c.  Assign Bernie an overall grade of A giving him the benefit of the doubt— perhaps he had personal problems during the term.

d.  Something else...

Scenario 6: Not c because of Guideline 2—only include achievement in the grade. We might choose a, b, or d for the same reason as Scenario 5—we don't know how great the overlap in content is between the two tests.

# ATI Report Card Grading Guidelines*

1. Assessments, achievement records, and grades should reflect student attainment of preestablished achievement standards, not the student's place in the rank order of classmates; that is, make final grades criterion referenced, not norm referenced.

2. Report evidence of student characteristics other than achievement, such as effort, class participation, compliance with rules, attitude, etc., separately from evidence of academic achievement; do not factor them into achievement grades.

3. Use assessments *for* learning as the basis for providing students with descriptive feedback they can use to see how to improve; do not factor them into report card grades.

4. When assigning grades, use the most consistent body of evidence available; that is, base all grades on verifiably accurate assessments of student achievement; discard any inaccurate assessments from grading records.

5. Base grades on the most current evidence of the student's level of achievement; that is, if more recent information about student achievement reveals new levels of attainment, thus rendering previous evidence outdated, then grades should be based on the newest evidence.

6. Do not enter missing or distorted evidence of achievement into gradebooks as zero; that is, do not interpret missed tests, scores attained by cheating, or assignments not handed in as evidence of the total absence of any learning. Rather, interpret those as a lack of evidence only, until turned in or retaken.

7. At any time during the grading period, be sure students know how their current level of achievement compares to the standards they are expected to master; this knowledge should arise from their consistent involvement in self-assessment, record keeping, and communication.

8. Arrange achievement records in the gradebook according to achievement target, not according to type or source of information such as type of assessment.

---

* For background on these guidelines, refer to Ken O'Connor's, *How to Grade for Learning* (Skylight, 2002), as well as the ATI textbook, *Student-Involved Classroom Assessment* (Chapter 13 on Report Cards) and the ATI interactive training video, *Report Card Grades: Strategies and Solutions*.

## Thinking About Assessment

### Activity 22: ATI Interactive Video, *Report Card Grading: Strategies and Solutions*

**Purpose:**     The Assessment Training Institute interactive training video series for use with school faculties includes one presentation that provides a commonsense overview of a practical set of classroom assessment quality standards. These are the same five standards addressed behind Door 3 in Part 3 of this guide and in all ATI professional development materials:

■ Clarify achievement targets.

■ Identify assessment users and uses.

■ Select a proper assessment method.

■ Sample student achievement with high-quality exercises.

■ Control for relevant sources of bias.

In this video and its associated trainer's guide, we provide the basis for a high-quality workshop experience for a faculty interested in an overview of how these standards lead to gathering accurate information about student achievement day to day in the classroom.

**Important Note:** While this program provides an easy to understand overview of sound classroom assessment practices, it cannot teach teachers to how to make those practices operational by itself. That requires further study of the principles of high-quality assessment.

**Time:**          About 2 hours

**Directions:**    Obtain a copy of the video and trainer's guide and follow directions provided in the guide.

**Closure:**       For those interested in learning more about these ideas and their application in their own classrooms, invite them to form learning teams to study and discuss the text *Student-Involved Classroom Assessment,* 3d ed. (Stiggins, 2001).

## Thinking About Assessment

### Activity 23: Panel Hears Exam Horrors

**Purpose:**    Many times dilemmas regarding test scores and grading occur because conditions for effective communication have broken down. This scenario provides a graphic example of what happens when such conditions are missing and gives leaders the chance to reflect on how to avoid these kinds of problems.

**Time:**    20 minutes

**Directions:**    "The Board of Education will hold further hearings today on the high school graduation test..." This statement could strike fear into any school leader's heart. The following case study gives you the opportunity to analyze what went wrong in a real situation and what might have been done to avoid the problem.

1. (5–10 minutes) Read the attached case, "Panel Hears Exam Horrors."

2. (10–15 minutes) Think about or discuss the following questions:
   a. Which of the following responsibilities of educators with regard to standardized tests (Stiggins, 2001, pp. 400–405 and below) went wrong?*
   (1) Protect the well-being of students.
   (2) Promote understanding within the community of the role of standardized testing in helping students learn.
   (3) Be constantly mindful of when standardized tests are likely to provide useful information and when they are not.
   b. What conditions for sound communication were violated?
   c. What should school officials (and teachers) do to avoid such problems?**

---

* Possible answers: Responsibility 1—fulfilling course requirements vs. being competent; math in grades 9 and 10 but not tested until grade 12; accuracy, only 4 points away; accuracy, clear targets; accuracy, what do "higher standards" mean (trickier, harder, or application of knowledge)?; student self-confidence. Responsibility 2—were students given adequate notice?

** Possible answers: Clarify what is meant by "higher standards." Make a clearer link between classroom assessments resulting in grades and the competency test—do they measure the same thing? How high a grade must be obtained to be reasonably sure a student will "pass" the competency test? Make sure students and parents have adequate notice. Establish a procedure to resolve discrepancies between multiple measures of the same skills and knowledge.

# Panel Hears Exam Horrors—Case Study*

With just seven weeks to go until graduation, a Clark Country high school senior with a 3.5 grade-point average is ready to drop out. Cindy Mason's daughter can't pass the math portion of the State's High School Proficiency Examination, and she's not alone. About 14 percent of the state's high school seniors are in the same predicament.

"My daughter's crying hysterically over this and she's ready to quit," Joan told State Board of Education members Thursday. "She can walk down the aisle, but she'll be walking on a false basis. She's not getting a diploma.". . .

Joan came specifically to tell the board that her daughter fulfilled all the recommended course work at her high school. Her math courses included basic math and pre-algebra. As a freshman and sophomore, that met state requirements. Now, as a senior, Joan's daughter is four points short of passing the math test. She's never had geometry, she's never had algebra, and at this point in the game, Joan thinks it's heartless to change the rules.

She didn't get much disagreement from the Board of Education. "I'm extremely sympathetic to what you're saying," said Bill Hanlon, a board member and career math educator. "But the state Legislature has mandated that we put this into effect."

Bill and other board members believe the testing was implemented too soon. He supports higher standards, but thinks the test should have been phased in after more stringent high school requirements had a chance to kick in.

And if students think this year was rough going, Bill has words of warning: "Wait until next year." The state's new standards, which take effect next year, include trigonometry—that could potentially make the exam more difficult. That will be coupled with students having to earn higher scores to pass. . . .

The set of circumstances prompted Bill to ask the board to consider several recommendations:

Allow the use of calculators on the test for special education students with individual education plans that permit them to use the device in math classes.

*Source: Reprinted from "Panel Hears Exam Horrors–Case Study," by L. K. Bach, 1999, *Las Vegas Review Journal,* 16 April. Reprinted by permission.

Add one more test opportunity before the end of the school year for seniors who haven't passed.

State law allows students five opportunities to take the test, but the fifth test this year won't be offered until June.

Lift the cap on the number of times a student can take the test. . . .

Tom McIntosh, state test director, briefed the board Thursday on the scores from the February round of graduation exams. Of 3,320 students tested in math, 2,366 failed. Of the 1,839 tested in reading, 1,095 failed. "The question is, is that too many kids?" Tom said.

Board member, Gary Waters said that while the numbers are sobering, they're also a sign to teens to take the test seriously. Before the graduation test was revised, less than 1 percent of students failed the exam.

## Thinking About Assessment

### Activity 24: When Grades Don't Match the State Assessment Results

**Purpose:** The case, "When Grades Don't Match the State Assessment Results," presents a phenomenon that is occurring with increasing frequency across the country—what happens when students consistently get high grades but fail to meet competency on a state test? This activity explores the reasons for this phenomenon.

**Time:** 10–20 minutes

**Directions:** Read the case and think about or discuss the following questions:

Why might the situation be occurring? Consider the extent to which conditions for sound communication are violated. Are other standards of quality assessment being violated?*

**Closure:** Discuss what you can do in your school/district to deal with this situation.**

## When Grades Don't Match the State Assessment Results—Case Study

"It seems important to let you know of a phenomenon I'm experiencing in my school as we deal with the data about students who do and do not meet standards on the state assessment in relationship to the grades they earn. While it remains true that most of the kids who are meeting standards are those who also get As, we are discovering a significant number of students who do get As who don't meet standards and a similar number who get rather poor grades who do meet the standards. What should we do?" (Personal communication to authors, 1997).

* Possible reasons: (1) The state assessment only includes achievement, while grades might include factors other than achievement, such as absences. (2) Class work may cover more than the priorities in the state assessment, so classroom assessments might measure different things than the state assessment. (3) The classroom assessments underpinning the grades aren't accurate. (4) It is unclear how the state performance standard cutoff relates to teachers' grading cutoffs. (5) They were given at different times and might not match with respect to the content students have encountered.

** Possible solutions: (1) Clarify state assessment and classroom learning targets. Do they match? If not, should they? Is instruction aligned? (2) Check classroom assessments for accuracy—do they meet the five standards of quality? (3) Calibrate classroom assessments to the state assessment so that teachers and students know the level needed to perform on classroom assessments to meet state standards.

## Thinking About Assessment

### Activity 25: Connecting Assessment with Reporting

**Purpose:**    To illustrate the connection among assessment, instruction, and meaningful reporting of student achievement.

Many times teachers feel that their required report card does not adequately reflect what students know and can do, but the exact reasons and what to do about it are often elusive. Beginning with the report card itself is usually not the best way to proceed. This case study illustrates a more productive approach to report card reform.

**Time:**    30–45 minutes

**Directions:**

Use the five standards of quality assessment as an overhead if needed, to orient teachers to the areas of quality assessment they will be examining.

1. Read the accompanying case study, "Connecting Assessment with Reporting," pages 275–276. Review the assessment model and revised report card.
2. Discuss the following questions:
   - What is the relationship between clear targets and good report card design? How was this relationship illustrated in this scenario?
   - What is the relationship between sound assessment and good report card design? How was this relationship illustrated in this scenario?

**Closure:**    Identify the barriers in your own building to attaining a higher level of consistency among teaching, learning, assessing, and reporting. What could be done to overcome them?

## Connecting Assessment with Reporting—Case Study

Recently, our kindergarten and first grade teachers implemented a new writing assessment model for primary students (see "Writing Progress Report"). This model involved applying developmental descriptors to the writing of young children so that growth in writing could be documented. Teachers looked for growth in the quality of ideas, organization, voice, word choice, fluency, and conventions. For example, conventions (called 'organizations' in the progress report) at the primary years might involve growth in orientation of pretend-writing on the page, spacing between pretend words and pretend-writing from left to right.

In addition to improving assessment at the early years, teachers felt the model also improved teaching and learning. For example, the staff felt that the language of the model helped them to articulate clear and appropriate learning targets for students so that they would know what to teach and how to track progress. The assessment tool drove curriculum and instructional strategy reforms that were seen by staff as increasing the quality of teaching and learning for kindergartners and first graders.

This created a direct link for teachers between assessment and curriculum. The perceived usefulness of the assessment information to influence instruction and to improve student learning furthered the teachers' use of the assessment model. The more they used it, the more perceived impact it had on student performance. This positive cycle powerfully improved the teaching and learning of writing at our school.

However, during parent–teacher conferences, teachers became frustrated with their ability to share information about student writing performance with parents via the district's report card. They felt the report card limited their reporting to information about printing and copying. This presented a frustrating institutional barrier in their efforts to further their application of writing assessment. After three trimesters of dealing with this mismatch, this group of teachers set out to improve the report card.

Teachers began by collecting a variety of report cards and grading continuums from other school districts. As a group, they viewed the Video Journal's production of "Reporting Student Progress." These sources fueled their early conversations about their goals and resulted in a first draft (see "K–1 Report Card"). During Fall and Spring parent–teacher conferences, teachers described each child's performance to their parents using the new report card. The report card, combined with collections of student daily work, classroom assessments, a formal district-wide writing assessment, and teacher descriptions, painted a clear picture of each student's development and achievement. Teachers were extremely pleased with the direct match between the language of the new report card and the formal and informal assessment information they were collecting during the year.

While our revised report card is not a high tech recording or reporting method, it is providing improved information to a variety of users. As teachers created it, they also constructed a high level of meaning for themselves about the information that it reports. While not at the same high level, the parent and administrative involvement in the process has raised our shared understanding of the report card and we too have constructed strong meanings for the information it reports. Through the process, parent, teachers, and administrators have further developed our conceptual understanding of the connections among teaching, curriculum, learning, assessment, and reporting. Our end product is a piece of paper, but the process created several equally important results along the way.

—Bill Nutting
Mt. Vernon School District, Washington (1997)

# Writing Progress Report

Student: _____

School Year: _____ Grade: _____    Teacher: _____

We believe that each child is unique and develops continuously at his/her own rate. Our goal is to provide the opportunity for each child to develop in a way that he/she might live cooperatively, successfully, and happily.

| | Exploring | Emerging | Developing | Independent | Expanding |
|---|---|---|---|---|---|
| Organization | Scribbles | Places strings of letters left to right, top to bottom | Randomly spaces between words | Routinely spaces words | Writes legibly |
| Organization | Mixes scribbles with some recognizable letters | Writes random recognizable letters | Forms most letters legibly and correctly | Forms all letters legibly and correctly | Writes legibly |
| Details | Draws a picture and labels it with personal symbols and/or tells about it | Sometimes uses writing as support for picture | Focuses on one main idea | Writes sequential simple sentences on one main idea | Writes a story with a beginning, middle, and end on one main idea |
| Details | Uses pictures and scribbles to express an idea | Combines pictures with text | Usually attends to detail in own text, pictures, or both | Supports ideas with details | Elaborates on main part of picture and/or text with interesting details |
| Voice | May express self through use of vivid or varied colors, thin or thick lines in pictures or scribbles | Picture/writing often reflects energy, characters with expressive faces/body language | Picture/writing usually recognized by someone who knows student | Picture/writing usually reflects uniqueness of individual | Uses expressions of personal style |
| Word Choice | Experiments with new words in dictation | Copies words from around the room | Chooses interesting words some of the time | Chooses interesting words most of the time | Chooses interesting words consistently |
| Spelling | Randomly places letters on paper | Begins pre-phonetic spelling mainly with consonants | Writes recognizable phonetically spelled words | Spells most common sight words | Spells commonly used words and some difficult words |
| Conventions | Writes part of a name | Writes name in upper or lower case letters | Capitalizes first name | Starts a few sentences with capitals; begin to use punctuation | Starts with capitals and ends with punctuation |

**Code for indicating progress by assessment periods: N=1st Grading Period; M=2nd Grading Period; J=3rd Grading Period**

Material reprinted with permission of Mount Vernon School District.

# K–1 Report Card

Student:_____     Teacher:_____

School Year:_____  Grade:_____

We believe that each child is unique and develops continuously at his/her own rate. We do not expect all children to reach the same levels of achievement at the same time. Our goal is to provide the opportunity for each child to develop in a way that he/she might live cooperatively, successfully, and happily.

| EXPLORING | EMERGING | DEVELOPING | INDEPENDENT |
|---|---|---|---|
| __ Scribbles<br><br>__ Draws a picture and labels it with personal symbols and/or tells about it<br><br>__ Uses pictures and scribbles to express an idea | __ Places strings of letters left to right, top to bottom<br><br>__ Sometimes uses writing as support for picture<br><br>__ Combines pictures with readable text | __ Randomly spaces between words<br><br>__ Writes sequential simple sentences on one main idea<br><br>__ Usually attends to detail in own text, pictures, or both | __ Routinely spaces words<br><br>__ Writes a story with a beginning, middle, and end on one main idea<br><br>__ Elaborates on main part of picture and/or text with interesting details |
| __ May express self through use of vivid or varied colors, thin or thick lines in pictures or scribbles<br><br>__ Experiments with new words in dictation | __ Picture/writing often reflects energy, characters with expressive faces/body language<br><br>__ Copies words from around the room | __ Picture/writing usually recognized by someone who knows student<br><br>__ Chooses words to make meaning clear | __ Picture/writing usually reflects uniqueness of individual<br><br>__ Chooses words to create a mood or build a picture for the reader |
| __ Randomly places letters on paper<br><br>__ Introduced to the vocabulary of 6-Trait Writing Model voice, word choice, organization, ideas, convention | __ Begins pre-phonetic spelling mainly with consonants<br><br>__ Often recognizes vocabulary of 6-Trait Writing Model | __ Writes recognizable phonetically spelled words<br><br>__ Regularily uses 6-Trait Writing Model vocabulary | __ Spells most common sight words<br><br>__ Comfortable talking about writing in terms of vocabulary on 6-Trait Writing Model |

Comments:

Material reprinted with permission of Mount Vernon School District.

## Applying the Skills

### Resource 8: Rubric for Grading

**What this resource is:** This resource is a rubric that adds detail to the guidelines for grading presented earlier. The rubric represents our best thinking at the current time on what constitutes sound grading practice—i.e., grading practices that best support assessment *for* learning. It includes several dimensions that cover sound grading processes and defines levels of quality for each.

**Ideas for making it useful:** To understand this rubric fully and use it well, both leaders and teachers need to engage in comprehensive study of sound classroom assessment practices. The rubric is included here to help leaders understand the complete "grading target" at which they are aiming.

Please use the rubric as a discussion starter for policy and practice rather than as a mechanism to rate teacher performance formally.

# Draft Rubric for the Grading Process*

| Criterion | Beginning | Developing | Fluent |
|---|---|---|---|
| **Organization of gradebook** | The evidence of learning (e.g., a gradebook) is entirely organized by assessment sources (tests, quizzes, homework, …). | The evidence of learning (e.g., a gradebook) is organized by assessment sources mixed with standards. | The evidence of learning (e.g., a gradebook) is completely organized by standards or benchmarks. |
| **Ingredients included in the grade** | Overall summary grades are based on a mix of achievement and non-achievement factors (e.g., timeliness of work, attitude, effort, cheating). Non-achievement factors have a major impact on grades.<br><br>Extra credit points are given for extra work completed; without connection to extra learning.<br><br>Cheating, late work, and missing work result in a zero (or a radically lower score) in the gradebook. There is no opportunity to make up such work, except in a few cases.<br><br>Borderline-grade cases are handled by considering non-achievement factors. | Overall summary grades are based on a mix of achievement and non-achievement factors, but achievement counts a lot more.<br><br>Some extra credit points are given for extra work completed; some extra credit work is used to provide extra evidence of student learning.<br><br>Cheating, late work, and missing work result in a zero (or lower score) in the gradebook. But, there is an opportunity to make up work and replace the zero or raise the lower score.<br><br>Borderline cases are handled by considering a combination of non-achievement factors and collecting additional evidence of student learning. | Overall summary grades are based on achievement only.<br><br>Extra-credit work is evaluated for quality and is only used to provide extra evidence of learning. Credit is not awarded merely for completion of work.<br><br>Cheating, late work, and missing work is recorded as 'incomplete' or 'not enough information.' There is an opportunity to make up work and replace an 'incomplete' with a score without penalty.<br><br>Borderline grade cases are handled by collecting additional evidence of student achievement, not by counting non-achievement factors. |
| **Consideration of assessment purpose** | Everything each student does is given a score and every score goes into the final grade. There is no distinction between "scores" on practice work (formative assessment) and scores on work to demonstrate level of achievement (summative assessment). | Some distinctions are made between formative (practice) and summative assessment, but practice work still constitutes a significant part of the grade, with little rationale for so doing. | Grades are based on summative assessments; when formative assessments are used summatively, students are aware of this and there is a compelling rationale for such use. |
| **Consideration of most recent evidence** | All assessment data is cumulative and used in calculating a final summative grade. No consideration is given to identifying or using the most current information. | More current evidence is given consideration at times but does not entirely replace out-of-date evidence. | Most recent evidence completely replaces out-of-date evidence when it is reasonable to do so. For example, how well students write at the end of the grading period is more important than how well they write at the beginning, and later evidence of improved content understanding is more important than early evidence. |

* Based on suggestions from Ken O'Connor, personal communication, 2003. Copyright 2004, ATI and Ken O'Connor.

| Criterion | Beginning | Developing | Fluent |
|---|---|---|---|
| **Summarizing information and determination of final grade** | The gradebook has a mixture of ABC, percentages, +/-, and/or rubric scores, etc. with no explanation of how they are to be combined into a final summary grade.<br><br>Final summary grades are based on a curve, or a student's place in the rank order of student achievement.<br><br>Final summary grades are based on calculation of mean (average) only. | The gradebook may or may not have a mixture of symbols, but there is some attempt, even if incomplete, to explain how to combine them.<br><br>Final summary grades are based on preset standards such as A=90–100% and B = 80–89%. But, there is no indication of the necessity to ensure shared meaning of symbols—i.e., there is no definition of each standard.<br><br>The teacher understands various measures of central tendency, but may not always choose the best one to accurately describe student achievement. | The gradebook may or may not have a mix of symbol types, but there is a sound explanation of how to combine them.<br><br>Final summary grades are based on preset standards with clear descriptions of what each symbol means. These descriptions go beyond A = 90–100% and B = 80–89%; they describe what A, B, etc. performance looks like.<br><br>The teacher understands various measures of central tendency (average, median, mode) and understands when each is the most appropriate one to use to accurately describe student achievement. |
| **Assessment Quality** | There is little evidence of consideration of the accuracy/quality of the individual assessments on which grades are based.<br><br>Quality standards for classroom assessment are not considered—or—the teacher has trouble articulating them. | The teacher tries to base grades on accurate assessment results only, but may not consciously understand all the features of a sound assessment.<br><br>Some standards of quality are adhered to in judging the accuracy of the assessment results on which grades are based. The teacher can articulate some of these standards—or—uses standards for quality assessment intuitively, but has trouble articulating why an assessment is sound. | Grades are based only on accurate assessment results. Questionable results are not included.<br><br>The teacher can articulate standards of quality, and can show evidence of consideration of these standards in his/her classroom assessments (clear and appropriate learning targets, clear and appropriate users and uses, choosing the best assessment method, good sampling, and avoiding potential sources of bias and mismeasurement). |
| **Student Involvement** | Grades are a surprise to students because (1) students don't understand the bases on which grades are determined; (2) students have not been involved in their own assessment (learning targets are not clear to them, and/or they do not self-assess and track progress toward the targets); or (3) teacher feedback is only evaluative (a judgment of level of quality) and includes no descriptive component. | Grades are somewhat of a surprise to students because student-involvement practices are too limited to give them insights into their own performance. | Grades are not a surprise to students because (1) students understand the bases for the grades received; (2) students have been involved in their own assessment throughout the process (they understand the learning targets they are to hit, self-assess in relation to the targets, track their own progress toward the targets, and/or talk about their progress); and/or (3) teacher communication to students is frequent, descriptive, and focuses on what they have learned as well as the next steps in learning. Descriptive feedback is related directly to specific and clear learning targets. |

281

## Applying the Skills

### Resource 9: A Standard Cover Letter to Parents

**What this
resource is:**
Parents report they appreciate proactive efforts on the part of the school to communicate with them about important matters, including school testing. Whenever possible, communicating with parents preceding test administration helps put the test in context and build support for the school assessment program. When not possible or practical, a letter home from the school after the test has been taken is essential.

The sample letter that follows is for a norm-referenced test and provides information from the following list. The letter can be adapted for a standards-based assessment or a diagnostic assessment, and can also be adapted to include other information specific to that assessment or based on the local interests of parents:

- A brief explanation of the test, including the purpose of the assessment, the grade levels to be taking the test, the amount of time the test will take, etc.
- What learning targets are assessed, and how those targets relate to the total district curriculum
- How the test items are scored
- What assessment methods are used
- How the results will be reported and used
- What strategies parents can use to help students improve
- And for more information, contact...

**Ideas for
making
it useful:**
Refer back to the assessment audit conducted in Resource 7 in Competency 6. The grids created in that activity could act as the information foundation for any communication that goes home to parents about tests being given at school.

Date

Dear Parent,

Last May your tenth-grade student took the _____ Test of High School Skills along with all other tenth graders at other high schools in ABC School District. This combination of tests is designed to measure your student's general progress in fundamental high school skills as compared to that of a national comparison group called the "norm" group. It is administered by the district for the purpose of identifying students who are low in skill levels and therefore perhaps not on track to pass the state test administered in the senior year. As you may know, a passing score on that test is required for graduation, and our intent is to identify those students who need additional help in preparing for that test.

The test taken in May had three sections: reading, language use, and mathematics. The items are drawn from a general national curriculum, and are not specifically designed to match the curriculum in either ABC School District or the state of _____. They are traditional multiple-choice tests, and students mark their response to each question on a separate answer document. The answer sheets are then machine scored by _____, the leading test publisher in the country. The results arrived in the summer and we are providing them to you now.

Tests of this kind come with many different score reports. But the score to examine most closely is the NPR. It stands for National Percentile Rank and tells you the percent of students in the norm group who scored below that score. So, if your student is at the 50th NPR, it means that 50 percent of the students in the norm group had fewer items correct than your child. The 50th percentile is the score that would be earned by a *typical tenth grader*. Because test scores of this type are not always exact indicators of a student's skill level, the district will consider other information, including other test scores, student GPAs, and individual teacher comments and observations before determining which students will be offered additional assistance.

Additionally, these test results will be used to examine strengths and weaknesses in our district curriculum and instructional practices. If you have any questions, please contact the _____ at _____.

Sincerely,

Principal
or
Assistant Superintendent
for Curriculum

# Competency 9

# The leader understands the attributes of a sound and balanced assessment system.

Assessment-literate school leaders know what needs to be balanced in a local assessment system. First, they attend to the balance of assessments *of* learning that check achievement status at a given point in time, including both classroom status checks and those conducted using standardized tests, with classroom assessments *for* learning, specifically designed to involve students and to inform them about their own progress. Each serves a different purpose. Each offers unique contributions to instructional decision making. And each requires its own support resources, professional development, and integration into school improvement. Second, they look for a balance of achievement targets. If the grade level or course curriculum derived from state standards predominantly reflects *knowledge* targets at the expense of *reasoning, skill, and product* targets, an imbalance in what students learn results (Stiggins, 2001). Third, they monitor balance of assessment methods (selected response, essay, performance assessment, and personal communication), which is in part achieved through a proper balance of learning targets in the written curriculum. And fourth, they ensure a balance of communication methods, which allows students, parents, and other stakeholders to gain access to timely and understandable information about student achievement.

School leaders also need to examine the balance between what is assessed at the state level and what is assessed at the local level. The state testing program may seem so comprehensive that the need for a local assessment system may not be apparent. However, just as classroom assessment is not likely to meet all information needs regarding attainment of state and district standards, by the same token, the state's assessment system may not provide all the information district decision makers need about student achievement. Especially in a time of heavy focus on accountability testing, we need to ensure our state and local systems are working in concert to afford useful information about state and local achievement priorities.

## Thinking About Assessment

**Activity 26:** Who Uses Assessment Information, and How?

**Purpose:** To get participants thinking about balancing assessments *of* and *for* learning in the classroom, the variety of decisions made on the basis of classroom assessment information, and the importance of the student as decision maker.

**Time:** 30 minutes

**Directions:** Have participants work in groups. Hand out the worksheet on the next page, and review the instructions. Make sure they understand that they are to be thinking about *classroom* assessment data—the information generated by assessments coming from the classroom, not from large-scale assessments.

Give them about 3 minutes of quiet time to write their responses individually to question 1 and then about 10 minutes to share their responses in groups. Then give them 5 minutes to discuss at their tables their thoughts about question 2.

**Closure:** Conduct a large-group debrief by asking the following questions:

- What are some of the decisions that students make?
- What are some of the decisions that (any other roles you choose) make?
- What conclusions can you draw about classroom assessment based on this activity?

Points to elicit or raise:

- Classroom assessment data must be of high quality because important decisions that affect students' well-being are made on its basis.
- Anyone conducting an assessment must know at the outset who will use the information and how it will be used.
- Students are the most important of the decision makers (an interesting opinion to discuss).

# Who Uses Classroom Assessment Information, and How?

A key to quality assessment is to know the purposes for which the assessment data is to be used. Who will use the data? What decisions will they make on the basis of the data? Anyone planning or administering an assessment must first answer these questions.

**Instructions:**

In this activity, you will choose the role of an important decision maker who uses *classroom* assessment data, and then list the decisions your "role" might make on the basis of the data.

Beginning with the person whose birthday is closest to today and moving clockwise, assign the following roles: student, parent, teacher, principal, coach, grandparent, guidance counselor, college admissions officer.

Spend 3 to 5 minutes on question 1, then share your list with others at your table. When all roles have shared, discuss conclusions you may have drawn about classroom assessment data (question 2).

1.  **My role is a** _____. The decisions I might make on the basis of classroom assessment data include the following:

2.  While discussing the decisions listed by all members of your group, please pay attention to thoughts you have about the decision makers and about the quality of classroom assessment. **What conclusions can you draw from this activity?**

## Thinking About Assessment

### Activity 27: Merging Local and State Assessment Systems

**Purpose:** We've advocated that a local assessment program function as a system, with each component sharing a common purpose, working toward the same goal of improved student learning. Assessments that do not contribute to that end or act in harmony with the system as a whole should be eliminated. This activity extends the systems-thinking approach to assessment by asking team members to consider what is necessary to achieve a level of balance and synergy between state and local assessment systems.

**Time:** 1 hour

**Directions:** First, gather the grids your team used to conduct an assessment audit in Resource 7. That activity helped map the "big picture" of assessment in your school or district. In addition, gather information about the state assessment system, including test and item specifications if available, examples of the various assessments and methods used, and sample reports from state assessments to the various levels: district, school, teacher, and student. Then consider the following:

Remember that it is difficult for any single test to deliver accurate, reliable, and meaningful information if the test is spread too thinly among multiple purposes. With that in mind, answer the following questions:

■ What is the purpose(s) of the state test?

Is it to satisfy accountability legislation?

To serve as indicators of system quality?

To ascertain attainment of state standards by large groups of students?

To improve curriculum and instruction?

To certify individual student mastery?

To function as a gatekeeper for student placement or promotion/graduation decisions?

Other?

■ Given the purpose(s), what information is provided by the state system?

■ What (and whose) information needs are being met by that information?

■ What information does it not provide? Whose needs are going unmet in the state system?

■ Is the information provided deemed adequate for the purpose(s)?

Now go back to the "big picture" of assessment in your school/district and compare it to the answer to the last question. If information needs are unmet by the state tests, are they being met currently by a district or school assessment? Are there subjects that seem over-tested while others are not tested at all? Is there redundancy between the information yielded by state tests and information from district assessments?

What information should your local assessment system provide? To whom? For what purposes? Answers to these questions can guide your choices of what to test locally and how to test it.

**Ideas for making it useful:**

No doubt there are many other questions your study team could pose in thinking about how to get the most from a system that integrates state and local assessment. Our purpose in this activity is to illustrate the opportunity local leaders have to improve balance and quality, even when the state system drives the majority of public focus and attention.

## Competency 10

## The leader understands the issues related to ethical and inappropriate use of student assessment and protects students and staff from such misuse.

School leaders are responsible for protecting the well-being of students whose achievement is assessed either by means of standardized tests or through classroom assessment. This standard of ethical practice underpins all of the previous nine competencies, and is accomplished when leaders promote interpretation, use, and communication of results that leads to appropriate inferences about student learning and proper action on behalf of student success. Leaders are obliged in all contexts to help avoid and discourage misinterpretation, misuse, and miscommunication of assessment results.

School leaders also have a responsibility to protect the confidentiality of individual student assessment results, obtain parental consent for certain assessments prior to the assessment being given, and follow procedures that protect test security. They also need to ensure that students with special needs be provided with assessment accommodations appropriate for their circumstance and consistent with their own IEP (OSPI, 1996; Stiggins, 2001). Allowing the widest range of students possible to participate in school testing programs provides the most accurate picture of system performance, and gives as many students as possible the opportunity to show what they know.

Monitoring test preparation practices is another important part of the leader's ethical responsibilities. Although we know that the best test preparation comes from a high-quality curriculum and good teaching, there is a great deal of pressure today to raise test scores, and so it becomes paramount that our staffs understand the differences between ethical and unethical practices. Ethical practices are aimed at raising student achievement; some unethical practices bypass increasing achievement and go directly to raising test scores.

Some state tests measure a narrow slice of their state content standards; by assessing only that which is easily measured, the tests do not address many important content standards (CISA, 2001). In such cases, school leaders need to guard against the practice of narrowing the curriculum to teach only to those standards

289

easily tested at the state level. This can skew the curriculum balance in favor of learning at the knowledge level, at the expense of how to reason, perform skillfully with that knowledge, and create quality products (Chappuis and Chappuis, 2002).

Listed here are standards of responsible practice* that should guide professional actions. Effective school leaders follow these guidelines and provide assistance to teachers to ensure that they do the same:

1.  Interpret, use, and communicate results in a fair manner that is consistent with the assessment's limitations and with full awareness of the implications of the decisions to be made for students and their academic success.

2.  Inform all assessment users of the reasons for the assessment (including all decisions to be made), as well as its limitations and dangers of potential misinterpretation.

3.  Provide understandable score reports that include guidelines for proper interpretation and caution against potential misinterpretations.

4.  Communicate all information needed to ensure proper interpretation and use of results. If a norm-referenced test is used, the norms used to compare student results must be clearly and completely described. If a standards-referenced test is used, standards must be clearly and completely described as well. In all high-stakes assessment contexts, standard error of measurement should be reported and explained along with scores.

5.  Use assessment results in ways that maintain student confidence in themselves as learners and that motivate them to keep striving to succeed academically; that is, use assessments in ways that prevent students from giving up in hopelessness.

6.  Accommodate the special needs of students with academic gifts and challenges in test administration, interpretation, and use.

7.  Encourage decision makers to tap multiple sources of information about student achievement to inform instructional decisions; as the potential impact of the decision increases in importance, so does the need to tap multiple sources.

8.  Avoid making, and actively discourage others from making, inaccurate reports, unsubstantiated claims, inappropriate interpretations, or other false or misleading statements about assessment results.

9.  Inform users of procedures for appealing results, requesting review of scores or rescoring, and rights of access to assessment results.

*Adapted from the "Code of Professional Responsibilities in Educational Measurement" of the National Council on Measurement in Education (Washington, DC: NCME, 1995).

10. Address improprieties in assessment development, administration, scoring, reporting, or use in a forthright manner, to prevent misinterpretations or misuse.

11. Protect the privacy rights of individuals and institutions involved in assessment.

12. Discourage unethical, dishonest, or inappropriate preparation of students for tests, such as reliance on practices that inflate test scores without promoting greater learning. (Guidelines for principals and teachers for proper test preparation are included with the Activities for this competence.)

13. Promote public understanding of standards of sound assessment practice to develop community support for proper assessment and communication of results.

## Thinking About Assessment

### Activity 28: "Is This Responsible?"

**Purpose:** This activity is for use with a building staff to stimulate thinking and discussion about responsible practices before, during, and after standardized testing. We recommend that you use this list as a springboard for your own needs; consider modifying it so that it reflects the kinds of tests your teachers administer and includes those practices you want to discuss with them.

**Time:** 30–60 minutes

**Directions:** Have participants read each practice on the chart, "Is This Responsible?" pages 293–295, and then mark each as "Responsible," "Irresponsible," or "It Depends." Let participants discuss the reasons for their answers with partners or in small groups. Then conduct a large-group discussion. Identify practices on which the whole group has consensus, and then discuss those practices on which there is more than one opinion. Or, you could hand out your answers and have discussion center on clarifying why each practice is either responsible or irresponsible, or conditions that are required to be in place for the practice to be one or the other.

**Closure:** Hand out a list of appropriate practices developed for your building or district testing situations.

**Directions:** Mark each practice as "Responsible," Irresponsible," or "It Depends." If you choose "It Depends," be prepared to describe the context(s) in which the practice is responsible and the context(s) in which it is irresponsible.

## Is This Responsible?

| PRACTICE | RESPONSIBLE | IRRESPONSIBLE | IT DEPENDS |
|---|---|---|---|
| Tell students what the test results will be used for. | | | |
| Use locally developed tests that parallel the content of an upcoming standardized test to help students get ready. | | | |
| Define on the test form words students don't understand. | | | |
| Discuss with students how the test will be administered, in advance of the test. | | | |
| Incorporate into the curriculum all subject-area objectives measured by an upcoming test. | | | |
| Teach test-taking skills. | | | |
| Use published test preparation material that promises to raise scores on a specific standardized test. | | | |

| PRACTICE | RESPONSIBLE | IRRESPONSIBLE | IT DEPENDS |
|---|---|---|---|
| During the test, pronounce words used in the test. | | | |
| Review skills, strategies, and concepts previously taught just before administering a standardized test. | | | |
| Limit curriculum and instruction to the skills, strategies, and concepts included on a standardized test. | | | |
| Review standardized test question answers after the test. | | | |
| Give help to those students who are confused during the standardized test. | | | |
| Exclude eligible students from taking the standardized test. | | | |
| Reproduce part of the test to help students understand it after they've taken the test. | | | |
| Comment on the quality of student work during the test. | | | |
| Hint that a student should change an answer. | | | |

| PRACTICE | RESPONSIBLE | IRRESPONSIBLE | IT DEPENDS |
|---|---|---|---|
| Read a part of the standardized test to a student to help him or her understand it better. | | | |
| Keep students focused and on task during the test. | | | |
| Teach directly to the state standards that are represented on a standardized test. | | | |
| Teach students to apply a performance assessment scoring rubric before a high-stakes assessment. | | | |
| Change a student's grade based on recent test evidence revealing a higher level of achievement. | | | |
| Report invasions of student test score privacy issues. | | | |
| Hand score a sample of student standardized test papers to evaluate the accuracy of electronic scoring services. | | | |

## Applying the Skills

**Resource 10:** Guidelines for Test Preparation and Administration

**What this resource is:** Two lists of actions principals and teachers can take to enhance the testing atmosphere in the school. The lists are taken by permission from "Ethical Standards on Testing: Test Preparation and Administration," developed by members of the Washington Educational Research Association (WERA) in 1999 and revised in 2001.

**Ideas for making it useful:** Read through each list and determine which practices are already in place in your building or district. Decide which to implement. Additionally, you may want to find similar documents produced by national organizations and by organizations within your state:

American Educational Research Association, American Psychological Association, National Council of Measurement in Education. (1985). *Standards for educational and psychological testing*. Washington, DC: APA.

American Educational Research Association. (1992). *Ethical standards of the American Educational Research Association*. Washington, DC: Author.

American Federation of Teachers, National Council on Measurement in Education, National Education Association. (1990). *Standards for teacher competence in educational assessment of students*. Washington, DC: Author.

National Council of Measurement in Education, Ad hoc Committee on the Development of a Code of Ethics. (1995). *Code of professional responsibilities in educational measurement*. Washington, DC: Author.

# Guidelines for Test Preparation and Administration

### The Principal's Role

There are a number of things the principal can do to enhance the testing atmosphere in the school:

1. Inform both students and parents about what each test does and does not do, when and how it will be administered, and how the results will be used. Indicate the importance of tests for students, staff, and the school. Stress the importance of school attendance on the scheduled testing dates.

2. Encourage the implementation of appropriate test-wiseness teaching and review. Teaching test-wiseness skills should be independent of subject matter being tested and should include an understanding of test books, use of answer sheets, item response strategies, time management, listening, and following directions.

3. Let parents know about upcoming tests and what they can do to encourage their children's performance.

4. Work with teachers to develop a building testing schedule. Attempt to maximize the efficiency of the building's physical layout and staff resources.

5. Pay careful attention to building schedules during the testing period. Avoid planning assemblies, fire drills, maintenance, etc., during the testing period.

6. Develop a plan to keep tests and answer sheets secure before and after administration, and ensure that all are returned properly.

7. Arrange, where possible, for teachers to have proctoring help in administering tests. Ensure that tests are carried out according to ethical and legal practice.

8. Provide a policy statement or handbook to all involved with test administration spelling out proper and improper testing procedures.

9. Create a process to check out any suspicions or allegations of cheating.

10. Require a detailed written explanation about why a student was not tested or the reason a score was not figured into a school's average.

11. Encourage teachers' participation in district inservice sessions on assessment.

12. Ensure that all students are tested. Review all test accommodations, including exclusion as a last resort, made for students with special needs. Ensure that accommodations and exclusions are consistent with specific testing program guidelines.

13. Ensure that there are no interruptions in classrooms during the testing period, including custodial tasks, intercom calls, delivery of messages, etc.

14. Work with the test coordinator and classroom teachers to schedule and staff makeup days for students who miss parts of the test. This might include bringing in a substitute or finding other ways to use building staff creatively to administer makeup test in an appropriate setting.

15. Share test results with staff. Neither the testing program nor the results are "owned" by any particular grade. The results are an indication of how well things are going in the school generally. Staff members need to work together to ensure that the testing process is a smooth one. School improvement is a team effort.

# Guidelines for Test Preparation and Administration

## The Teacher's Role

Students will do their best on tests if they find an encouraging and supportive atmosphere, if they know that they are well prepared, and if they know that they will do well with hard work. To create a situation that will encourage students to do their best, teachers should:

1. Attend inservice workshops on test administration.

2. Develop an assessment calendar and schedule.

3. Prepare students well in advance for assessment by teaching test-wiseness skills. Independent of subject matter being tested, teach and review test-taking skills that include an understanding of test books and use of answer sheets, item response strategies, time management, listening, and following directions.

4. Develop a list of which and how many students will be tested, and when they will be tested. Determine students for whom special-needs accommodations may be necessary.

5. Develop a list of students who will be exempted from testing and the reason for the exemption. The list must be reviewed and approved by the principal or test administration committee. Parents must be notified and alternative assessments identified.

6. Develop plans for the administration of makeup tests for students absent from the scheduled testing period.

7. Prepare and motivate students just before the test.

8. Prepare to administer the test, with sufficient materials available for all students to be tested.

9. Prepare classrooms for the test. Arrange for comfortable seating where students will not be able to see each others' test materials, but will be able to hear test directions. Eliminate posters or other materials that may be distracting or contain information that could be used with the test.

10. Alert neighboring teachers to the testing schedule and ask their help in keeping noise levels to a minimum.

11. Arrange a separate, supervised area for those students who finish early and may cause a distraction for other students.

12. Read the test administration manual carefully, in advance. Administer the test according to the directions.

13. Meet with proctors to discuss their duties and responsibilities. Carefully and actively proctor the test.

14. Arrange for appropriate breaks and student stress-relievers.

15. Follow the rules for test security and return all test material to the test administrator.

## Thinking About Assessment

### Activity 29: A Self-Analysis for School Leaders

**Purpose:**    Up to this point you have largely worked with your leadership study team members. This activity asks you to reflect individually on the 10 competencies using the following three questions:

1. Each of the 10 competencies for educational leaders offers many ways for principals to demonstrate proficiency. With the list of the 10 competencies in front of you, examine each one in relation to your knowledge and actions as a school leader. Try to attach specific examples to each competency that you carry out as the assessment leader in the school.

2. Using the worksheet, "Assessment Competencies for Educational Leadership," page 302, rate yourself on the 10 competencies. What areas stand out as your strengths? Which one(s) could you target for improvement?

3. Look at your areas of strength and areas in which you'd like to improve, and compare those rankings with the school/district profile created at the end of Part 3 of this guide. You can use the chart on pages 303–305 that cross-references the doors with the 10 competencies. What similarities do you see between the systems analysis and your own individual analysis? What major differences are there? How could these two ratings be combined to further clarify the assessment priorities of your school/district?

# Assessment Competencies for Educational Leaders

1. The leader understands the standards of quality for student assessments and how to ensure that these standards are met in all assessments.
   Low 1_____ 2_____ 3_____ 4_____ 5_____ High

2. The leader understands the principles of assessment *for* learning and works with staff to integrate them into classroom instruction.
   Low 1_____ 2_____ 3_____ 4_____ 5_____ High

3. The leader understands the necessity of clear academic achievement targets, aligned classroom-level achievement targets, and their relationship to the development of accurate assessments.
   Low 1_____ 2_____ 3_____ 4_____ 5_____ High

4. The leader knows and can evaluate teachers' classroom assessment competencies and helps teachers learn to assess accurately and use the results productively.
   Low 1_____ 2_____ 3_____ 4_____ 5_____ High

5. The leader can plan, present, or secure professional development activities that contribute to the use of sound practices.
   Low 1_____ 2_____ 3_____ 4_____ 5_____ High

6. The leader accurately analyzes assessment information, uses the information to improve curriculum and instruction, and assists teachers in doing the same.
   Low 1_____ 2_____ 3_____ 4_____ 5_____ High

7. The leader can develop and implement sound assessment and assessment-related policies.
   Low 1_____ 2_____ 3_____ 4_____ 5_____ High

8. The leader creates the conditions necessary for the appropriate use and reporting of student achievement information, and can communicate effectively with all members of the school community about student assessment results and their relationship to improving curriculum and instruction.
   Low 1_____ 2_____ 3_____ 4_____ 5_____ High

9. The leader understands the attributes of a sound and balanced student assessment system.
   Low 1_____ 2_____ 3_____ 4_____ 5_____ High

10. The leader understands the issues related to the unethical and inappropriate use of student assessment and protects students and staff from such misuse.
    Low 1_____ 2_____ 3_____ 4_____ 5_____ High

| Competency | Relates to Door | Activities | Resources |
|---|---|---|---|
| 1. The leader understands the standards of quality for student assessments and how to ensure that these standards are met in all assessments. | 3. Assessment Literacy | 5. Understanding Standards of Classroom Assessment Quality, pg. 130<br>6. ATI Interactive Video *Creating Sound Assessments*, pg. 131<br>7. Auditing Classroom Assessments for Quality, pg. 132<br>8. Developmental Continua for Teachers, pg. 153 | 1. Confidence Questionnaire, pg. 163 |
| 2. The leader understands the principles of assessment *for* learning and works with staff to integrate them into classroom instruction. | 1. Clear targets<br>2. Users/Uses<br>3. Assessment Literacy<br>4. Communication | 1. Building the Foundation, pg. 8<br>3. "Emily's Story," pg. 60<br>9. Classroom Assessment for Learning, pg. 170<br>10. Principles of Assessment *for* Learning, pg. 176<br>11. Converting Learning Targets, pg. 179<br>12. Ways That Teachers and Students Use Formative Assessment, pg. 183<br>13. Using Feedback to Set Goals, pg. 191 | 2. Student Survey, pg. 188<br>3. Using Test Results, pg. 196<br>4. Student Self-Assessment and Goal-Setting, pg. 200 |
| 3. The leader understands the necessity of clear academic achievement targets, aligned classroom-level achievement targets, and their relationship to the development of accurate assessments. | 1. Clear targets<br>3. Assessment Literacy | 14. Deconstructing Standards, pg. 209<br>15. Using Interviews to Hire, pg. 217<br>16. Auditing Your Classroom Curriculum, pg. 219 | 5. Implementing the Written Curriculum, pg. 205 |

| Competency | Relates to Door | Activities | Resources |
|---|---|---|---|
| 4. The leader knows and can evaluate teachers' classroom assessment competencies and helps teachers learn to assess accurately and use the results productively. | 3. Assessment Literacy | 17. Should Teachers Be Held Accountable for Assessment Competence, pg. 223 | |
| 5. The leader can plan, present, or secure professional development activities that contribute to the use of sound assessment practices. | 3. Assessment Literacy | 18. Analyzing Your Professional Development Program, pg. 227<br>19. Learning Teams for Assessment Literacy, pg. 231 | 6. How Principals Can Support Learning Teams, pg. 238 |
| 6. The leader accurately analyzes student assessment information, uses the information to improve curriculum and instruction, and assists teachers in doing the same. | 2. Users/Uses<br>3. Assessment Literacy<br>4. Communication | | 7. Preparing an Assessment Inventory, pg. 248 |
| 7. The leader can develop and implement sound assessment and assessment-related policies. | 5. Policies | 20. Using School/District Policies to Support Quality Assessment, pg. 254 | |
| 8. The leader creates the conditions necessary for the appropriate use and reporting of student achievement information, and can communicate effectively with all members of the school community about student assessment results and their relationship to improving curriculum and instruction. | 2. Users/Uses<br>3. Assessment<br>4. Communication | 21. Grading Scenarios, pg. 264<br>22. ATI Interactive Video *Report Card Grading*, pg. 269<br>23. Panel Hears Exam Horrors, pg. 270<br>24. When Grades Don't Match the State Assessment Results, pg. 273<br>25. Connecting Assessment with Reporting, pg. 274 | 9. A Standard Cover Letter to Parents, pg. 282 |

| Competency | Relates to Door | Activities | Resources |
|---|---|---|---|
| 9. The leader understands the attributes of a sound and balanced student assessment system. | All 5 Doors | 2. Examining Your Assessment Beliefs, pg. 57<br>4. Creating An Assessment Profile, pg. 112<br>26. Who Uses Assessment Information, pg. 285<br>27. Merging Local and State Assessment Systems, pg. 287 | |
| 10. The leader understands the issues related to the unethical and inappropriate use of student assessment and protects students and staff from such misuse. | 2. Users/Uses<br>3. Assessment Literacy | 28. Is This Responsible?, pg. 292 | 10. Guidelines for Test Preparation and Administration, pg. 296 |
| Competencies 1–10 | | 29. A Self-Analysis for School Leaders, pg. 301<br>30. Connecting Classroom Assessment Balance, pg. 310 | |

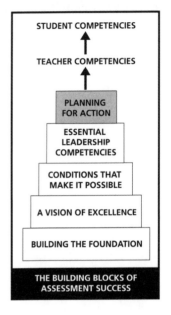

## 5

*A system that is in balance will ensure that the right kind of assessment is used for the right purpose, and that assessment will be used to continually improve student learning. Through the use of high-quality assessments **of** and **for** learning, linked to the targets of instruction, all students will be able to show what they know and can do.*

## *Part Five*

# PLANNING
# FOR
# ACTION

The final part of this guide focuses on helping you synthesize the thinking and work of your leadership study team from Parts 1 through 4. That synthesis will lead to a plan of action that takes your vision of quality assessment and moves it toward reality. At this point, you have developed some ideas about the current status of your assessment system. You may also have formed opinions about the level of your own assessment knowledge and skills, and about the professional development needs of your leadership team and teaching staff. Before acting on those conclusions, there is one final Activity to complete.

Throughout this guide we've encouraged you to think systemically, to see the whole picture when planning for improvement in your assessment system. This is especially helpful when looking at the many school/district policies related to assessment, when thinking about the teacher hiring, evaluation, and staff development functions in your district and their relationship to sound assessment, and in looking at the total assessment program. The mission and purpose of assessment, what you believe assessment should accomplish, the grading and reporting systems, and the information needs of all stakeholders are just some of the system components. The final Activity, pages 310–314, asks that you consider the current goals of your school/district from a systems perspective by examining the connections between those goals and activities and an initiative that promotes assessment balance and quality through planning and professional development. How does creating a balanced assessment system and developing assessment-literate staff fit into the current scope of work and priorities of your school and/or district? How will one affect the other? How can we best communicate with staff about the relationship between existing and new priorities?

## Thinking About Assessment

**Activity 30:** Connecting Assessment Literacy to Other School Improvement Initiatives

**Purpose:** Planning for assessment balance and quality, including professional development in assessment literacy, can be seen as "just one more thing we should do, in addition to differentiated instruction, curriculum mapping, improving teaching in the content areas, aligning to standards...," or whatever the current school improvement goal happens to be. We need to be able to connect assessment literacy and assessment *for* learning to these other initiatives in ways that help others understand the relationships among them.

This activity helps your leadership study team identify the logic that links assessment literacy with common initiatives:

- Developing local standards-based assessment systems, aligned with state standards
- Aligning instruction with standards
- Differentiating instruction
- Curriculum mapping
- Closing the achievement gap
- Improving instruction in the content areas
- Improving teacher quality
- Developing standards-based report cards

We've taken two of these initiatives—"Aligning Instruction with Standards" and "Closing the Achievement Gap"—and have provided examples of the possible connections between these initiatives and developing assessment literacy.

**Time:** 30–60 minutes, depending on the number of initiatives to be analyzed.

**Directions:** **Step 1.** Working individually and then as a team, make a list of the school improvement initiatives that are priorities in your school or district. Set this list aside for later use.

**Step 2.** Choose either "Aligning Instruction with Standards," or "Closing the Achievement Gap." Working alone or as a team, brainstorm your answers to the following question: *What role would/could a foundation of assessment literacy and the effective use of quality classroom assessment play in the success of this initiative?* If you needed to explain how assessment underpins the effectiveness of the initiative, what major point(s) would you make?

**Step 3.** Compare the logic flow between your points and the points we make in our examples. It doesn't matter if they match; it only matters that you've thought it through and begin to see concrete connections. Reflect on and discuss the similarities and differences between the two lists.

**Step 4.** Work with the other school improvement initiative from Step 2 and repeat Steps 2 and 3.

**Step 5.** Compare the lists of talking points that you generated for both school improvement initiatives. What similarities do you see? Aside from a few initial entries unique to each initiative, do you see commonalties across them? If you study the connections among all of those listed and a foundation of assessment literacy, you will find that strong connections can be made for each one. This activity helps make it clear that many school improvement initiatives can reach their potential only when accompanied by sound classroom assessment.

**Step 6.** Select one of your own school improvement initiatives that you listed in Step 1. Brainstorm a list of reasons why sound classroom assessment is essential for that effort as well. The goal is to state the connection between your local initiative and assessment literacy in such a clear manner that others can also see and understand how assessment literacy can help form a foundation of success.

## *Aligning Instruction with Standards*

**For use in Step 3**

Make the following points to connect a foundation of assessment literacy to this school improvement priority:

- Clearly articulated statements of student learning (content standards and benchmarks) provide a clear focus on what is most important for students to know and be able to do. A grade-by-grade curriculum aligned to state standards focuses the instruction.

- In the standards-aligned classroom, teachers do not teach by proceeding page by page though the textbook, but rather select what to teach based on the curriculum. As students progress, teachers need to select, modify, or develop classroom assessments based on the curriculum. They must know which specific learning target each item on every test they give is intended to measure. If they don't, their standards-aligned teaching will not be accompanied by standards-aligned assessment. They will not be working with accurate information about student learning for summative or formative purposes—assessments *of* learning and assessments *for* learning will lead to inaccurate decisions on the part of teachers, students, and parents.

- Therefore, each teacher needs to understand the following:
  a. How to build accurate assessments (the five standards of quality): translating content standards and benchmarks into instructionally useful statements; having a clear idea of the purposes for every classroom assessment; building sound classroom assessments that match targets and purposes (target–method match); sampling; and avoiding potential sources of bias and distortion.
  b. How to involve students in their own assessment to maximize student achievement and motivation.
  c. How to communicate about student achievement to others in an effective and timely manner. This includes, at the classroom level, how to provide descriptive feedback to students.

- The most effective and efficient way to deliver professional development in classroom assessment is through establishing learning communities in which adults can learn new strategies and apply them in the classroom.

## *Closing the Achievement Gap*

**For use in Step 3**

To help others understand how a foundation of assessment literacy underpins attempts to close achievement gaps, the following points apply:

- Black and Wiliam's (1998) research shows that one of the best ways to close the achievement gap is to improve classroom assessment. Their three recommendations are to improve the quality and accuracy of classroom assessment, increase descriptive feedback, and increase student involvement in assessment. They state that teachers and students must be able to answer three questions about student learning: "Where am I going? (standards-aligned instruction, with the standards clearly communicated to students); "Where am I now?" (descriptive feedback to students about the quality of their work and student self-assessment about the quality of their work); and "How can I get there?" (teaching strategies designed to act on information about where students are in their learning relative to the standards, and student mastery of strategies to improve their own learning). These are foundations of assessment literacy.

- For reform efforts in closing the achievement gap to succeed, professional development needs to be focused on topics required to implement standards-based classrooms—understanding standards, being skillful with instructional methodologies that best promote learning, and using both assessment *of* and *for* learning to accurately assess and effectively promote learning. Accurate classroom assessment is an essential part of the mix.

- There is evidence that every dollar invested in improving teacher competencies returns more in student achievement than from any other intervention.

- Educators need the following knowledge and skills:
  a. How to build accurate assessments (the five standards of quality): translating content standards and benchmarks into instructionally useful statements; having a clear idea of the purposes for every classroom assessment; building sound classroom assessments that match targets and purposes (target–method match); sampling; and avoiding potential sources of bias and distortion.
  b. How to involve students in their own assessment to maximize student achievement and motivation.

    c. How to communicate about student achievement to others in an effective and timely manner. This includes, at the classroom level, how to provide descriptive feedback to students.

- The most effective and efficient way to deliver professional development on assessment is through establishing learning communities in which adults can learn new strategies and apply them in the classroom.

# Action Planning for Assessment Balance and Quality

Now that your team has created a vision of quality assessment, considered the conditions that are necessary to make it possible, analyzed the leadership skills needed to implement and support the vision, and thought about the connections among assessment literacy and current school improvement priorities, it is time to plan the next steps.

Start by considering the next three questions you probably recognize from Part 4 of this guide:

- Where are you trying to go?
- Where are you now?
- What will you do to close the gap?

As we have seen, these three questions help students learn to self-assess and set goals for their own improvement. To answer the first question, the learning expectations have to be clearly defined and communicated so the student knows where he or she is trying to go. The second question is a summative question, seeking a point-in-time summary about where the student is right now relative to the intended learning. And the third question prompts action. It relies on a repertoire of strategies students can call on to close the gap between where they are and where they need to be. In short, the series of three questions relies on clear expectations, a vision of what quality and success look like, and a sense of control and responsibility by students for the personal actions they will take to help them hit the target.

The same three questions can serve as a planning framework for schools and districts as they strive to raise student achievement and build better assessment systems in service of that goal. Now you can use your leadership study team experiences to answer them.

Consider the first question, "Where are you trying to go?" The answer to this question is found in your thinking and discussions in Part 1 and Part 2 of this guide regarding your vision of a perfect assessment system, about the essential ingredients in such a system, and particularly about your beliefs regarding balanced and quality assessment. The answer to this question describes where you want your school/district to be in the future relative to student assessment.

315

The second question, concerning the current status of your system, or where you are now, was addressed in Part 3. When you analyzed your school/district using the profile at the end of Part 3 describing the Five Doors to Excellence, you drew a picture of the current status of your assessment system. You identified what work has already been done, in what areas, what work is underway, and what work remains. Other indicators of work yet to be done may also have emerged along the way through team discussions or from other sections of this guide. The analysis of your own professional knowledge and skills relative to the 10 competencies in Part 4 may also influence how you answer the second question regarding the current status of your local assessment system. By completing the analysis and creating the profile, you established where you are right now in relation to your final destination, the vision your team has created. Your team's profile may point to the need for professional development, or it may point to the need for a clearer, well-written curriculum, or to the need to communicate more accurately and efficiently about student achievement. Each leadership team will be in a different place, with perhaps multiple priorities. Now what you need are specific answers to the third and final question: "What will you do to close the gap?"

## Closing the Gap

Now you must transfer your team's analysis of the current system and priorities for a new system to a written plan of action. Throughout this guide we have presented ideas and strategies for helping you close the gap between the reality of your current assessment system and one that is grounded in balance, quality, and student involvement. The work you must do now will vary based on the profile you created. Some leadership teams will be able to take action on their own; others may want to bring into the process a larger group of district or school stakeholders. Still others may first need to educate their peers or the instructional staff about the need for and promise of assessment balance and quality.

But whatever the content, completed action plans have the potential to languish on a shelf, unimplemented. There could be a lack of shared ownership that causes the plan to be abandoned, a lack of funding or committed leadership, or simply too many plans for one organization to follow. Like the district curriculum guide that can collect dust on top of the file cabinet, there is no absolute guarantee that ensures action plans will fulfill their promise. But just as you can raise the probability that the written district curriculum is also the taught, tested, and learned curriculum, you can also increase the likelihood that your action plans for assessment will succeed. Here's how:

- Ensure your plan is grounded in the clear vision your team refined over the course of its study, using well-articulated beliefs about assessment as the foundation for that vision.
- Use the Five Door profile analysis to focus on results by identifying long-term goals and specific, achievable milestones to chart the progress of your plan.
- Develop clear strategies aimed at reaching the goals and milestones with the required resources identified and allocated.
- Identify the staff development required for teachers and administrators and plan for it to be readily available.
- Recognize and communicate to others that the plan is aimed at improved student learning, making it even more difficult to leave on a shelf.

Most school leaders are familiar with strategic planning with well-defined procedures that result in plans of improvement. If your school or district has a preferred planning process used successfully in the past, or has a series of planning templates for documenting the goals and objectives, or follows a policy that guides the makeup of a planning team, we encourage your leadership team to put those tools to use here. Success of the plan is important; flexibility in its content, creation, and documentation is important to that success. If you have no preferred process, let us propose one for you.

Our goal has been to keep the planning as straightforward as possible, relying in large part on the school/district profile in Part 3 that documents the current status of your assessment system relative to your vision of the future. As a result of that self-analysis, your team has completed much of the information gathering already, and it is now time to gather all of that work and analysis and begin to draft a plan of action. What you gather in preparation could include the following:

- The team's final written assessment vision that has been refined over time
- The school/district profile created through the analysis of the Five Doors
- Any of the self-analysis tools (The 9 Principles of Assessment for Learning, The 10 Assessment Competencies for School Leaders, etc.)
- Any information produced through the "Thinking About Assessment" activities or "Applying the Skills" resources from this guide.

If you made notes in the margins of the guide during discussion or activities, now would be a good time to compile them into a usable summary. District policies, and the chart on pages 303–305 that cross references the Five Doors with the 10 assessment competencies for school leaders and the activities and resources in this guide will be helpful tools. Also, Activity 4 at the end of Part 3 asked your team to complete the "School/District Assessment Self-Analysis" to create a profile of the current status of your assessment system. The final section of that self-analysis, titled "Leadership for Assessment Reform," will also be helpful in planning your next steps. This set of nine items takes a "big picture" view of the status of your assessment system from a leadership perspective, and profiles items such as the existence of a written, comprehensive assessment plan, coordinated local/state testing schedules, stakeholder involvement in planning, and the assessment literacy of local leaders. Considering these issues will also be helpful in finalizing your action plan.

## Action Planning Templates

To complete your action plan we have provided planning templates for each of the Five Doors described in Part 3. Remember, these are some of the questions asked behind each door. Each implies its own action plan if the answer is NO.

### 1—Clear Targets

- Do we have well-defined achievement goals for students?
- Are they connected across grade levels and within subjects?
- Are they taught by teachers who have themselves mastered the learning targets they are to teach their students?

### 2—Uses and Users

- What are our current sources of achievement information about students?
- What information do we need and not have?
- Are we meeting the information needs of all users?
- Have we balanced classroom assessment and standardized testing?
- Have we considered and defined the purposes for all of our assessments?
- Do we know how to avoid the misuse of assessment information?

### 3—Assessment Literacy

- Have we analyzed the level of assessment literacy in our instructional staff, administrators, and local community?
- Are classroom assessments aligned with state and district standards?
- Are we assessment literate? If not, what is our plan for developing assessment literacy where it is needed?

### 4—Communication

- Are we communicating effectively about student achievement?
- Do our grading practices help or hinder in that regard?
- Are we using a systems approach in reporting student progress that adheres to the principles of effective communication, including multiple methods of communicating?

### 5—Policies

- What policies guide practices that have the greatest impact on student learning?
- Do we have policies that support quality assessment, including fair and ethical practice?
- Do our policies work as a system to drive good practice relative to student assessment?

The top section of each of the five templates that follow (pages 321–325) crosses the various roles and levels in the organization of a school system. It is designed to help your team think about all of the different levels and positions in the organization that could be called on to contribute to the plan's success. The intent is to foster thinking that reaches from the classroom to the boardroom in the design of the action plan. As an example: think about the work you need to do around achievement targets behind Door 1. Within each cell of the table, enter what responsibilities fall to each player at each level. What is the school board's job relative to achievement standards, if any? The superintendent's? Determine who in the system needs to do what to accomplish work related to Door 1.

The bottom half of each template is the action planning tool where you specify exactly what is to be done to create assessment balance and quality. Your team may have one goal for each of the Five Doors, or several goals for each, depending entirely on the profile created through your school/district analysis. The activities in support of each goal for each of the Five Doors can be captured here, describing the intended outcome, the specific tasks required to achieve the outcome, the person(s) responsible, the resources required, and the timeline for accomplishment. Copy as many pages as needed per door to accommodate the scope of work.

# ASSESSMENT OF AND *FOR* LEARNING
## Door 1 – Clear Targets

### Roles and Responsibilities

| Position | District Level | School Level | Classroom Level |
|---|---|---|---|
| School Board | | | |
| Superintendent | | | |
| Curriculum Director | | | |
| Principals | | | |
| C & I/Prof. Dev. Support Staff | | | |
| Teachers | | | |

### Action Plan Goal

| Proposed Action(s) | Intended Outcome | Specific Task(s) | Evidence of Accomplishment | Person(s) Resp. | Resources Required | Due Date |
|---|---|---|---|---|---|---|
| | | | | | | |
| | | | | | | |
| | | | | | | |
| | | | | | | |

# ASSESSMENT OF AND *FOR* LEARNING
## Door 2 – Uses/Users

## Roles and Responsibilities

| Position | District Level | School Level | Classroom Level |
|---|---|---|---|
| School Board | | | |
| Superintendent | | | |
| Curriculum Director | | | |
| Principals | | | |
| C & I/Prof. Dev. Support Staff | | | |
| Teachers | | | |

## Action Plan Goal

| Proposed Action(s) | Intended Outcome | Specific Task(s) | Evidence of Accomplishment | Person(s) Resp. | Resources Required | Due Date |
|---|---|---|---|---|---|---|
| | | | | | | |
| | | | | | | |
| | | | | | | |

# ASSESSMENT OF AND *FOR* LEARNING
## Door 3 – Assessment Literacy

## Roles and Responsibilities

| Position | District Level | School Level | Classroom Level |
|---|---|---|---|
| School Board | | | |
| Superintendent | | | |
| Curriculum Director | | | |
| Principals | | | |
| C & I/Prof. Dev. Support Staff | | | |
| Teachers | | | |

## Action Plan Goal

| Proposed Action(s) | Intended Outcome | Specific Task(s) | Evidence of Accomplishment | Person(s) Resp. | Resources Required | Due Date |
|---|---|---|---|---|---|---|
| | | | | | | |
| | | | | | | |
| | | | | | | |
| | | | | | | |

# ASSESSMENT OF AND FOR LEARNING
## Door 4 – Communication

## Roles and Responsibilities

| Position | District Level | School Level | Classroom Level |
|---|---|---|---|
| School Board | | | |
| Superintendent | | | |
| Curriculum Director | | | |
| Principals | | | |
| C & I/Prof. Dev. Support Staff | | | |
| Teachers | | | |

## Action Plan Goal

| Proposed Action(s) | Intended Outcome | Specific Task(s) | Evidence of Accomplishment | Person(s) Resp. | Resources Required | Due Date |
|---|---|---|---|---|---|---|
| | | | | | | |
| | | | | | | |
| | | | | | | |

# ASSESSMENT OF AND *FOR* LEARNING
## Door 5 – Policies

## Roles and Responsibilities

| Position | District Level | School Level | Classroom Level |
|---|---|---|---|
| School Board | | | |
| Superintendent | | | |
| Curriculum Director | | | |
| Principals | | | |
| C & I/Prof. Dev. Support Staff | | | |
| Teachers | | | |

## Action Plan Goal

| Proposed Action(s) | Intended Outcome | Specific Task(s) | Evidence of Accomplishment | Person(s) Resp. | Resources Required | Due Date |
|---|---|---|---|---|---|---|
| | | | | | | |
| | | | | | | |
| | | | | | | |

## *Additional Planning Considerations*

The five action planning templates linked to the Five Doors provide a planning framework that you may broaden to include assessment issues not directly raised or covered in detail in this guide. Following are other issues your team may want to consider either in the development of the action plan or for future review and planning.

### *The Comprehensive Assessment Plan*

The action planning process and templates in this guide will help your team focus on improving assessment balance and quality while emphasizing the role assessment *for* learning can and should play in the total system. Although similar in some respects, it is not the same as developing a school/district comprehensive assessment plan. A comprehensive assessment plan helps manages the assessment business of the school or district and acts as a guide for all issues related to testing, assessment, and monitoring the progress of all students. Issues such as appropriate student placement in special programs, testing accommodations for special populations, total system costs, test materials maintenance and security, technical and legal issues, student promotion and retention, and the information needs, sources, and models for program evaluation are examples of topics addressed in a comprehensive assessment plan. Those types of issues may or may not find their way into your assessment *for* learning action plan; if they do not, remember that they can and should be addressed and communicated to staff in some way.

### *Helping Policy Makers Understand Balance and Quality*

We've worked in this guide at the school/district policy levels, trying to make sure policies drive sound practice and support quality assessment at those levels. But there are other levels of policy we might also want to consider trying to influence in the same way. Policy makers, not just at the local school board level but also at the state and federal level, need a deep understanding of assessment issues if they are to assist schools and districts achieve balance and quality. Knowing the limitations of standardized testing, and also knowing the quality information and data that assessment-literate teachers can produce about individual students is an important start for policy makers at these levels. Further, they need to understand the role of professional development in improving schools and in achieving standards-based systems. Without that, educators will continue to be left without opportunity to learn and apply in the classroom what we know works when assessment is used as part of instruction. The parent/community guide published by ATI, *Understanding School Assessment* (Chappuis and Chappuis, 2002), can be used as a resource in helping policy makers.

### Communicating and Monitoring the Plan

The success of many reform efforts is due as much to the collaboration used to develop the plan and the effective communication of the plan to all stakeholders as it is to the actual goals and content of the strategic plan. Your leadership team should consider strategies for creating support for improvement plans both small and large by asking the following questions:

- Who needs to be either involved in the planning effort or informed along the way?
- Should there be different levels of involvement, from direct decision making to advisory in nature?
- Whose advice do we want/need relative to our plan?
- Once written, is it clear that a leadership plan is in place that is across levels: district, school, and classroom?
- Is there a communications component of the plan that will be uniformly applied to reach all stakeholders? Will those stakeholders, including the school board, be regularly updated on the progress of the plan?

### Reconciling Current and Future Systems

Some action plans may seek both to improve present conditions in the current assessment system and to create and plan for future conditions in a new system. Some advocate differentiating these purposes into one set of plans that focuses on present-day operations, maintaining a short-term view of improvement, and a second set of plans with an emphasis on the long term, concentrating on creating the new system as described in the team's vision (Blanchard and Waghorn, 1998). The two sets can then be intentionally merged into one comprehensive plan by a team familiar with both.

## Evaluating the Action Plan

The assessment system itself, when functioning properly, provides data for program evaluation, continuous improvement, and school/district accountability, while also providing teachers, students, and parents the information they need on a daily basis to positively affect learning. Your own action plan is a statement about what parts of that system need to get better. You may have sequenced it in stages, stepping out the activities so that progress can be more easily monitored and reported. Thinking about what data you can collect as evidence of accomplishment along the way is important to document as part of the plan.

It is likely that in many plans there will be goals and objectives related to staff acquiring the knowledge and skills necessary for the vision to become reality. Professional development in classroom assessment will be at the center of many plans. While there is compelling evidence that deep student involvement in classroom assessment can increase student learning, we strongly recommend that all who implement assessment literacy professional development programs design and conduct their own local program evaluations. These evaluations can be both formative and summative. Formative evaluations help program directors monitor and adjust their professional development efforts as they go. The purpose of evaluation in this case is program improvement. Summative evaluations provide evidence of effectiveness to those who fund the professional development efforts or are responsible for their success. These evaluations serve to inform judgments of overall program effectiveness. Evaluators can conduct meaningful evaluations by focusing evidence gathering at any of a variety of levels. Here are some examples.

## Case Study of an Individual Teacher or a Few Teachers

Evaluation results can be derived from the in-depth study of a single teacher or just a few teachers. Precisely what did these teachers experience and what effect did it have on their classroom assessment practices? A clear portrait of individual teachers' experiences can provide information on what worked and what did not. Because evaluation resources are being invested in understanding a few specific experiences, one can examine in detail how and why the professional development effort worked or didn't. In this case, generalizability of results is sacrificed for depth of understanding.

However, generalizability of results can be enhanced by including teachers from a range of contexts (grade levels and content areas). This kind of evaluation can be conducted by following teachers as they develop their assessment literacy. Or, it can center on the teachers' design and implementation of action research studies focused on student-involved classroom assessment (described in the next subsection).

### The Study of a Learning Team

A slight variation on this plan focuses the evaluation on all members of a single local learning team. Here again, the power of the investigation resides in the depth of insight that it can yield, not the breadth. The objective is to generate a composite picture of the learning, experimentation, growth, and impact of a group of teachers working together. The strength of this approach is the lessons it can teach about the power of collaborative learning. How did the group define success? What procedures did they follow? What were their norms for interaction? What went on at team meetings? What evidence of greater assessment literacy emerged? What kinds of experimentation resulted? What was the extent of success and challenges? What were the joys and disappointments?

### The Study of a School District

Information might be pooled on the collective experience of a sample of students, teachers, administrators, and teams across a school district. Why did professional development begin? Was there a leadership commitment? What did it take to secure a district commitment? Who was involved in the program and why? What events took place? What did they cost? What was their impact on classroom assessment quality? Efficiency? Student, teacher, or community dispositions? Student achievement? In this case, assuming that resources are limited, depth of information is sacrificed for the sake of results that generalize across individuals, classrooms, and schools.

## Classroom Action Research—The Study of Impacts on Students

It can also be instructive from a program evaluation perspective to study and understand the impact of an assessment literacy development program by studying its effects on the classroom learning experience of the students whose teachers implement a student-involved classroom assessment environment. Precisely what happened to those students and what impact did that experience have on their achievement and dispositions? This kind of action research evaluation invests its resources in obtaining rich and deep understanding of program effects by using a high-resolution microscope. But again, those results may not generalize beyond those students studied.

## Two Evaluation Focal Points

At any of these levels, program evaluations can be designed to document the nature of the professional development *processes*, or events as they unfold, and/or document the *effects* or *impacts* of those events on teachers or students. While evaluations can focus on either, we believe that the most powerful evaluations cover both.

### Process Evaluation

Process evaluation documents the nature of the professional development intervention that actually was implemented. Who did what, when, and where? Did actual interventions align with what was supposed to occur? If the program "worked," precisely what worked? Without this information, you will be unable to replicate the same effective program in the future. If the professional development intervention did not work, then the results of a process evaluation provide an information base from which to make procedural adjustments.

In the case of assessment literacy development programs, the process evaluator seeks to answer procedural questions such as these:

- What procedures were used to introduce the ideas of balanced assessment systems, student-involved assessment, and the use of learning teams as the professional development process?
- How many learning teams were formed?
- What was their composition?
- What materials were available for use, were actually used, and to what extent?
- What were the teams' schedules of events?
- What happened at team meetings?
- What kinds of ongoing facilitation did teams need?
- How many learning teams were completed?
- What proportion of participants actually experimented with student-involved assessment in their classrooms?
- What student-involved classroom assessment procedures did teachers actually experiment with in their classrooms?
- What was the cost of program implementation?

To generate answers to these and similar process questions, program evaluators must maintain open lines of communication with those working to manage the learning team process and with the learning teams themselves. This may require developing a simple reporting system, with specific procedural information flowing to the program director for summary across teams. Evidence might come from team meeting minutes, training logs or diaries, or direct participation in or observations of team meetings.

### Evaluation of Impact

Program effects typically unfold over time, as the professional development experience under study provides participants with new insights, ideas, and experiences. So program evaluations are likely to be most helpful in shaping program improvement and making summative judgments if they collect, summarize, and interpret evidence at the beginning, during, and at the end of a learning experience. For this reason, we urge program evaluators to plan to document progress along the way to be sure that things proceed as intended. They then must gather evidence verifying that the intervention delivered what it promised—higher levels of assessment literacy and confidence.

Program evaluators have a variety of potential sources of impact information from which to choose to gather the evidence:

- Increased assessment literacy
- Increased teacher confidence
- Increased assessment efficiency
- Increased assessment quality
- Increased student confidence
- Impact on student achievement
- Learning teams as professional development

## In Closing

Through the use of high-quality assessments *of* and *for* learning, linked to the targets of instruction, all students will be able to show what they know and can do. A system that is in balance will ensure that the right kind of assessment is used for the right purpose, and that assessment will be used to continually improve student learning. We have focused the contents of this guide on our belief that strong classroom assessment is the heart of any assessment system.

But it is through a combination of assessments, working in a coordinated fashion, that students can truly prosper and where all information needs can be met. Your work and the work of your colleagues in pursuit of assessment balance and quality will benefit teachers, schools, and communities, but will benefit most especially the students we all serve.

# References

American Federation of Teachers, National Council on Measurement in Education, and National Education Association. (1990). Standards for teacher competence in educational assessment of students. *Educational Measurement: Issues and Practice, 9*(4), 30–32.

Amrein, A., and Berliner, D. (2003). The effects of high-stakes testing on student motivation and learning. *Educational Leadership, 60*(5), 32–38.

Arter, J. A., and Busick, K. U. (2001). *Practice with student-involved classroom assessment.* Portland, OR: Assessment Training Institute.

Arter, J. A., and Nutting, B. (1998). *Student assessment mini-lessons for your staff.* Portland, OR: Northwest Regional Educational Laboratory.

Arter, J., Stiggins, R., Duke, D., and Sagor, R. (1993). Promoting assessment literacy among principals. *NASSP Bulletin, 77*(556), 1–7.

Assessment Reform Group. (1999). *Assessment for learning: Beyond the black box.* Cambridge, UK: University of Cambridge.

Atkin, J. M., Black, P., and Coffey, J. (2001). *Classroom assessment and the National Science Standards.* Washington, DC: National Academy Press.

Black, P., Harrison, C., Lee, C., Marshall, B., and Wiliam, D. (2002). *Working inside the black box: Assessment for learning in the classroom.* London: King's College.

Black, P., and Wiliam, D. (1998). Inside the black box: Raising standards through classroom assessment. *Phi Delta Kappan, 80*(2), 139–148.

Blanchard, K., and Waghorn, T. (1998). *Mission possible.* Columbus, OH: McGraw Hill

Bloom, B. (1984). The search for methods of group instruction as effective as one-to-one tutoring. *Educational Leadership, 41*(8), 4–17.

California School Boards Association. (1999). *Targeting student learning: The school board's role as policymaker.* Springfield, IL: Illinois Association of School Boards.

Center on Education Policy. (2003). *From the capital to the classroom: State and federal efforts to implement the No Child Left Behind Act.* Washington, DC: CEP.

Chappuis, J., and Chappuis, S. (2002). *Understanding school assessment: A parent and community guide to helping students learn.* Portland, OR: Assessment Training Institute.

Chappuis, S., and Stiggins, R. J. (2002). Classroom assessment for learning. *Educational Leadership, 60*(1), 40–43.

Commission on Instructionally Supportive Assessment. (2001). *Building tests to support instruction and accountability.* Arlington, VA: American Association of School Administrators.

Guskey, T. R. (2002). Computerized gradebooks and the myth of objectivity. *Phi Delta Kappan, 83*(10), 775–780.

Ingersoll, R. M. (1999). The problem of under-qualified teachers in American secondary schools. *Educational Researcher, 28*(2), 26–37.

Jacobs, H. H. (1997). *Mapping the big picture: Integrating curriculum and assessment K–12.* Alexandria, VA: Association for Supervision and Curriculum Development.

National Education Association: Assessment Training Institute. (2003). *Balanced assessment: The key to accountability and student learning.* Student Assessment Series, G. W. Cutlip, Series Ed.. Washington, DC: National Education Association.

O'Connor, K. (2002). *How to grade for learning.* Arlington Heights, IL: Skylight.

Office of Superintendent of Public Instruction. (1996). *Designing a district assessment system.* Olympia, WA: OSPI.

Pellegrino, J., Chudowsky, N., and Glaser, R. (2001). *Knowing what students know: The science and design of educational assessment.* Washington, DC: National Academy Press.

Schmoker, M. (2002). The real causes of higher achievement. *SEDLetter, 14*(2). Retrieved July 2002 from the World Wide Web: http://www.sedl.org/pubs/sedletter/v14n02/1.html

Stiggins, R. J. (2001). *Student-involved classroom assessment,* 3d ed. Columbus, OH: Prentice Hall/Merrill; distributed by Assessment Training Institute, Portland, OR.

Stiggins, R. J. (2002). Assessment crisis! The absence of assessment *for* learning. *Phi Delta Kappan, 83*(10), 758–765.

Washington Educational Research Association. (2001). White paper. Ethical standards in testing: Test preparation and administration. University Place, WA: WERA

# About the Authors

**Steve Chappuis** has been a teacher, counselor, and school and district administrator. His leadership experiences include serving as a junior high principal, a senior high principal, and executive director responsible for supervision of schools and principals. As an Assistant Superintendent for Curriculum and Instruction he implemented a standards-based instructional program that included comprehensive assessment plans and policies and professional development in classroom assessment. Steve is also the coauthor of *Understanding School Assessment: A Parent and Community Guide to Helping Students Learn* (2002).

**Rick Stiggins** created the Assessment Training Institute in 1992 for the purpose of supporting educators as they face the challenges of day-to-day classroom assessment. He is committed to helping teachers learn to gather accurate information about student achievement and use that information to benefit (not just grade and sort) their students. He encourages teachers to involve students deeply in classroom assessment, record keeping, and communication in order to build their confidence and academic success. His awardwinning book, *Student-Involved Classroom Assessment,* 3d ed. (2001), designed for professional development in school-based learning teams, is used extensively in schools across the country.

**Judy Arter** is a nationally recognized expert in performance assessment. Her background includes the development of statewide writing assessments, large-scale and classroom-based items and performance assessments, and interactive training videos. Prior to joining Assessment Training Institute, Judy directed Northwest Regional Educational Laboratory's (NWREL) assessment unit. Her list of recent publishing credits include *Practice with Student-Involved Classroom Assessment* (2001), the companion workbook to Rick Stiggins' textbook, and *Scoring Rubrics in the Classroom: Using Performance Criteria for Assessing and Improving Student Performance* (2001), coauthored with Jay McTighe.

**Jan Chappuis** has been a teacher, curriculum and assessment specialist, and independent assessment trainer and consultant. She has more than a decade of experience in providing dynamic and hands-on staff development in classroom assessment. Jan leads ATI professional development efforts in writing assessment and student-involved assessment strategies. She is coauthor of *Understanding School Assessment: A Parent and Community Guide to Helping Students Learn* (2002), and a presenter and codeveloper of the training video, *Student-Involved Performance Assessment.*

# CD-ROM/DVD Contents
## Activities, Resources, and PowerPoint Presentations on the CD-ROM

### Thinking About Assessment: Activities

Activity 1:   Building the Foundation for Understanding Quality Assessment
Activity 2:   Examining Your Assessment Beliefs
Activity 3:   "Emily's Story"
Activity 4:   Creating an Assessment Profile for Your School/District
Activity 5:   Understanding Standards of Classroom Assessment Quality
Activity 6:   ATI Interactive Video, *Creating Sound Classroom Assessments*
Activity 7:   Auditing Classroom Assessments for Quality
Activity 8:   Developmental Continua for Teachers
Activity 9:   Classroom Assessment *for* Learning
Activity 10:  Principles of Assessment *for* Learning: A Self-Analysis
Activity 11:  Converting Learning Targets to Student-Friendly Language
Activity 12:  Ways That Teachers and Students Use Formative Assessment
Activity 13:  Using Feedback to Set Goals
Activity 14:  Deconstructing Standards into Classroom-Level Achievement Targets: Practice for School Leaders
Activity 15:  Using Interviews to Hire Teachers with Content Knowledge and Assessment Competence
Activity 16:  Auditing Your Classroom Curriculum
Activity 17:  Should Teachers Be Held Accountable for Assessment Competence Through Evaluations?
Activity 18:  Analyzing Your Professional Development Program
Activity 19:  Learning Teams for Assessment Literacy
Activity 20:  Using School/District Policies to Support Quality Assessment
Activity 21:  Grading Scenarios
Activity 22:  ATI Interactive Video, *Report Card Grading: Strategies and Solutions*
Activity 23:  Panel Hears Exam Horrors
Activity 24:  When Grades Don't Match the State Assessment Results
Activity 25:  Connecting Assessment with Reporting
Activity 26:  Who Uses Assessment Information, and How?
Activity 27:  Merging Local and State Assessment Systems
Activity 28:  "Is This Responsible?"
Activity 29:  A Self-Analysis for School Leaders
Activity 30:  Connecting Assessment Literacy to Other School Improvement Initiatives

### Applying the Skills: Resources

Resource 1:   Confidence Questionnaire
Resource 2:   Student Survey to Study Assessment *for* Learning Practices in the Classroom
Resource 3:   Using Test Results to Self-Assess and Set Goals
Resource 4:   Student Self-Assessment and Goal-Setting Activities
Resource 5:   Implementing the Written Curriculum
Resource 6:   How Principals Can Support Learning Teams

Resource 7:  Conducting an Assessment Audit
Resource 8:  Rubric for Grading
Resource 9:  A Standard Cover Letter to Parents
Resource 10:  Guidelines for Test Preparation and Administration

## PowerPoint Presentations

Part 2: *A Vision of the Perfect Assessment System*
Part 3: *Five Doors to Excellence in Assessment*

## DVD Presentation

*Assessment* for *Learning: A Hopeful Vision of the Future*